MW00992420

LIKE A GREAT FEUDAL LANDLORD

Mercer University Press

Endowed by

Tom Watson Brown

and

The Watson-Brown Foundation, Inc.

LIKE A GREAT FEUDAL LANDLORD

How Architecture and Slavery Created the World of the Upcountry Planter

Heidi Amelia-Anne Weber

MERCER UNIVERSITY PRESS
Macon, Georgia

MUP/ H1017

Published by Mercer University Press
1501 Mercer University Drive
Macon, Georgia 31207

27 26 25 24 22 5 4 3 2 1

Books published by Mercer University Press are printed on acid-free paper that meets the requirements of the American National Standard for Information Sciences—Permanence of Paper for Printed Library Materials.

Printed and bound the United States.

This book is set in Adobe Caslon Pro.

Cover/jacket design by Burt&Burt.

ISBN 978-0-88146-822-9
Cataloging-in-Publication Data is available from the Library of Congress

For my parents

Judge Frederic Gordon and Patricia Banghart Weber

CONTENTS

ABBREVIATIONS

Archives Abbreviations

Department of Rare Books and Special Collections, Princeton University Library—DRBSC

Emory University Manuscript, Archives, and Rare Books Library—EU-MARBL

Hargrett Rare Books and Manuscripts Library, University of Georgia Libraries-HRBML

Library of Congress, Manuscripts Division—LOC, MD

North Carolina Division of Archives and History—NCDAH

South Carolina Archives and History— SCAH

South Carolina Historical Society, Manuscripts Division—SCHS, MD

South Caroliniana Library, Manuscripts Division, University of South Carolina—SCL, MD

Southern Historic Collection, Manuscripts Division, University of North Carolina—SHC, MD

Special Collections, Robert Muldrow Cooper Library, Clemson University—JCCP, SC, RMCL

US Army Military History Institute—USAMHI

Winterthur Library, Winterthur Archives—WL, WA

Papers/Collections Abbreviations

Adger and Bowen Families Papers, South Caroliniana Library, Manuscripts Division—ABFP, SCL

Baldwin County, Georgia. Deed Book J—BCDBJ

Colonel David C. Barrow Papers, Hargrett Rare Books and Manuscripts Library, University of Georgia Libraries—CDCBP, HRBML

Richard Bennehan Letters Miscellaneous, North Carolina Division of Archives and History—RBLM, NCDAH

Burge Family Papers, Emory University Manuscript, Archives, and Rare Book Library—BFP, EUMARBL

Bryce Family Papers, South Caroliniana Library, Manuscripts Division—BFP, SCL, MD

Henry Kirke Bush-Brown Papers, Library of Congress, Manuscripts Division - HKBBP, LOC, MD.

Robert M. Cahusac Papers, South Carolina Historical Society, Manuscripts Division—RMCP, SCHS, MD

Matthew Calbraith Butler Papers. South Caroliniana Library, Manuscripts Division—MCBP, SCL, MD

John Caldwell Calhoun Papers, Special Collections, Robert Muldrow Cooper Library, Clemson University—JCCP, SC, RMCL

John Caldwell Calhoun Papers, South Caroliniana Library, Manuscripts Division—JCCP. SCL, MD

John C. Calhoun. *The Papers of John C. Calhoun X: 1825-1829.,* ed. Clyde N. Wilson and W. Edwin Hemphill. Columbia, S.C.: University of South Carolina Press, 1977—*Volume X*

John C. Calhoun. *The Papers of John C. Calhoun XI: 1829-1832.,* ed. Clyde N. Wilson. Columbia, S.C.: University of South Carolina Press, 1978—*Volume XI*

John C. Calhoun. *The Papers of John C. Calhoun XIV: 1837-1839.*, ed. Clyde N. Wilson. Columbia, S.C.: University of South Carolina Press, 1981—*Volume XIV*

John C. Calhoun. *The Papers of John C. Calhoun XVI: 1848-1849.*, ed. Clyde N. Wilson. Columbia, S.C.: University of South Carolina Press, 2001—*Volume XVI*

Cameron Family Papers, Southern Historical Collection, University of North Carolina—CFP, SHC

Bennehan Cameron Family Papers, Southern Historical Collection, University of North Carolina Press—BCFP, SHC

Duncan Cameron Will, Durham County, Record of Wills, Vols. A, B. North Carolina Division of Archives and History—DCW, DC, NCDAH

Duncan Cameron Will, 1853, Wake County, Record of Wills. Inventories, Settlement of Estates, 1850-1855. Vols. 27, 28. North Carolina Division of Archives and History.

Paul C. Cameron Papers, Civil War Collection, Orange County, North Carolina Division of Archives and History—DCW, WC, NCDAH

Paul C. Cameron Petition for Amnesty File, North Carolina Division of Archives and History—PCCPAF, MCDAH

Elizabeth S. Winthrop Chandler Papers, South Caroliniana Library, Manuscripts Division—ESWCP, SCL, MD

Civil War Collection, North Carolina Division of Archives and History—CWC, NCDAH

Civil War Collection, Orange County, North Carolina Division of Archives and History—CWC, OC, NCDAH

Civil War Miscellaneous Collection, US Army Military History Institute—CWMC, USAMHI

Thomas Green Clemson Papers, South Caroliniana Library, Manuscripts Division. Copies of the original letters that are housed at Clemson University—TGCP, SCL, MD

Anne Cameron Collins Papers, Southern Historical Collections, University of North Carolina—ACCP, SHC

Ellis Merton Coulter Historical Manuscripts, Confederate States of America, Hargrett Rare Books and Manuscripts Library, University of Georgia Libraries—EMCHM, HRBML

Telamon Cuyler Collection, Hargrett Rare Books and Manuscripts Library, University of Georgia Libraries—TCC, HRBM

Telamon Cuyler Collection, Georgia Governor's Papers, Hargrett Rare Books and Manuscripts Library, University of Georgia Libraries—TCCGGP, HRBML

Fairntosh Plantation, National Register of Historic Places Inventory-Nomination Form, Durham County, North Carolina. North Carolina Division of Archives and History—FPNRHI, NCDAH

Fort Hill-Pickens County Research File, South Carolina Archives and History—FHPCRF, SCAH

Hammond, Bryan, and Cumming Families Papers, South Caroliniana Library, Manuscripts Division—HBCFFP, SCL, MD

Harry Hammond Papers, South Caroliniana Library, Manuscripts Division—HHP, SCL, MD

James Henry Hammond Papers, Library of Congress, Manuscripts Division, Microfilm. JHHP, LOC, MD.

James Henry Hammond Papers, South Caroliniana Library, Manuscripts Division—JHHP, SCL, MD

James Henry Hammond Papers, Southern Historical Collection, University of North Carolina -

Harry Hammond Papers, South Caroliniana Library, Manuscripts Division—HHP, SCL, MD

Hampton Family Papers, South Caroliniana Library, Manuscripts Division—HFP, SCL, MD

Preston Hampton Revolutionary Pension and Bounty Land Warrant Application Files, National Archives Microfilm Publication, Revolutionary Pension and Bounty Land Warrant Application Files 1800-1900, roll #1177 Hamner, Henry—Hancks, Abraham - PHRPBLWAF

Sarah (Sally) Strong Baxter Hampton Papers, South Caroliniana Library, Manuscripts Division—SSBHP, SCL, MD.

Wade Hampton Papers, Southern Historical Collection, Manuscripts Division, University of North Carolina—WHP, SHC, MD

Harrisburg Civil War Round Table, US Army Military History Institute—HCWRT, USAMHI

Historic American Buildings Survey. Ainsley Hall, South Carolina—HABS, AH

Historic American Buildings Survey. Clinton, Jones County. Lowther Hall—HABS, JC, LH

Historic American Buildings Survey. Milledgeville Vicinity, Baldwin County, Tucker, Daniel R.

House (Lockerly), Survey No. GA-1151, Data Sheet #2—HABS, MV, BC

Historic American Buildings Survey. Milford. Governor John L. Manning Plantation—HABS, M

Historic American Buildings Survey, "Millwood" (Wade Hampton Mansion) Ruins, Habs No. SC-256, Part I, Historical Information—HABS, MR

James Jones Papers, South Caroliniana Library, Manuscripts Division - JJP, SCL, MD.

Ledger Papers, South Caroliniana Library, Manuscripts Division—LP, SCL, MD

Manning Family Papers, South Caroliniana Library, Manuscripts Division—MFP, SCL, MD

John L. Manning Biographical Information, Compilation for Class of Ex-1837. Preparation Material for General Catalogue of Alumni, Officers and Honorary Graduates of Princeton University, Department of Rare Books and Special Collections, Princeton University Library—OHGPU, DRBSC, PUL

John L. Manning File, Department of Rare Books and Special Collections, Princeton University Library - JLMF, DRBSC

John Laurence Manning Papers, South Caroliniana Library, Manuscripts Division.

John L. Manning Paperwork. Filed with Princeton University for the compilation of the Princeton University General Biographical Catalogue 1746-1916. Princeton University Library—PUGBC, PUL

Maverick and Van Wyke Papers, South Caroliniana Library, Manuscripts Division. MVWP, SCL, MD.

Virginia Gurley Meynard Papers, South Caroliniana Library, Manuscripts Division—VGMP, SCL, MD.

Milford Plantation, Sumter County Research File, South Carolina Department of Archives and History—MRSCRF, SCDAH

Milford Plantation, 1839-1969. Private File of Dr. Rodger Stroup. The South Carolina History Center—MP, RS, SCHC

Robert Mills Papers, Library of Congress, Manuscripts Division. RMP, LOC, MD

Millwood, National Register of Historic Register of Historic Places—Nomination Form, South Carolina Department of Archives and History— MNRHPHP

Millwood-Richland County Research File. South Caroliniana Division of Archives and History—MRCRF, SCDAH

Montmorenci. Winterthur Library, Winterthur Archives— MWLWA

Johnson M. Mundy Papers, South Caroliniana Library, Manuscripts Division. JMMP, SCL, MD.

National Register of Historic Places Inventory—Nomination Form, Fort Hill, Pickens County File. South Carolina Department of Archives & History—NFFH, SCDAH

North Carolina Historical Commission Papers, North Carolina Division of Archives and History—NCHCP, NCDAH

Northampton County, Wills, 1764-1950, Calvert-Clemens. North Carolina Division of Archives and History—NCW, CC, NCDAH

Henry Junius Nott Papers, South Caroliniana Library, Manuscripts Division—HJNP, SCL, MD

Official Records of the War of the Rebellion (CD-Rom)—ORWR

Orange County, North Carolina Deeds. Book 28. North Carolina Division of Archives and History—OCNCD, NDAH

Orange County Deed Book, North Carolina Division of Archives and History—OCDB, NCDAH

Orange County Wills, Book F. North Carolina Department of Archives and History—OCWBF, NCDAH

Person County, North Carolina Deeds, Book O. North Carolina Division of Archives and History—PCNCD, NCDAH

Photographs. Montmorenci. Winterthur Library, Winterthur Archives—WL, WA

Polk Papers, North Carolina Division of Archives and History—PP. NCDAH

Edward Elmer Potter Papers, South Caroliniana Library, Manuscripts Division—EEPP, SCL, MD

Denmark Raleigh photographs, Montmorenci, Winterthur Library, Winterthur Archives—DRPMWLWA

Redcliffe, Aiken County, Research File, South Carolina Department of Archives and History -RACRF, SCDAH

Charles Rhodes Collection, US Army Military History Institute—CRC, USAMHI

William Tecumseh Sherman Papers, South Caroliniana Library, Manuscripts Division—WTSP, SCL, MD

Mary Amarinthia Snowden Papers, South Caroliniana Library, Manuscripts Division—MASP, SCL, MD

South Carolina Papers, South Caroliniana Library, Manuscripts Division—SCP, SCL, MD.

Sumter County Deeds—SCD

Sumter County Records—SCR

Sumter County Records and Deeds - SCRD

George Tattersall Papers, South Caroliniana Library, Manuscripts Division—GTP, SCL, MD

Daniel Heyward Trezant Papers, South Caroliniana Library, Manuscripts Division—DHTP, SCL, MD.

200 Meeting Street File, South Carolina Historical Society, Manuscripts Division—MSF, SCHS, MD.

Wake County Record of Wills, Inventories, Settlement of Estates 1850-1855, Vols. 27, 28, North Carolina Division of Archives and History—WCRWISE, NCDAH.

Warren County Estate Records 1772-1940, n.d. (Williams, W.K.A.—Wise), North Carolina Division of Archives and History—WCER, NCDAH.

Warren County Wills. North Carolina Division of Archives and History—WCW, NCDAH

William May Wightman Papers, South Caroliniana Historical Society, Manuscripts Division.—WMWP, SCHS, MD

Williams-Chesnut-Manning Families Papers, South Caroliniana Library, Manuscripts Division—WCMFP, SCL, MD.

PREFACE

Modern Americans struggle to comprehend how knowledgeable people of power justified enslaving people. It is something that we find deplorable. Yet, without the labor of their slaves, White plantation owners could not have acquired the wealth that enabled them to build their resplendent homes.

The upcountry regions of Georgia, South Carolina and North Carolina were not as renowned for their wealth as the low country. Yet, around the turn of the nineteenth century, planters embarked on growing cotton in these areas. Once they attained financial success, these men began building houses that reflected their social and financial status. These planters decided to use the Greek Revival architectural style as the status symbol of their generations' wealth. In an attempt to differentiate themselves from the previous generation of planters who built in the Federal style, while simultaneously trying to gain their own identity, these men embraced the Greek Revival architectural style for their houses. Though resplendent with their designs and interior details, these grand residences concealed a harsh reality. These planters' successes were forged on their slaves' labor and the beauty of these homes was truly tarnished by the stain of slavery.

This work is not a justification of these men's actions of owning slaves nor is it condoning it. The purpose of this book is the tell the history of these planters and the process by which they designed, built, and decorated their Greek Revival Plantation homes. In addition, it addresses how their slaves enabled them to construct and maintain such houses. These slaves never had a voice and were not recognized for their contributions. The upcountry planters of Georgia, South Carolina and North Carolina that are discussed in this book prospered from their slaves' cultivation of cotton and built their homes as a result. They selected Greek Revival to be their architectural style and embraced its historic ties with another ancient slave culture

My research to ascertain the significance of the houses, their architectural styling, and how they were designed to represent the landowners relied on journals, letters, and records left by these planters and their families. The planters selected for this book all fit three specific criteria: (1) their chief residence was in the upcountry of Georgia, South Carolina, and

North Carolina, (2) they grew cotton, and (3) they built their homes in the Greek Revival architectural style.

The initial chapters discuss the significance of Greek Revival architecture and the emergence of Greek Revival architecture in America, particularly in the upcountry region of the plantation South. The third and fourth chapters explore specific planters and their families who built in the Greek Revival style. The next three chapters explore the relevance of the interior design of the big house, the possessions displayed within as well as other relevant structures and assets. The exterior decorations, landscape architecture, additional buildings on the plantation as well as other houses are also discussed. These chapters also show the significance of slaves and slavery to these planters as well as to the market economy. This essential institution allowed these men to build and maintain their grand houses. The concluding chapters of this book focus on the destruction that came from the Civil War as these planters saw their slaves freed and their status as wealthy planters gone. Their world was dramatically turned upside down with the loss of their slaves.

These Greek Revival plantation homes served as a testament to the legacy of their owners and the culture that produced them. As such, these upcountry Greek Revival mansions were truly emblematic of the men who built and owned them.

ACKNOWLEDGMENTS

First and foremost, I would like to thank my parents, the Honorable Frederic and Patricia Weber, for all of their love, support, and guidance. They have always stood by me and supported me. From a very young age, they cultivated in me a love of history. They are my greatest inspiration and I know that I have made them proud. Although my parents are no longer here with us on Earth, I know that they are smiling down on me. My Dad was always my greatest supporter. My Mom was my faithful editor and I am lost without her and her help. I am grateful for all the support I have received from my three sisters, Patti Rittenhouse, Lee Whitby, and Gretchen Lauzon, and their families as well. My family and friends amaze me, and I am so grateful that they are always by my side.

I would also like to thank everyone who helped me at the South Caroliniana Library, the South Carolina State Archives, the Hargrett Rare Books and Manuscripts Library, the Georgia State Archives, Emory University Manuscript, Archives, and Rare Books Library, the North Carolina Division of Archives and History, the University of North Carolina libraries, the Military History Institute at Carlisle Barracks, Princeton University Library Department of Rare Books and Special Collections, the Library of Congress, the National Archives, the Winterthur Archives, Morgan County Archives, and at the plantation houses. I am grateful to the people at these locations who shared their in-depth knowledge and helped me in my research.

I have been so fortunate to have been encouraged by the great teachers that I had in my life, the incredible professors under whom I studied, my amazing colleagues, and the wonderful friends who have given their unfaltering support. Mrs. Elizabeth "Scottie" Hontz, Mr. George Kaiser, Dr. James N. J. Henwood, Dr. John G. Muncie, Dr. Marie Donaghay, Dr. Leonne Hudson, Dr. Kenneth Bindas, Dr. Charles Crawford, Dr. Gary Pavek, Aunt Jeanette Hammerstone, Carol Ramagosa, and Brian LeHuray have all helped me in their own individual ways. Thank you! I would also like to thank David Roberts, the Burn Family, Bob Ramagosa, Jean Pavek, Tom and Barbara Madsen, Chris Hemmer, the Sparta V.F.W. Post, John Drake, Gary and Claude Larson, Sylvia and Ron

Petillo, Michael Hanifan, Craig Merrill, and other great friends who have supported me in the publication of this book.

This has been a long process and I thank everyone who has been with me along the way. I am truly grateful.

Mom and Dad—this is for you!!!

CHAPTER 1

WHY GREEK REVIVAL?

Increased cotton production and sales in the late nineteenth century, made possible by slave labor, created a new generation of wealthy and prosperous citizenry in Georgia, South Carolina, and North Carolina, particularly in the upcountry regions. Impressive Greek Revival mansions found on the upcountry plantations of Georgia, South Carolina and North Carolina are a vestige of a bygone era. Yet, in the early part of the nineteenth century, these estates—and their owners- were pillars of the community. With the wealth generated by their cotton plantations and the unpaid labor of slaves, these planter sought to build regal homes that would reflect their economic power and social status. These planters set the criterion of status for the South and their mansions reflected their positions of power. At the root of this societal classification were their slaves.

Their newfound economic prosperity was exhibited in their appropriation of the Greek Revival plantation home which became a mirror of sorts, reflecting the planter himself. The Greek Revival architectural style was not distinct to upcountry Georgia, South Carolina and North Carolina, as it existed throughout the entire United States. The design originated and was used in ancient Greece and Rome. It was then revived in the eighteenth and nineteenth centuries in Europe. Transported from abroad, this architectural style was first used in the public sector in Philadelphia. By most accounts, the Bank of Pennsylvania in Philadelphia was the initial Greek Revival structure built in the United States. It was completed in 1801.[1] From this point on, this style made its way to the private sector. Successful Northern capitalists built their homes in the Greek Revival architectural style. The imposing pillars

---

[1]Gelernter, *Cultural*, 134.; Hamlin, *Account*, 63.; Lancaster, *Bluegrass*, 79.; Nash, *First*, 141.

which lifted the massive portico, key features of this architectural design, created an image of majesty and might, in essence, power, that appealed to the new Southern aristocracy.

Greek Revival made its way from the Philadelphia region and throughout America.[2] Yet it attained a place of distinction in the antebellum South. The planter class embraced this architectural style for a variety of reasons. Greek Revival was functional and practical for the weather with its wide porticos that offered shade in the hot Southern summers, yet still aesthetically appealing. The houses were designed with open rooms that had tall ceilings for better air circulation to help alleviate the heat and humidity of the summers in the South. Mark Gelernter, in his *A History of American Architecture*, explains that "the Greek idea spread to the southern plantation homes where…freestanding colonnades were long employed for climate control in this region. Updating the plantation house in the new style required little more than constructing the columns and entablatures with more accurate Greek proportion."[3]

Greek Revival architectural was not just practical, but also, and was more importantly, symbolic, representing power and influence. It became a symbol of the slaveocracy of the nineteenth century almost in the same manner it was in ancient times. Southern planters embraced this style, but it had added meaning to those in the upcountry. The upcountry planters were well versed in the history of ancient Greece. They had studied the language, scholarship, architecture, and practices, as well as other aspects, of this civilization. Upcountry cotton planters from three of the traditional plantation states, Georgia, South Carolina, and North Carolina, used Greek Revival as a testament to their social standing, and the houses and their content and other possessions to define them as economic, social, and political leaders. These upcountry planters grew cotton in regions not always considered "cotton" areas and defined their social status through architectural choices. These men bound themselves to the legacy of ancient Greece, idolizing its

---

[2]Hopkins, *Creating*, 90.; Truettner, *Aspirations*, 24.
[3]Gelernter, *Cultural*, 136.

characteristics, ideologies, slavery, and even their version of democracy. The beliefs and ideologies found in ancient Greece had many appealing aspects to the Southern cotton planter. Slavery was entrenched in both societies. Upcountry planters were educated in the works of ancient Greek scholars and leaders. To them, the Greek civilization and government represented much of what they sought for their own. Aside from slavery, and although it might seem ironic, the planters found Athenian democracy appealing in that there was a sense of independence. They often shared the same beliefs. As Aristotle had proclaimed in his *Politics* that "...the lower sort are by nature slaves and it is better for them as for all inferiors that they should be under the rule of the master."[4] Upcountry planter James Henry Hammond echoed this same ideology in his "Mudsill Theory." Although elite Southerners found the history of ancient Greece appealing, they were also cognizant that they were eventually defeated by people who resided in territory to the north.[5] Perhaps the Southern planters felt that they had built a civilization that was strong enough to endure or maybe they just assumed that this was not to be their fate. However, it was ultimately. The Greek Revival house held a symbolic place to the cotton planter. Though some contemporary scholarship has examined various aspects about the importance of this housing style, this work explores the complex significance of the upcountry Greek Revival home as emblematic of the planter as a slaveholder because neither the wealth or the upkeep required to build and maintain such homes would have been possible without the unpaid labor of slaves.

For Northern industrialists, Greek Revival was symbolic of the wealth they had generated by the free market economy. However, for Southern cotton planters, this architectural design represented the status they had attained based on the labors of the enslaved. By embodying the ideas of ancient Greece, like that of slavery and democracy, upcountry Georgia, South Carolina, and North Carolina planters sought to make Greek Revival their style, as it was different from what was built

---

[4]Aristotle, *Book One.*

[5]Moore, "Attitude," 26.

by their fathers' generation. They also made individual modifications to the designs so that it was personal.

Greek Revival architecture was usually associated with the coastal or low-country South planters who grew wealthy over generations from the production of rice, indigo, tobacco and sea-isle cotton. In the early years of the nineteenth century, the upcountry regions of Georgia, South Carolina, and North Carolina prospered in the early years of the nineteenth century, however, from the cultivation of green seed cotton, which helped drive the markets. Many, like James Henry Hammond, John Caldwell Calhoun, and Judge John Harris, were prosperous planters as well as active politicians. They built elaborate Greek Revival plantation homes to mark their distinction from the more recognized or noted low country planters which have captured so much of the attention of historians.[6]

---

[6] For some examples of scholarship on low-country planters and plantations, see: Ralph Bailey, *A History of the South Carolina Lowcountry Plantation Landscape, 1663-1920: An Example of the Use of Plats and Plat Collections* (Charleston, S.C.: University of Charleston and The Citadel, 1997).; Douglas W. Bostick, *Sunken Plantations: The Santee Cooper Project* (Charleston, S.C.: The History Press, 2008); Jack P. Greene, Rosemary Brana-Shute and Randy Sparks, eds., *Money, Trade, and Power: The Evolution of Colonial South Carolina's Plantations* (Columbia, S.C.: University of South Carolina Press, 2001); N. Jane Isley, William P. Baldwin and Agnes Lelenad Baldwin, *Plantations of the Low-country: South Carolina 1697-1865* (Westbrook, ME: Legacy Publications, 1985).; Matthew Mulcahy, *Hubs of Empire: The Southeastern Lowcountry and British Caribbean* (Baltimore, MD: Johns Hopkins University Press, 2014); Lawrence Sanders Rowland, Alexander Moore and George C. Rogers, Jr., *The History of Beaufort, South Carolina: 1514-1861* (Columbia, S.C.: The University of South Carolina Press, 1996); Samuel Gaillard Stoney, *Plantations of the Carolina Low Country* (reprint of 1938 edition) (Charleston, S.C.: Carolina Art Association, 1955).; Drew A. Swanson, *Remaking Wormsloe Plantation: The Environmental History of a Lowcountry Landscape* (Athens, GA: University of Georgia Press, 2012); James H. Tuten, *Lowcountry Time and Tide: The Fall of the South Carolina Rice Kingdom* (Columbia, S.C.: The University of South Carolina Press, 2010); Steven Paul Whitsitt and Tina Skinner, *Lowcountry Plantations: Georgia & South Carolina* (Atglen, PA: Schiffer Publishing Ltd., 2010); Gordon S. Wood, *Empire of Liberty: A History of the Early Republic, 1789-1815* (Oxford: Oxford University Press, 2009)—particularly pp. 510-513.

Greek Revival architecture, although used throughout the United States, had particular appeal to many upcountry planters. It represented a renewal of the ideals embodied by the ancient Greeks, who firmly adhered to a division of society as well as the need for and use of slavery. Additionally, the upcountry cotton planter of the nineteenth century sought to differentiate himself from the planters of the previous generation, who used the Federal style of architecture. In a way, the Federal style was symbolic of democratic ideals whereas Greek Revival denoted the ideology of states' rights. The simplistic Federalist style reflected more of the tone of the era in which it was popular. As the American nation was being forged, attention had to be focused on democratic ideals, not superfluous displays of wealth. The Greek temple-like structures were a means of exhibiting an independent style. It reflected the desire to show independent ideologies as well as wealth. The upcountry cotton planters embraced the democratic ideologies of the ancient Greeks as well as the institution of slavery. These men were contradictory as they promoted republican ideals yet embraced the institution of slavery. They selected this architectural style, which was far grander than the previous generations' Federal style, but also because it was symbolic of rising power. The advocates of the states' rights political theory embraced this imposing architectural style and its relationship to the ancient slaveholding civilization. The massive pillars which upheld the house's pediment gave an impressive appearance, one distinctly of power. Throughout the South, large scale cotton planters embraced this architectural style. It stood as a testament to the wealth generated from the slave labor that produced their cotton crops. It had not been the architectural style of the tobacco, rice or indigo planter, for it was their generation's style. This was the architectural design that the upcountry cotton planters embraced. These men modified Greek Revival to conform to their ideals; but it also served as a valuable measure of who the man was that built the house.

With the prosperity generated from cotton cultivation, the upcountry planters of these states saw in their Greek Revival plantation house a lasting legacy to their power and societal status. Many planters sought to emulate various aspects of the ancient Greek society. Slave ownership and this architectural style were two of the most identifiable.

The warmer climate found in the South afforded a longer growing season, which resulted in an agrarian-based economy and society. With the tendency towards single staple crops, the plantation system emerged. Once a planter possessed the necessary acreage to operate in a profitable manner, the decision to construct a home on the confines of his property was an extraordinary one. Moving the family from the town borders or from the temporary structures in which they dwelled required great consideration. Choosing the site for the main house was a deliberate process undertaken with great care. Living on the land meant that the planter and his family would be isolated from towns and close neighbors, so many built their homes near rivers or roads (later near rail lines), which provided transportation for both people and goods to the market.[7] The main house was frequently constructed on top of a hill so that the family could overlook the property and revel in their possessions.[8]

In his seminal work, *Greek Revival Architecture in America: Being An Account of Important Trends In American Architecture And American Life Prior to the War Between the States* (1944), Talbot Hamlin proclaimed that "...the history of Greek Revival architecture in the southern states is a confused story of local influences, of conservatism in taste, and a sudden and late flowering."[9] By embracing this revival form of architecture, the upcountry planter was liberating himself from the established traditions in American building. The planters and their architects made their house designs personal, adding to the basic temple form to reflect their individual desires. Once the planters started moving away from the Federal style and building in Greek Revival, this design took on a different connotation to these Southerners. They molded an architectural style to conform to their societal needs and beliefs. Hamlin argued that "...the Greek Revival of the South stood for...the attempt to create a new and American architecture."[10] These planters altered the basic design and made it personal. In essence, it

---

[7]R. L. Allen, "Letters," 21.; E. Burke, *Pleasure*, 21.; Bremer, *Impressions*, 285.; Faust, *Mastery*, 1.; Severens, *Distinctive*, 30.; Woodman, *King*, 15.

[8]Bierce, "Frontier," 65.; J. F. Smith, *Houses*, 18.

[9]Hamlin, Account, 192.

[10]*Ibid*, 212.

came to be symbolic of the slaveholding South rooted in the very institution of slavery itself.

A revolution in agriculture took place in the late eighteenth and early nineteenth centuries. While many planters remained interested in the cultivation of tobacco, rice, and indigo, others began to consider the potential of the cotton crop. The transition to cotton as a primary crop was gradual but facilitated by the invention of the cotton gin which allowed the fiber to be quickly processed.[11] As a result, cotton could move more rapidly from the fields to the marketplace. Cotton regenerated the economy, pushing the American South into the forefront of world cotton producers.[12]

Backed by the illusion of a sense of financial stability emerging from cotton profits and the accompanying benefits of the cotton gin, large-property planters in Georgia, South Carolina and even North Carolina began concentrating their efforts on home construction on a more grand scale. Planters like Paul C. Cameron, James H. Hammond, and Wade Hampton II detailed in their personal letters their desire to build better homes with their greater financial security.[13] Gone were

---

[11]Gates, *Farmer's*, 7-8.; Freehling, *Anti-Confederates*, 17.; Although Eli Whitney obtained a patent in 1794, many planters copied his design and produced their own versions on the confines of their properties.

[12]Wright, *Political Economy*, 91. It is claimed by W. B. Seabrook, President of the Agricultural Society (1844) that the first cotton gin used in South Carolina, however, was designed and implemented by Ogden Holme, found in Harry Hammond, "Agriculture in South Carolina," HHP, SCL, MD, 5.

[13]To view examples of fluctuating cotton prices, see various *New Orleans Price Current, Commercial Intelligence and Merchants' Transcript*, Cameron Family Papers, Southern Historical Collection, University of North Carolina-Chapel Hill.; Various letters from the Cameron Family Papers, Southern Historical Collection, University of North Carolina-Chapel Hill, i.e. Kevin Hamilton to Duncan Cameron, January 8, 1836, May 11, 1836, May 19, 1836, and August 15, 1836.; Letter, unknown name to Paul C. Cameron, November 22, 1860.; Bryce, Henry & Walter Information on British Cotton Market sent to James Henry Hammond, Charleston, August 30, 1834, JHHP, SCL, MD, digital collection.; Sidney Crane, Account of Genl. Wade Hampton, January 19, 1833, HFP, SCL, MD.; Letter, William P. Brooks to James Henry Hammond, November 17, 1831, JHHP, SCL, MD.; Letter, [?} to Hon. Wade Hampton, March 13, 1832, HFP, SCL, MD.; Letter, George F. Platt to David C. Barrow, CDCBP, HRBML.

the days of transient-like edifices. Now the men of great holdings expressed their prosperity through their familial dwellings. To ensure continued profits, they practiced better land rotation and avoided packing up and abandoning their lands in search of virgin areas. Planters prioritized building a strong foundation for their families and Greek Revival set the tone for their era, which began approximately in 1820 and ended around the time of the outbreak of the Civil War.[14] At the very core was their ownership of human beings. Slaves and their labor generated the wealth necessary to fund the construction of their houses and the maintenance of their status.

The planters, aided by their architects, carefully considered the design, construction and decoration of the big house. Once built, the grand home was to be a legacy, kept within the family for as long as they were able to maintain the property. The residence was to be unique and as distinctive as the family who built it. As John B. Irving wrote in 1844 in the "Sporting Epistle From South Carolina" that the plantation house was "...well adapted to the wants of the family for which it was built..."[15] It would commemorate the planter and his posterity.[16] Carefully designated with a name, the house was more than simply a hereditary piece of property. It was a namesake. The contents of the plantation, inclusive of the chattel, were to be passed down.[17]

---

[14]Andrews, *Ambition*, 103.; Gowans, *Images*, 267-268.; Lane, *Romantic*, 8.; Parsons, *Inside*, 107.; Patrick, "Ecclesiological," 117.; For greater detail on the plans, architectural drawings and photographs of Federal Style homes, see John Linley, *The Georgia Catalog: Historic American Building Survey* (Athens, Georgia: The University of Georgia Press, 1982), 30-95, Chapter 5 - *The Federal Period* as well as Mills Lane, *Architecture of the Old South: Colonial & Federal* (Savannah, Georgia: The Beehive Press, 1996).

[15]Irving, "Sporting."

[16]"Account of Wade II," HFP, SCL, MD.; B. Collins, *White*, 167.; Grootkerk, "Artistic," 33.; Irving, "Sporting."; Severens, *Distinctive*, 4.; Letter, L. Berkman to Hon. James Henry Hammond, April 16, 1859, JHHP, SCL, MD.

[17]Avirett, *How*, 21.; "Ga., 1860, physician" in *Advice*, ed. Breeden, 59.; Letter, James Henry Hammond to Harry Hammond, February 19, 1856, JHHP, SCL, MD.

Location on the property was but one of many considerations in the building of the plantation house. By nature of its geophysical positioning, the southeastern United States is prone to intense humidity and high temperatures. With limited options to combat the extreme weather conditions, houses were structurally set up to alleviate some of this burden. Open rooms, with a great distance from floor to ceiling, provided a capacious area and better circulation of the inland, humid summer air.[18]

If this architectural style was, as Roger G. Kennedy asserted in his *American Greek Revival* (2010), "...the social and political statement of a popular state of feeling and...an aesthetic phenomenon,"[19] then how did these upcountry planters differentiate themselves from the others who built in this design? In essence, these men shared many similar motivations with their Northern brethren, specifically adopting this architectural style as a means to display their wealth. However, it was a distinct type of wealth, one forged by virtue of slaves laboring in the cotton fields. Although low country planters used this architectural style as well, the upcountry planters sought to truly make it emblematic of their cultural, social and political position in the United States. It was a means of securing their place among the American elite.

The examination and analysis of various familial letters, diaries, journals, and plantation records, show that these upcountry cotton planters took the popular Greek Revival architectural style and modified it to represent their cultural and societal placement. Since most upcountry planters were often not as revered as the low country planters, even as their wealth and power was equal, the legacy of their reputation as being inferior remained. By building their plantation estates and townhouses in the Greek Revival style, they put themselves in the same social classification as low country planters. Greek Revival architecture was a tie to the past and it bound them to ancient Greece and its slave society. These men linked themselves, if not justified, their alliance to this ancient society and its adherence to slavery through this

---

[18]"Editorial Correspondence," *Charleston Courier*.; Hamlin, *Account*, 203.; Linley, *Catalog*, 97.; J. F. Smith, *Houses*, 18.; Tucker, "On," 561.; Wieneck, *South*, 12-13.

[19]Kennedy, *Revival*, 14.

architectural style. What truly differentiated these upcountry cotton planters' Greek Revival homes from those constructed by Northern businessmen was that they were built by slave labor. The essence of the home was defined by the crop and those who toiled in the fields to cultivate it. Southern Greek Revival took on its own meaning. Upcountry planters sought to define their place in the economic and political world. Since they were late comers to the planter elite, they used this architectural style to place themselves in this category. Yet they clearly defined that they were from a new generation of planter. Their world was cotton and it was the slave who ultimately defined the planter and his possessions.

Sectionalism of the 1850s found its way into many aspects of life outside of politics. Though specific architectural styles were found in both the North and South, people from these geographic regions interpreted them in their own way. James C. Bonner contended in his article that Southern cotton planters expressed their crop-specific agricultural dependency through the construction of buildings on their property. Planters wanted everyone who saw their home and its surrounding structures to know its connection to a specific crop, which determined their status. They decided to build generously proportioned structures to help tell this story, and Greek Revival appeared to be the favorite because it best displayed their wealth and power, with the undertone that this profit was made at the hands of the enslaved.[20]

While some planters in Georgia could afford to build the Greek Revival style mansions that reflected their affluence, such homes were out of reach for most planters. Sometimes, a bumper crop of cotton would result in enough money for a farmer to build a fine house, but he was unlikely to maintain such a level of income. Many planters could only afford modest wooden homes without glass windows and contained little more than dowels to rest their clothing.[21] However, when the cotton market boomed in the 1830s, many planters set themselves

---

[20]Bonner, "Landscape," 5 and 7.

[21]E. Burke, *Pleasure*, 32 and 38.; Gowan, *Images*, 278.; Parsons, *Inside,* 108-109, and 113. Although Charles G. Parsons' account of his Southern travels reflects Northern bias, his descriptions of the modest homes are highly detailed.

to the task of creating magnificent and lavish homes, built on the land that was bringing them their wealth.

Prior to the 1830s, Georgia cotton planters had prospered from the sea-isle cotton, which was grown in the low country. The planters who took the chance to grow cotton in the more northern regions did not draw the same attention. Because many of their private papers were destroyed in the Civil War or discarded throughout the years, historians have struggled to study the true significance of the house to the planter himself. However, the patterns of the lives of these cotton planters of the more middle and northern regions of Georgia were dramatically different then their lowland counterparts.

As in most societies, family was important to South Carolinians. Marriage records indicate that social and politically prominent families intermingled their bloodlines.[22] Planters married within their own social and economic circle, which created an intricate pattern of interconnected plantation homesteads. Upcountry South Carolina planters also saw Charleston as a place to maintain a town because having a second home helped secure the status of the family name throughout plantation culture. Intermarriage of the prominent families was essential in Charleston society and these townhouses helped extend their social standing in plantation society.[23] The rapid growth and cultivation of cotton, combined with machinery to make the product market-ready, transformed the economic conditions of South Carolina and shifted in the concentration of wealth. Although rice still generated riches, cotton soon made new masters of the world of the upcountry.[24]

North Carolina was not as well-known as South Carolina for its plantation culture and society. Geographically situated between the affluent states of Virginia and South Carolina, in the antebellum era the state actually received the negative reference as a "valley of humiliation

---

[22]Clemens, ed., *Marriage*, ix and general review of the records, looking at specific family names.; Tasistro, "Theatrical," 190.

[23]Rogers, Jr., *Pinckneys*, 23.

[24]Hewatt, *Progress*, 118 and 119.; Rogers, Jr., "Transition," 87-88.; A. G. Smith, *Readjustment*, 1958), 2-3.; A. G. Smith, "Order," 95.; Stoney, *Low-Country*, 41.

between two mountains of conceit."[25] As within the other southern states, social status was reflected in the architectural style of the plantation homes. However, there was not a large planter class in North Carolina, as they comprised only six percent of the total population of the state.[26] As a result, there were fewer who engaged in the growing of cotton and building Greek Revival mansions.

Tobacco had been the bumper crop for North Carolina throughout the eighteenth and early nineteenth centuries. Rapidly stripping the land of its rich nutrients, tobacco crops limited the lifespan of the fields. Most plantations were not large enough to allow for crop rotation, so many tobacco farmers simply relocated. Farmers in North Carolina who planted crops appropriate to their field sizes were more successful. Cotton was grown in the state, but not to the extent it was in other Southern locations. Few planters here attained the social and economic status that cotton planters found within Georgia and South Carolina. Farmers and planters lived mostly in modest wooden structures without any extravagance.[27]

With agricultural modernizing agents at work within the state, a new momentum in construction took hold in the 1830s. Cotton had a positive impact on the economy of North Carolina as well. With a sense of newfound prosperity, planters started to build homes with character instead of basic functionality. Following the Greek Revival trend, most new houses were center hall structures, flanked by rooms on each side.[28]

The ownership of humans as property presents a fundamental moral dilemma for us today. How can a man who believed himself a

---

[25]Draper, "Southern Plantations," 2.; Frederick Law Olmstead in his *Journeys And Explorations in The Cotton Kingdom, Volume I,* speaks of how "North Carolina has a proverbial reputation for the ignorance and torpidity of her people…" (190). Louise Wigfall, as quoted in Mary Elizabeth Massey, *Refugee Life in the Confederacy* (Baton Rouge: Louisiana State University Press, 1964), 79, proclaimed it was her opinion that she "always thought North Carolina was not good for much…"

[26]Lefler and Newsome, *State,* 421.

[27]Bishir, "Proper," 48 and 49.; Robert, *Tobacco,* 15 and 17.

[28]Bishir, "Spirit," 131, 136 and 138.

gentleman and a pillar of his community, have taken away the essence of a human being, that of belonging to oneself? These cotton planters prided themselves as being politically, socially, and culturally astute. They were also men of influence who displayed their wealth through their possessions. Their cotton was grown by their slaves; their houses were built on the fruits of their labor. In essence, their status was reliant upon the labor of their slaves. The symbol of that status, the magnificent Greek Revival homes, were in fact marred by the reality that the homes were made possible only by the inhumane treatment of chattel property. There is a mythology that surrounds these homes, one that was created in the Reconstruction era and has been perpetuated. The beauty of these homes was an illusion that masked the cruelty of slavery.

The big house that stood as the summit of the property defined the plantations. Symbolic of the planters' tendency towards patriarchy, the home was the most prominent feature, dwarfing the surrounding structures that housed functional outbuildings, provided living accommodations for the slaves and contained operational material and livestock. The local population relied upon the planter.[29] Slavery allowed the planter to be a patriarch, as did the vast holdings of his plantation. Their dependence upon him enhanced this notion. Of the three states discussed, South Carolina was the one that enforced patriarchy to the highest degree. The legacy of familial lands, passed down through generations, in addition to the deeded chattel property, aided in the creation of such an atmosphere. The master provided the barest sustenance for his slaves.[30] The "big house" was intentionally grand in comparison to the smaller, plainer outbuildings, and this contrast dramatized the planter's authority. As reflected by Christopher Gustavus Memminger, "the Slave Institution of the South increased the tendency to dignify the family. Each planter is in fact a Patriarch-his position compels him to be a ruler in his household…"[31]

Ideologically, slavery was a capitalistic enterprise. Though slavery was primarily a Southern institution, Northerners benefitted from it as

---

[29]Joseph, "Black Hands," 59.
[30]Avirett, *How*, 6 and 21.; DeSaussure, *Old*, 31.
[31]Genovese, Made, 4.

well. "...slavery was indispensable to national economic development," Seth Rockman explains, "as access to slave-grown commodities and to markers in slave-agriculture regions proved essential to the lives and livelihoods of Americans far removed from the plantation South."[32] Rockman's historiographic article is filled with references to scholarship that examines the ideology of slavery in a capitalist sense.

Southern planters want their homes to project the refinement, dignity, and nobility commensurate with their family's social status. Therefore, families gave great consideration to the decoration of the rooms and the furnishings., for they sought to portray the genteel family. The Greek Revival architecture of the homestead also symbolized the power and wealth generated from slave labor which was reinforced through the social hierarchy of the estate.[33]

The reality was that most Southerners barely eked out an existence; yet a minority created a world that represented what was called the "Old South." The legacy and the allure of the plantations of the Old South are part of a deeply rooted American myth, fostered by the nostalgia produced in the post-bellum era of restoration when only a minority of planters were able to hold on to their majestic Greek Revival mansions. These big residences were unlike the tidewater or low country rice, indigo and sugar estates; these were the product of cotton money. Eighteenth century low country plantation houses were built in the Federal style. This architectural style defined the revolutionary and post-revolutionary generations. As American high society evolved in

---

[32]Rockman, "Future."

[33]The South Carolina State House, though not a private dwelling, is a magnificent Greek Revival structure originally designed with a front pediment that contained sculptures. Six of the nine images were of slaves toiling in both the cotton and rice fields, thus tying the style of architecture with the institution of bondage. Refer to John M Bryan, *Creating the South Carolina State House* (Columbia: University of South Carolina Press, 1999); The Henry Kirke Bush-Brown Papers, Library of Congress, Manuscripts Division; Christie Zimmerman Fant, *The State House of South Carolina, An Illustrated Historic Guide* (Columbia, South Carolina: R. L. Bryan, 1970), 116-118; and Letter, Johnson M. Mundy to Mary E. Mundy, February 20, 1861, JMMP, SCL, MD.

the nineteenth century, those of means followed the trends of Greek Revival. This marked a distinction.

The story of these upcountry planters who built homes in the Greek Revival architectural design, a style that they embraced as their own, has not fully been told. The planters of the upcountry regions of these states were distinct from their low country brethren, especially since they generated their wealth from cotton rather than other crops. For example, most plantation money in North Carolina had been acquired during the eighteenth century from tar and tobacco; cotton was rarely cultivated in this state since it was a somewhat perilous venture given the climatic and soil conditions. Those who resided in the upcountry region of the state who experimented in the risky endeavor of growing cotton were distinctive and distinguishable. Although the two planters selected for this study, William Williams and Paul C. Cameron, owned multiple plantations within their home state of North Carolina as well as others in deep South locales, they grew wealthy from the boom crop of the era at their upcountry plantations.

Extant letters, records, diaries, and plantation journals allow scholars a glimpse of the intimate world of these cotton planters and suggest the significance their grand homes held for them and their families.[34] Most of James Henry Hammond's, Paul C. Cameron and family, and John Caldwell Calhoun's correspondence and journals survived the vast destruction of the war, allowing us extraordinary insight into their world, especially with regard to the plantation, inclusive of its house, land, and slaves. Wade Hampton II and his family's letters are also very detailed, offering a glimpse of what he valued most in life. Editorial correspondence, articles of visits to the plantations, as well as corre-

[34]There is, of course, some challenge here. Many family papers and letters, as well as county and state records, were destroyed during the course of William Tecumseh Sherman's Atlanta Campaign, the March to the Sea and the Carolinas Campaign in addition to Potter's Raid. In fact, Wade Hampton II's son, Wade Hampton III, wrote about the loss of familial papers when Millwood was destroyed in a letter after the war. He stated "...when my house was robbed & burned by Sherman's, all my papers which were in it, shared the same fate." Letter, Wade Hampton III to General, no date, HFP, SCL, MD.

spondence between individuals outside of these families helps to outline the importance, and relevance that stemmed from the overall appearance of the house as well as the sphere of influence of the planter himself.

Although many of the planters who built these homes, like William Williams, John C. Calhoun, and Wade Hampton II, were no longer living by the time the Civil War commenced, their legacies were ever present. Some of their grand homes were destroyed, but others still stand and continue to represent this elite class and the brutal era of enslavement. The challenges of the years of war led to loss on many levels, whether it was fine décor, furniture, lives, or property in general. However, the harsh reality is that the remnants of these plantations are a lasting reminder of the brutal institution of slavery. The pillars that still stand at Millwood, for example, reflect an age of oppression.

These planters, who stood as the representatives of the slave-owning, cotton-producing Old South plantations, found themselves at the crossroads of a new order. Their world, their way of life and many of their possessions which had always defined them, passed into oblivion.

When the era came to a close, it was done with an air of certitude, so that it would not resurface. With the 13th Amendment and the end of the Civil War, the world of the Southern plantation owner collapsed. Without the slaves to provide unpaid labor to farm the land and maintain the homes, most lost their wealth and their fine possessions and their grand Greek Revival houses. They were masters of vast properties based on slave-generated labor. Many of these men and their families maintained their prestige, but not as masters of slave run cotton lands.

Though the plantation system would continue in a form, it would never again be one maintained through the labor of chattel slavery and directed by a class of planter elite who dominated Southern society, culture and politics.

CHAPTER 2

GREEK REVIVAL ARCHITECTURE IN AMERICA

Architectural styles in the United States tend to follow the trends found in Europe. Although the Greek Revival style used in American antebellum homes was not unique, plantation houses in this style spurred a mythology of the White landowners' gentility and charm. Steeped in the historical traditions of ancient Greece, this nineteenth century representation sought to embody the legacy left behind by this former glorious civilization. The southern cotton planter aristocracy embraced this history and molded an architectural style to conform to the needs of the slave-generated wealth that they had accumulated. Greek Revival became symbolic of the upcountry cotton planter class of Georgia, South Carolina, and North Carolina.

Greek architecture, particularly that of temples, is geometrically precise. A carefully planned use of line and structure brought forth a perfect proportionality.[1] As builder Alexander Jackson Downing proclaimed in his *The Architecture of Country Houses*, "...the purest of Greek architecture...are at once highly symmetrical and beautiful..."[2] Each building was constructed for not only the aesthetic, but for the functional as well. Climatic conditions factored into the design. The intended purpose of the portico was to alleviate the burdens of powerful sun, heat, and humidity.[3]

Realities of ancient Greek architecture held truths for Southern buildings to come. Great monuments such as the Parthenon, symbolized the status and eminence of Greek society and government. The ability to place so much of the nation's resources into the construction of such elaborate edifices helped to denote its alleged societal superiority. Although these great structures were visually appealing and served their designated purpose, many were deficient in their planning. Allur-

---

[1]Downing, *Country*, 22.; Greenough, "American," 206.; Tucker, "On," 560.
[2]Downing, *Country*, 29.
[3]Tucker, "On," 560 and 561.

ing in its appearance, the Parthenon was structurally inferior and contained numerous errors in its overall design.[4] To construct the resplendent, inadequacies occurred. Though flawed in structure, many of these markers have stood the test of time, though perhaps somewhat diminished by weather, war, and wear. Their survival is a reminder of the prominent legacy of the ancient Greece. This ideology transcended time and found its way into the American planter culture. The planters hoped to establish a lasting power and sought to leave a reminder of their reign. Their Greek Revival house was to remain for generations and serve as a symbol of this planter class.

As had been in the ancient empire of Greece, structures and landscapes stood as testament to the South's prestige and endurance. The Southern planter elite embraced these ancient traditions.[5] The upcountry planters sought to have a lasting civilization. They further evolved their ideologies and concepts about ancient Greece, designating themselves as a modern representation of sorts. The independent dominion maintained a plantation was seen as the embodiment of Plato's ideal structuring of government and society.[6] The lure of the legacy of ancient Greece and her history was a strong one. Archibald Alison, in his contribution to the January 8, 1846 edition of Nashville, Tennessee's *The Daily Orthopolitan,* proclaimed "the taste of Athens continued to distinguish its people long after they had ceased to be remarkable for any other or more honorable quality...to this day the lovers of art flock...to the Acropolis, and dwell with rapture on its unrivalled beauties..."[7] The stately buildings of Greece held great aesthetic appeal, radiating both beauty and power.[8] The efforts of the Southern planter class actualized this legacy.[9]

The planter class further evolved their ideologies and concepts about Greece, designating themselves as a modern representation of sorts. The framework of the ancient realm was seen as rigidly structured

---

[4]Burchard and Bush-Brown, *Social,* 36 and 37.; Scranton, *Greek Architecture*, 30.
[5]Greenough, "American," 209.; Mumford, *Darcy Lectures*, 35-36.
[6]Cardwell, "Plantation House," 5 and 16.
[7]Alison, "Architecture."
[8]Greenough, "Structure," 115.
[9]Greenough, "American," 209.

and organized. Southern high society, too, placed itself at the zenith of societal order as well as the model for maintenance of a semblance of peacefulness and harmony. The independent dominion maintained on a plantation was seen as the true embodiment of Plato's ideal structuring of government and society.[10]

The library shelves of the great planters included Plato's works, particularly *The Republic*, along with many others works by the celebrated masters.[11] These nineteenth century men studied the classics with vigor and absorbed many of the ancient ideals. For example, Plato, in *The Republic*, writes that the leader who "...rules those who are really simple and just, while they serve their ruler's interests because he is stronger than they, and his subjects promote his happiness to the complete exclusion of their own."[12] Aristocratic Southern planters embraced this idea that they, the strong leaders, rightfully ruled over the simple (the slaves), who would accept his autocracy with no thought to their own happiness.[13] Following this line of thought, the planter could claim to be helping the slave by guiding him through what would be an unproductive life without this much needed assistance and by enlightening his "inferior" status.[14] The rigid, organized social framework of ancient Greece also appealed to the Southern planters who wished to elevate their status, believing it would lead to a semblance of peace and harmony between the slave and master. Planters embraced the logic that leaders were the most concerned about national interests, a concept found in Plato's writings. The individual who "governs" did so embodying all that is found within their civilization.[15]

---

[10]Cardwell. "Plantation Houses," 5 and 16.

[11]Coit, Portrait, 383. Ms. Coit cited Calhoun's book list as found in Clemson College Papers. In contacting the reference librarian at Clemson University, he told me that this list was no longer available. This book was also on the shelf of James Henry Hammond's Redcliffe.

[12]Plato, *The Republic*, 25.

[13]Cardwell, "Plantation House," 5 and 6.

[14]Calhoun, "Remarks," in Volume XIV, 4.; Letter, James Henry Hammond to William G. Simms, April 19, 1854, JHHP, LOC, MD.

[15]Baker, *Political Thought of Plato and Artistotle*, 109.

The planter and slave maintained a unique relationship with each other, one in which the master believed he was aiding the slave, guiding him through what would be an unproductive life without this much needed assistance.[16] Not surprisingly, slaves had no choice but to acquiesce to the social order imposed by their masters. Slave owners knew they needed to keep their chattel inferior in order to make their plantations profitable. There was a cognitive dissonance in this process; on one hand, the White masters needed to believe that their slaves were not fully human so they could justify continuing to hold them in bondage. On the other hand, many slaveholders did acknowledge that their slaves were more than just property. Walter Johnson writes that "slaveholders were fully cognizant of slaves' humanity-indeed, they were completely dependent upon it."[17] Ultimately, this was ironic since planters maintained that chattel were property. Hence, these planters' thoughts were convoluted. Slaves had to produce for their masters in multiple ways. Despite the ways they may have acknowledged their slaves' humanity, slaveholders needed slavery to be self-perpetuating to ensure both their profits and their continued was of life. In *The Half Has Never Been Told*, Baptist writes that slavers equated "...slavery's expansion with its prosperity, with the growth of their own wealth and power..."[18] In order for slave owners to be successful, slavery needed to be a self-perpetuating system. This in itself is abhorrent, something that we cannot comprehend in modern day.

Ancient Greece found its place in the dominion of the Southern cotton planter, in the political, social and architectural realms. Ideologies and theories shared in Plato's *The Republic* were ones that the upcountry cotton planter applied to his life. The essence of the big house was of great significance to the planter. The plantation house was also symbolic of the South's quest for permanence. Though perhaps some architectural styles were used both north and south of the Mason-

---

[16]Fragment from Henry Kirke Brown's Notebook, December 1855, HKBBP, LOC, MD.; Grund, *Aristocracy*, 149.; James Henry Hammond, "Speech on the Admission of Kansas" in *Slavery Defended*, 122-123.; "Slavery in the Southern States," 353.

[17]Johnson, *River*, 207.

[18]Baptist, *Half*, 346.

Dixon line, those in the South embodied the slaveholding, planter aristocracy-dominating world that guided the thoughts, practices and actions of this distinct region of the country. Guy A. Cardwell expanded on these concepts, while looking at the plantation home in terms of both historical and literary perspectives. Cardwell assessed, "these actual mansions, like the houses in Southern fiction, occupied a central position in a series of linked analogies. Each plantation aimed at being more-or-less self supporting little worlds modeled after some ideal on the order of Plato's republic [sic]. The plantation house was a dramatic center; it brought everything to a focus."[19]

Temples were one of the key structures that dominated the skyline of ancient Greek city-states, particularly that of Athens. These structures were consecrated to a specific deity or at least as a locale from where people could worship.[20] People ventured to these temples for guidance and as a means of attaining assurance from a force that was beyond their control in order to answer their needs. In the nineteenth century, the planter and his home served in a similar capacity. Planters offered financial assistance and advice to their neighbors, particularly those of lower economic standing. People came to their plantation homes in order to attain this guidance.[21]

Many aspects of these piedmont cotton planters' homes and properties were the embodiment of the legacy of ancient Greece. These vast columned homes stood as testaments to the planter as well as this exalted ancient civilization. E. T. Shaffer explains that South Carolina Governor John L. Manning's Milford "...linked the life of the Old South with a glory that was Greece..."[22]

Greek Revival architecture served as a rejoinder to the simplistic, nationalist style found with the preceding era's structural design. This Southern antebellum version derived its roots not from Americana but from the historical legacy left from when Pericles ruled over Athens. Steeped in the religious tradition of the pantheon of mythological

---

[19]Cardwell, "Analogical," 5.

[20]Scranton, *Greek Architecture*, 9.

[21]B. Collins, *White*, 37.

[22]Shaffer, *Gardens*, 184.

Greek gods, the temples constructed to their honor reflected the undercurrents of monumental power. With Greece serving as the representative, the plantation house built in the Revival format epitomized these notions.[23] Optimism expressed through Greek Revival infused a promise of a great American empire, like that of the glorious antediluvian civilizations.[24] Ancient Greece was also imbued with a tradition held dear to the Southern planters, that of slavery. Deemed as the "corner-stone" by South Carolinian James Henry Hammond, slavery was reflected both in the ideals espoused in ancient Greece and the antebellum southern United States.[25]

This architectural style found its place in America initially in the North, specifically in Philadelphia.[26] Public structures were the first ones built in this design. Gradually, prosperous individuals embraced this style for their private domiciles. Nationalism, democratic trends, warfare, and culture were reasons why Greek Revival took hold, yet there was not one decisive impetus.

The essence of Greek architecture allowed for interpretation. In sharp contrast to the formal styles of the preceding era, the new ornate detailing heightened emotional expression. In sharp contrast to the formal Federal styles of the preceding era, the new ornate detailing heightened emotional expressions. Although Southern plantation owners did not overlook previous architectural styles, Greek Revival architecture allowed them to assert their class and status.[27] Greek Revival homes on Southern plantations were reminiscent of classical temples. Following the traditional manner, the pillars upholding the front pediment reflected the various column orders. The columns at the front of a Greek Revival plantation home sometimes echoed the ornate Corinthian,

---

[23]Ellis, "Greeking," 1.; Greenough, "American," 206.; Gowans, *Images*, 267-268.; Linley, *Catalog*, 30 and 97. For a brief overview of Athenian architecture during the Age of Pericles, refer to Wallace Everett Caldwell, *The Ancient World* (New York: Rinehart & Company, Inc., 1949), 239-244.

[24] Peck, "Parlor," 239.

[25]Hammond, "Letters," 388.

[26]Lane, *Louisiana*, 96.

[27]Hamlin, *Account*, 188.; Latrobe, *Journal*, 139.

basic Doric, or Tuscan (a Roman column) style.[28] In addition to the historical foundations of the style, the porticoed house functioned as a measure of protection from the the sun.[29] Weather and temperature were big factors in the design and selection of architectural styles.[30]

The evolution of Greek Revival architecture in United States required many different facets. One such component revolved around the knowledge of Greek structures and forms. Archaeological excavations enabled architects to learn from their findings and constructed their own interpretations of the structures of antiquity.[31] But Greek Revival architecture was far more than just a facsimile of the original structures themselves. Thomas U. Walter, the fourth architect of the U.S. Capitol, expressed this in a 1 January 1841 article in *The Journal of The Franklin Institute* proclaiming "the Popular idea that to design a building in Grecian taste is nothing more than to copy a Grecian building, is altogether erroneous…"[32] This was but one attempt to dispel American adoption of Greek architecture styles was merely a duplication. With great zeal, architects across the nation sought to create their own version of these ancient temples. Americans embarked on the creation of their own Grecian format.[33]

The nineteenth century upcountry cotton planters wanted to differentiate themselves from earlier masters. Cotton was their crop; the successful growth of cotton done through slave labor had generated a source of wealth for them.[34] With their own crop, these planters wanted to display their independence through a different architectural style from the previous generations' Federal style. They sought to represent their stature and affluence through a permanent means. With prosperity came the desire to portray one's wealth and status. The house was among the most substantial and eternal of possessions through which

---

[28]Linley, *Catalog*, 99 and 105.; Perkerson, *Columns in Georgia*, 6.; O. P. Smith, *Domestic*, 19.; Tuthill, *Condition*, 83.

[29]Lane, *Romantic*, 8.

[30]"The Rev. Dr. Storrs," *The New York Times.*; Tucker, "On," 560.

[31]Buchard and Bush-Brown, *America*, 93.; Peck, "Parlor," 239.

[32]Walter, "Architecture," 12.

[33]Greenough, "American," 206.

[34]Ford, *Deliver*, kindle edition (no page numbers are visible).

the planter could display the perpetual reminder of his power. Large and grand, the big house stood as a measure of many things. The essence of its design, that of Grecian (Greek Revival), provided great depth to its overall meaning. Ancient Greece had been an impressive as well as an enduring power, one that the Southern planter aspired to emulate and imitate.[35] Grecian structures left a distinguished legacy, a recollection of the prestige of the glorious era, as represented in their architecture. the planter class aspired to follow the model, but to never allow their civilization to succumb to another authority. Cotton planters bound themselves to this architectural style for many reasons. There was solace in the vestiges of ancient Greece.

Though not all architects readily embraced this style, several eighteenth and nineteeth century authors published lavishly illustrated volumes that helped spur the explosion of Greek Revival architecture in America and Europe. One of the most notable, Stuary and Revett's *Antiquity of Athens*, was a five-volume set written over sixty-eight years (1762-1830) and based upon their own personal observations and explorations Greece.[36] Published in England, these monographs made their way to America, but were available only at great cost. Stuart and Revett were not the first to publish the findings from their personal excavations of Greek sites but their work inspired others.

Impassioned by the prospect of revealing the splendor of this temple form, Julien-David Le Roy (Le Roi) conducted his own research and produced *Le ruines des plus beaux monuments de la Grece* (1758), hoping to attain the accreditation for giving impetus to this new style.[37] Though LeRoy's book preceded *The Antiquities of Athens,* Stuart and Revett's series set the precedent for the great Greek-style architectural books and inspired architects in England and the United States to try to capture the essesence of ancient Greece. Others then set out to produce similar works, among them Stephen Riou's *The Grecian Order Of Architecture, Delineated and Explained from the Antiquities of Athens.* Riou published this work soon after the release of the first volume of

[35]Seebohm and Woloszynski, *Oaks*, 16.

[36]Lane, *Romantic*, 8.; Wiebenson, *Sources*, 10, 18 and 74.

[37]Watkin, *Athenian*, 14.

The Antiquities of Athens. The contents of his book closely following the trends established by Stuart and Revett.[38]

The Stuart and Revett books were aesthetically appealing, filled with landscape portraits with the structures as they had stood and in partial decay, as they appeared when these men made their observations. They incorporated pen and ink sketches of the architectural features of the various structures as well as of the plans. *Volume The Second*, published initially in 1787, highlighted the Temple of Minerva (Athena)—the Parthenon. Stuart and Revett included in their description the key figures who enabled the construction of the monumental temple, that of Pericles, Callicrates, Ictinus and Phidas.[39] In addition, they also incorporated the evaluations made by previous explorers of the likes of Sir George Whaler and Dr. Jacob Spon. When these men arrived in Athens in the late 17th century, the Parthenon looked similar to its original appearance. Their accounts detailed the Venetian attack in 1687 that effectively diminished the temple's overall composition and appearance.[40] Stuart and Revett incorporated Whaler and Spon's findings with that of their own personal observations as to ascertain many of their conclusions about ancient Greek architecture.

Although Stuart and Revett found some of their predecessors' discoveries helpful, there were those that they met with disdain. They assailed Sir William Chambers' appraisals, proclaiming that they had "…so little foundation in real facts…"[41] Julien-David Le Roy was not exempt from such criticism either. Stuart and Revett challenged his

---

[38]Stephen Riou's work, published in 1768, has proven difficult to find. It seems that only a few of the original versions exist in the United States. Although the Library of Congress lists the book in their holdings, searches in the General Reading Rooms, Rare Book Reading Room and Folios proved futile. No staff member, after conducting multiple lengthy searches, from any of these locations was able to locate the book.

[39]Stuart and Revett, *Second*, 1. It has proved a difficult task to view the original copies of these works. At the Library of Congress, they were unable to provide these original volumes to me in the various reading rooms, although they are in the catalog. In searching for original copies, I came across one location, a book dealer who is selling the five volumes, which retail for $37,338.60.

[40]*Ibid*, 3.

[41]Stuart and Revett, *Third*, x.

surveying appraisals of structures in the beginning of their *Volume The Third*, claiming that Le Roy erred in his assessments.[42]

The Antiquities of Athens series was resplendent with its vivid imagery, transporting the reader to the sites of these architectural masterpieces. The drawings of the temples were done with great precision so as to delineate the detailed craftsmanship in the pediments, cornices, columns and other parts of the structures. The various depictions as well as plans of the different temples, such as the Parthenon and the Temple of Theseus, helped to represent the overall essence of ancient Greek architecture.[43] It was from these drawings that many American architects got their inspiration and gained impetus for the Greek Revival house. In viewing these drawings, one can see the transformation of the Greek temple into the cotton plantation big house, stunning with its columns and pediment. Though James Stuart and Nicholas Revett's books were not the sole texts published in the eighteenth and nineteenth centuries that highlighted ancient Grecian architecture, their influence appeared to have the most profound effect.[44]

The initial pattern books used by American architects, builders, and carpenters were all from abroad, thus making them all the more costly. Many who learned these trades did so at the hands of studying these valuable sources.[45] At last, in 1818, Philadelphian John Bioren published the nation's initial pattern book. However, most still relied on the European books.

In his defining work *The Builder's Assistant Containing The Five Orders Of Architecture, for the Use of Builders, Carpenters, Masons, Plasters, Cabinet Makers and Carvers*, the foreign-born John Haviland helped introduce Americans to the column orders, which are so critical to the Grecian style.[46] This work inspired American architects, designers and builders to produce their own guide books. Various architectural books flooded the market with both plates of stylistic options as

---

[42]*Ibid*, viii.

[43]Stuart and Revett, *Second*, 9, 10 and 11.; Stuart and Revett, *Third*, 5 and 6.

[44]Lane, *Romantic*, 8.

[45]Letter, B. Henry Latrobe to Robert Mills, July 12, 1806, RMP, LOC, MD.

[46]Haviland, *Assistant*, iii.; Lane, *Romantic*, 25.

well as personal treatises by the architect himself on the relevance and significance of these styles. Asher Benjamin, a New England builder, created various guides in order to provide instruction in designing buildings and houses. It was not until the sixth edition of his *The American Builder's Companion* (1827) however, that he truly brought to light all the details and finery of Greek Revival architecture. Benjamin's emphasis on the column orders was enhanced by the incorporation of the mythological-historical stories as motivation the designation for each.[47] His work also incorporated plates in addition to the mechanics as to how to construct the various components of modern Grecian adapted architectural style.

Another influential book published and used in the United States was Andrew Jackson Downing's *The Architecture Of Country Houses* (1827) in which he pointed out that "...a good house...is a powerful means of civilization."[48] The planter class clearly embodied this notion. The Greek Revival home, their specified choice of architectural style, was a symbol of their world, their power, and their lifestyle. Downing went on to further his thesis, citing that "...the individual home has a great social value for a people" as well as that "...there is moral influences in a country home..."[49] Downing himself was no advocate of the upcountry planters' favorite style as he believed it served a limited purpose though it was tasteful in its application. However, his expression about the relevance of the house itself was found firmly planted in the ideology of these men of the South.[50]

Interestingly, Downing refers to "...another hand" and incorporated the commentary made by this unidentified person about Greek architecture. "Again, we have the pure Greek temple...This can be used in a special way (having its individual expression). It is the most simple, rational, and harmoniously elegant style..."[51] He continues, "buildings which have but one object, and which require one expression

---

[47]Benjamin, *Builder's*, 31-32.
[48]Downing, *Country*, xix.
[49]Ibid.
[50]Ibid, 21 and 41.
[51]Ibid, 20 and 29.

of that object, cannot be built in a style better adapted to convey the single idea of their use than in the Grecian temple form."[52]

Column orders, or types, were one of many features of ancient Greek architecture presented in these texts. These column orders found a significant home in the Revival style. A modest and unadorned style, the Doric brought forth a smooth or straight capital appearance. This antiquated column style is the most traditional of all the orders. Its volute classifies the Ionic order, a slightly more ornate feature not in the Doric style. Thirdly, and last of the true Greek line, is the Corinthian. The most elaborate and adorned in form, Corninthian columns are enhanced with the curvature found in the tips of the sculpted acanthus leaves.[53] Asher Benjamin, in his *The American Builder's Companion*, proclaimed that "the Corinthian order is proper for all buildings, where elegance, gaiety and magnificence are required..."[54] In many instances, the upcountry cotton planters used this type of column to adorn their plantation homes. Architect Nathaniel F. Potter clearly specified that he planned to use the Corinthian order for the pillars at the entrance of John L. Manning's plantation, Milford.[55]

Greek "fever" took a strong hold over American architects as well as their employers. Although not all embraced this modernized version of the ancient style, its popularity rapidly exploded on the American scene. Benjamin Henry Latrobe, one of the architects of the Capitol building in Washington, DC, himself proclaimed, "I am a bigoted Greek in the condemnation of the Roman architecture...the Grecian style can be copied without impropriety..."[56] Although many of Latrobe's works were public structures, he recognized how defining the Greek Revival edifice was of its proprietor. When reflecting upon one such bank, he claimed that it was "...a pure specimen of Grecian simplicity in design, and Grecian permanence in execution, the existence

---

[52]Ibid, 22.

[53]Benjamin, *Builder's*, 33.; Haviland, *Assistant*, 3 and 8.; O. P. Smith, *Domestic*, 19-21.; Tuthill, *Condition*, 83.

[54]Benjamin, *Builder's*, 35.

[55]Potter, "Specifications."

[56]Latrobe, *Journal*, 139.

and taste of this building is due, not to the architect, but to a man…"[57] Greek Revival was definitive.

The columns, the pediments and facades signified the emergence of a new distinction in architectural style. Soon, American streets included public structures of the Greek Revival form. Greek Revival rapidly became the favored style initially for judicial and governmental structures. Two prominent examples of this are the United States Capitol and the South Carolina State House, both of which, at points, had plans, though perhaps not truly under consideration, that incorporated images of slaves into the architectural design.[58] The plans for both structures underwent many changes. The U.S. Capitol extension plan of 1853, as designed by United States Army Captain Montgomery C. Meigs, called for pediments to define the new wings being added to the original structure. This commenced a careful search for the appropriate symbols designated for placement in the pediments, particularly amidst the mounting sectional tension within the nation over slavery.[59]

In 1855, abolitionist Henry Kirke Brown was the first sculptor to send design plans to Montgomery C. Meigs for the pediment of the House of Representatives wing. In his proposal, the central figure was the female embodiment of America, who dwarfed all other symbols of this country. Among those images was that of a slave atop a bale of cotton, the so-called "Thinking Negro."[60] Meigs advised Brown to remove this sculpture from his pediment upon the initial submission of this plan.[61] The nation as a whole could not tolerate such a figure gracing its national capitol that stood precariously geographically located

---

[57]Latrobe, "Anniversary," 81.

[58]Savage, *Standing*, 32 and 38.

[59]Somma, *Apotheosis*, 17.

[60]Fragment from Henry Kirke Brown's Notebook, December 1855, HKBBP, LOC, MD.; Photograph of Enlargement of 'Thinking Negro' sculpture and First Pediment Design for the House Wing, HKBBP, LOC, MD.; The model for the pediment for the House wing of the U.S. Capitol composed by Henry Kirke Brown is no longer in the possession of the Library of Congress. All that remains are the photographs that Brown had taken of the pediments.

[61]Fragment from Henry Kirke Brown's Notebook, December 1855, HKBBP, LOC, MD.

between North and South.[62] Henry Kirke Brown however found acceptance for his slave sculpture from a smaller audience in South Carolina for the new State House.

Architectural plans for the new South Carolina State House were similar to the structure that stands today in Columbia. There was one major difference found in the design sketches for the pediment not included in the final product.[63] Hired to sculpt two medallions to adorn the capital building in order to honor two of her native sons, Henry Kirke Brown moved to South Carolina in 1859.[64] The men of power within the state were pleased with his work upon completion and then called upon him to extend his stay in the Palmetto state so that he could to produce a pediment.[65] Once again Brown had a chance to create a pediment in which he could place the true representations of the region. Upon the submission of his plans in 1860, Brown received a favorable response from state leaders, like the "...Hampton's [sic], Manning's [sic]..."[66] It was the powerful men of the planter class who granted their ascensions to the pediment design. Much like their Greek Revival homes that had been built as a result of slave labor, their capitol would now stand as a testament that Greek Revival and slavery were bound together. Both Wade Hampton II and John L. Manning resided in Greek Revival homes; now their capital building would reflect their homesteads in the usage of this same architectural style.

---

[62]When Henry Kirke Brown submitted his revised plans for a pediment sans the slave figure, his proposal was rejected. See: Letter, M.C. Meigs, Captain of Engineers in Charge, to Honorable Jefferson Davis, Secretary of War, March 20, 1865, HKBBP, LOC, MD..; Letter, written by Honorable Jefferson Davis, Secretary of War, March 26,1856, HKBBP, LOC, MD.

[63]After South Carolina seceded and Fort Sumter was attacked, the state began using her financial resources for other means and had to suspend work on the Capitol building. See: Letter, R. W. Gibbs to Henry Kirke Brown, May 13, 1861, HKBBP, LOC, MD.

[64]Letter, John R. Niernsee to H. K. Brown, Esq., April 2, 1859, HKBBP, LOC, MD.; Photographs of the marble medallions of Robert Y. Hayne and George McDuffie, HKBBP, LOC, MD.

[65]William Morris Davis, "Heroism in Art," HKBBP, LOC, MD.

[66]Letter, J R Niernsee to H. K. Brown, March 10, 1860, HKBBP, LOC, MD.

Originally the fronton was to be carved with different representations of the state. "...Hope, Justice and Liberty..." were central to the pediment, flanked by slaves laboring in the fields and moving cotton bales. Rice and cotton, the source of great wealth in the Palmetto State, and the bondspeople who produced them, filled most of the gable. In the farthest corners was a slave on each side, who was in a relaxed position.[67] Plans to have slaves sculpted in the United States Capitol had been previously rejected, but the Greek Revival South Carolina State House was to have the source of her wealth, the slaves, as prominent fixtures on the building.[68] These figures, images of this institution and symbols of their labors, were not to be hidden within the context of the pediment; they were to be on prominent display. Each was to stand roughly ten feet in height.[69] South Carolinians were boasting that they held men and women in bondage by forever enshrining their labor force on the State House.

By juxtaposing freedom, equity and bondage, in one scene helped to portray the philosophy espoused by the planter class that these ideals were harmonious and congruent.[70] It was with their assent that this pediment was to be sculpted and carved, the capital building forever

---

[67]Letter, Johnson M. Mundy to Mary E. Mundy, February 20, 1861, JMMP, SCL, MD.; Letter, Jno. Niernsee to H. K. Brown, Jan. 19, 1860, HKBBP, LOC, MD.; Bryan, *Creating*, 52-53.; Image, "The New State House, The Capital Of South Carolina—From a Sketch By Our Special Artist," SCP, SCL, MD. (The pediment, however, is not clearly detailed in this sketch.); Photographs, Design for Pediment, State House, South Carolina, Right Hand Fragment and Left Hand Fragment, HKBBP, LOC, MD, Vol V: 1333 A, 1369 A and 1369B.; In the sixth issue of Confederate currency (April 1863-February 1864), one of the $10 bills (T304) also used an image of this South Carolina State House. Most of the original documentation, including the model of the pediment, regarding the plans for the South Carolina State House was destroyed in the grand conflagration that took place in Columbia on February 17, 1865 during the course of Federal occupation.

[68]Bryan, *Creating*, 48-49.; Savage, *Standing*, 32, 35 and 36.

[69]Letter, H. K. Brown to Henry D. Udall, May 1, 1860, HKBBP, LOC, MD.

[70]Fant, *Illustrated*, 116-118.

bearing the institution of slavery.[71] The South Carolina State House would be one of their great symbols to help emphasize the righteousness of this institution. Though Brown's goal was to depict slavery in a monument, his motivation was perhaps not quite the same as the planters. Brown wasn't using these statues to promote slavery; he was attempting to show the horrors of this institution through his artistry. Placing this symbol of Southern wealth and power on a Greek Revival structure would have cemented[72] the association of this architectural style and the institution of chattel slavery. Though this had long been shown before by the cotton planters' columned porticoed houses, the state capital would further cement the union of Greek Revival and slavery.

The intended pediment with its sculpture of slaves, however, was not to be. The Civil War brought a change in the allotment of funds within the state and halted the construction of the State House. Fortunately, the vision of the building with slaves embedded in the pediment too would fortunately be terminated.[73] Architect Henry Kirke Brown believed that the structure, upon completion, would be "...the finest building in the country not excepting the new Capitol at Washington."[74] The empty shell of the State House was all that would stand for the next few years. The pediment, as so designed to include slaves, would pass into a distant memory, mostly forgotten in history as well.

In 1860, the cotton planter class found another tie binding them and their institution of chattel slavery to Greek Revival architecture. When the South Carolina secession convention initially met on 17 December 1860, the delegates met at the First Baptist Church in Columbia.[75]

---

[71]Letter, J R Niernsee to H. K. Brown, March 10, 1860, HKBBP, LOC, MD.

[72]Davis, "Heroism," HKBBP, LOC, MD.

[73]Letter, James Jones to Governor Pickens, April 28, 1861, JJP, SCL, MD.

[74]Letter, Johnson M. Mundy to Mary E. Mundy, February 20, 1861, JMMP, SCL, MD.

[75]Blease, Destruction, 4.; Ordinance of Secession, SCP, SCL, MD.

Although secession was not officially declared there, the initial meeting took place in a symbolic structure—that of a majestic brick Greek Revival building.[76]

Greek Revival and slavery seemed to be inherently tied together. The connotations of this architectural design were intrinsically different to Southerners than its significance to their fellow Americans. To the men of wealth and power of the South, the institution that gave them their status found relevance, perhaps an interpretation, in this architectural style.[77]

In the private sector, architect George Hadfield put his training to work for plans for a member of the initial first family, effectively incorporating Greek Revival into the southern architectural style. Years after the passing of his mother, George Washington Parke Custis commissioned the British architect to draw plans for his Virginia home. Recognized as the preeminent classical piazza in a Southern place of residence, Arlington (commonly known as the Custis-Lee Mansion) embodied the tradition of ancient Greek design.[78] Thus began the 19th century architectural pursuit of fusing the Greek style into the Southern plantation homestead.

Though Hadfield brought the architectural style to the South in general, it was two other men who helped to fuse it on to the scene of Georgia, South Carolina and North Carolina. William Jay and Robert Mills were credited for truly molding this design to conform to the needs and wishes of prominent individuals of this region.[79] It would be in this area of the country that the great pillared cotton plantation

---

[76] Ordinance of Secession, SCP, SCL, MD..; Personal observations of the historical displays in the interior and the exterior of the First Baptist Church, 1306 Hampton Street, Columbia, S.C.; When Sherman's armies converged on the city on February 17, 1865, the soldiers sought out this structure. Allegedly a sexton directed the troops to another church, in an effort to save this building.

[77]Gowans, *Images*, 281.

[78]Lane, *Romantic*, 12.; Lane, *Virginia*, 174.; Nelligan, *Custis-Lee*, 2, 5 and 29.; Whiffen and Koeper, *Volume I*, 172. In researching the Custis-Lee Papers at the Library of Congress, I could find no records kept by George Washington Parke Custis regarding the building of this house.

[79]Cunningham, "South Carolina Architecture," MVWP, SCL, MD., 15; Hamlin, *Account*, 200.

homes were erected. Jay and Mills gave impetus to this style through their designs of city/town structures for many of the prominent families of the South as well as the state of South Carolina. Robert Mills' built his initial Greek Revival structure, the First Baptist Church of Charleston in low country South Carolina, which was the quintessential Greek Revival building, having meticulously followed the true Greek temple symmetry and arrangement.[80]

Among many of the great works constructed under Mills' tutelage, the Ainsley Hall mansion in Columbia, South Carolina epitomized all that Greek Revival architecture was to embody. Four majestic Ionic pillars that were crowned by a pediment graced the façade of the structure.[81] Though many of Mills' Greek Revival contributions were found in public structures, this is but one of his prominent private edifices.

Greek Revival was not only used in public structures as well as town houses but found itself used greatly by the upcountry planter class. As Greek Revival became more popular and began to stand as a symbol of this socio-economic class, many modified their existing Federal style structures by adding Greek-inspired columns and a pediment; Fort Hill, the home of John C. Calhoun, is one example of a Federal style home embellished with Greek columns.[82] Fairntosh, one of the Cameron family's North Carolina plantation homes, was modified into a Greek Revival structure with the addition of a columned veranda, which altered the overall appearance and character of the home.[83] Throughout the upcountry South, plantation houses were constructed in the Greek Revival form, whether built in the true architectural style or modified from their original style. Wade Hampton II painstakingly transformed his modest residence into one of the most magnificent Greek Revival homes of the era, one that was legendary for its beauty and grandeur.[84] Behind the scenes of these great changes were the

---

[80]Mills, *Statistics*, 411.

[81]HABS, AH.

[82]Cunningham, "South Carolina Architecture," MVWP, SCL, MD, 11-12.

[83]Letter, Jean Cameron Syme to Mary Anderson, May 31, 1827, CFP, SHC.

[84]Irving, "Sporting."

slaves whose unpaid labor supplied both the profit and the manpower such construction required.

The American architects who built these planters' mansions found themselves reliant upon the aforementioned various guidebooks produced here and abroad. For example, Nathaniel F. Potter, whose buildings included the Charleston Hotel as well as Milford, John L. Manning's plantation, readily acknowledged his use of these instructional books. In his "Specifications for a House to be Built in Sumpter [sic] district, South Carolina, for John L. Manning Esq.," Potter concluded the formal written specifications with "all the above plates referenced to are from Lafever's *Modern Architecture* of 1835."[85]

Private letters, diaries and the account books of these planters, however, did not always specify which architect designed a house or which design books may have been consulted. Researchers can only speculate as to the resources used, based upon other architectural and design examples. For instance, Redcliffe "...was designed and planned by the General himself, and constructed by mechanics under his direction."[86]

As Roger G. Kennedy pointed out in his *Greek Revival America* (2010), "the largest, most ambitious, and most sophisticated houses built during Greek Revival...are known to us by the names of their owners, not their architects...it does indicate that the American Greek Revival was the social and political statement of a popular state of feeling..."[87] He furthered this thought by proclaiming that "Greek Revival was a statement of power."[88] The architect himself was not considered to be significant because it was the planter who built his mansion. In addition, not only were the architects lost in the details but so were the humans held in bondage who were ultimately responsible for the construction of these Greek Revival homes.

Cotton planters in the upcountry of Georgia, South Carolina and North Carolina particularly took to this great architectural style. As cotton brought a sort of financial permanency, the planters opted to

---

[85]Potter, "Specifications."
[86]"Editorial Correspondence," *Charleston Courier.*
[87]Kennedy, *Revival*, 14.
[88]*Ibid*, 23.

remain on their tracts of land instead of moving to a new area. It was on these lands that they built these pillared mansions, which marked their place in this world. These planters intended for this world to last, with their families residing in their Greek Revival plantation homes forever guiding society. The Greek Revival mansion was symbolic of the wealth obtained by the planter through the slave cultivated cotton crop as well as the image he tried to portray. It was allegorical of the planter's financial status, his cultural and political standing but most importantly, as a master of slaves. This ideology had been entrenched in ancient Greek society; it found a place in the American South as well. These upcountry planters formed an attachment to this architectural style.

As Roger G. Kennedy assessed in his 1985 monograph, *Architecture, Men, Women And Money In America 1600-1860*, the planters, particularly John C. Calhoun, found their essence, their way of life in a world that was not to last, within these Greek Revival plantation houses. Kennedy espoused that "...to the southern reasoning and to the southern architecture of the time, there clings a scent of desperation..."[89] Further expanding on the inherent tie of architectural style and slavery, Kennedy stated that "...each house expressed an anxious supremacy over the passions of each owner..."[90] They wanted their way of life to last.

The transition to the growth of a shorter fiber cotton gave planters the opportunity to locate their plantations away from the low country. Thus, upcountry Georgia and South Carolina became "...the first great short-staple cotton region."[91] The men who opted to raise this crop in the upcountry embarked on this endeavor with aspirations of great returns. Not all attained great wealth and status, but there were men who did. Those who achieved planter status, as defined by a certain number of slaves, rose to the top of the social order. As Paul E. Johnson astutely proclaimed in *The Early American Republic: 1789-1829* (2007), that "plantation masters-both the southeastern nabobs and the cotton

[89]Kennedy, *Men*, p. 345.
[90]*Ibid*, 345.
[91]P. Johnson, *Republic*, 90.

planters of newer regions-were the acknowledged economic, social, cultural, and political elite of the South."[92] Essentially, these planters dominated all aspects of society as well as their own lands. Yet this new generation of planters needed to provide a display of their status, one to differentiate themselves from their parents' generation. The Greek Revival home was one such measure. It was representative of the wealth found among this new generation, both North and South. As this design made its way into the South, it gained significance among the cotton planter elite. As a final step to differentiate themselves from the low country, long-staple cotton planters, the upcountry planters constructed their homes in this architectural style, ultimately seeking to make it their own. Greek Revival soon after became recognized as the home of the upcountry cotton planter elite.

The Greek Revival house took on a unique role in the plantation South. Although this architectural style was found in both Europe and all over the United States, its tones reflected a unique status for those who reaped profits from the institution of chattel slavery. It became the icon of this labor practice, that of holding men in bondage, who cultivated cotton, as well as the successes generated for those who owned these individuals.[93] In his *Greek Revival America*, Kennedy emphasized that "the slave-owning South had its own Greek Revival, different from that of the North and very different in implications."[94] This assessment could be taken to another level in that this architectural style in fact was emblematic of plantation slavery in the South while representative of industry in the North.

Even before Greek Revival took such a hold over the nation's architects, T. Walter acknowledged that the essence of this style would morph itself into suiting the needs and images of institutions found within the nation.[95] Occurring simultaneously with the commencement of the cotton boom, the thrust of this architectural style rapidly became associated with slave-generated wealth.[96] Southern planters

---

[92]*Ibid*, 90.

[93]Gowans, *Images*, 281.

[94]Kennedy, *Revival*, 5.

[95]Walter, "Architecture," 12.

[96]Gamble, "Tradition," 45.

made the Greek Revival their own. Embodying the principles and legacies of this architectural style, they modified it to conform to the realm of the slave holding class.

Upcountry Georgia and Carolina cotton planters embraced this architectural style in their own way, attempting to differentiate themselves from the rice and indigo planters of the coastal regions. This architectural design became a measure of status for these men, for it marked them as being their own generation of planter, no longer using the Federal style of the previous era. Whether through modification or outright construction of a new home, the Greek Revival plantation house became symbolic of the upcountry Georgia, South Carolina and North Carolina cotton planter. These planters were knowledgeable of the ways of the ancient Greeks and embraced their practice of slavery. Planters were inherently bound to slavery, much like the ancient Greeks. Thus, they chose a symbol of this ancient society, the temple, and modified it to serve as a representation of themselves. Although found in many parts of the country, this architectural style was a definite component of the life of the upcountry planter. This defined his status.

CHAPTER 3

THE BUILDING OF GREEK REVIVAL PLANTATION HOUSES IN UPCOUNTRY SOUTH CAROLINA

The planters' decision to build a house in the Greek Revival format was not one that was taken lightly. Before the construction of the big house, the planter took many factors into consideration, like the production of successive crops. Some homes were built as new structures in this architectural style outright while other houses were modified from their original architectural designs and transitioned into a Greek Revival homestead. Making additions to the structure enabled the planters to go along with the trend of the times as well as with the style patronized by their fellow planters. The house was to be a lasting testament to the status of the man and his family a perpetual reminder of the power and prestige of the upcountry cotton planter.

Plantation life resembled a self-contained world. The planter attempted to be virtually self-reliant, and this helped to mold the type of man into whom the cotton planter evolved.[1] As John Townsend Trowbridge assessed in his *The South*, written during the course of his excursion through the South in the aftermath of the Civil War, that "the buildings of a first-class plantation form a little village by themselves."[2] In reality, planters were far from self-reliant. The world in which they built their plantations existed solely because of the slaves whose labor produced the crop, cotton, which generated their wealth and provided them with these fortunate lives.[3] The life of a slave was sacrificed to give the planter his authority. As Walter Johnson advocated in his *Soul By Soul: Life Inside The Antebellum Slave Market* (1999), "...every slaveholder lived through the stolen body of a slave."[4] Johnson also astutely

[1]Calhoun, "Remarks," in *Volume XIV*, 84.; Wertenbaker, *Founding*, 6.

[2]Trowbridge, *The South*, 483.

[3]Baptist, *Half*, 118.; Glymph, *Bondage*, 49.

[4]Johnson, *Soul*, 214.

asserted that as "slaveholders became visible as farmers, planters, patriarchs, ladies, and so on, by taking credit for the work they bought slaves to do for them."[5] As a leader on the plantation itself as well as in the community and the state, his status as a powerful figure was clearly represented and defined.

One such means of enforcing this designation was through the house. The lands might have been familial with an existing structure upon them, but the Greek Revival house identified the antebellum cotton planter. In attempting to make himself unique from his predecessors, the upcountry cotton planter of this generation opted to define himself through the prestige and vigor of the Greek Revival structure. The Greek Revival home was a symbol of power and it was used to distinguish the upcountry planter. These men sought to use this style of architecture as a means of independence. They moved away from the legacy of the previous planters' Federal architectural style so that they gained their own identity.

With the development of the Carolina colony in the seventeenth century, the English crown acquired fertile lands ripe for cultivation. The numerous rivers were duly noted in early documentation of the region, which provided prodigious promise of vast agronomy of water-dependent crops.[6] In time, this all came to fruition. The great wealth of South Carolina was initially acquired from the production of crops like rice. Colonial and post-Revolutionary farmers cultivated this crop, from which many generated a healthy income. As Edward E. Baptist highlighted in his *The Half Has Never Been Told* that "low-country Carolina planters were the richest elites in the revolutionary republic."[7] Rice, however, gradually gave way to a new bumper crop around the time of the turn of the century. Planters soon found that wealth and prosperity were to be gained from cotton as well.[8] The cotton gin was instrumental in this since it aided getting cotton to market more efficiently and expeditiously.

---

[5]Ibid, 102.
[6]Wilson, "Province," 22 and 28.
[7]Baptist, *Half*, 4.
[8]Ramsey, "Impact," 63.

Region-specific varieties of cotton generated markets and proved to be regionally specific. "Sea island" cotton, grown on the cost, was of the greatest premium.[9] Although this cotton and two other types were cultivated, the most commonly grown variety was the "mulkeen" or "yellow" type. Since it was readily made into cloth, mulkeen cotton was highly profitable.[10] It was from raising this variety of the fiber that some of the greatest wealth and plantations prospered.

South Carolina planters embraced cotton as their new future. In *Deliver Us from Evil*, Lacy K. Ford explained that cotton "...lured many...into staple production since cotton production required a much smaller capital outlay than rice or sugar."[11] Although rice was still cultivated along the waterways of the state, cotton eclipsed all other crops. By the early nineteenth century, cotton plantations were common and planters with the greatest land holdings reaped the highest rewards in the market place.[12] Like many of the plantation crops, the cultivation and production of cotton was labor intensive, even with the use of the efficient cotton gin. Slaves were the essential work force, necessary for the planting, cultivation, picking and processing of the fiber. The need for more slaves to work the fields increased as more cotton was planted.[13]

Much of the land of the state were adequate enough to produce bountiful crops. Agriculture experts "...the sandy and spongy..." soil that was "of deep and soft mold..." that was a mixture to produce the best cotton yield.[14] South Carolina's terrain was filled with a variety of soil types as well as vegetation, plant life and flora. By its nature, the state is divided into two distinct regions. The northern portion of the state, which incorporates the western area as well, is deemed the upcountry. Planters and farmers in this vicinity made their living off mostly subsistence crops, growing foodstuffs as well as harvesting their

---

[9]Mallet, *Meteorological*, 22.

[10]Ramsey, "Impact," 65.

[11]Ford, *Deliver*, kindle edition (n.p).

[12]Rogers, Jr., "Transition," 87-88.

[13]Letter, James Henry Hammond to William M. Wightman, June 7, 1840, WMWP, SCHS, MD..; Olmsted, *Kingdom*, 156.; A. G. Smith, "Order," 98.

[14]Chambers, "Treatment," 12.

northern neighbors' prime commodity, tobacco. With the rapid growth and cultivation of cotton, combined with the machinery that facilitated making the fiber market-ready, the economic conditions of South Carolina were transformed. Although rice still generated wealth, affluence and prosperity were gained through the growth of cotton. The low country bred moneyed and landed gentry who rose to prominence in the state, especially in the realms of government and economics. However, prosperity extended well beyond this portion of the state, for even those of the upcountry started to benefit from this flourishing crop.[15] Powerful individuals emerged with vast wealth and prestige. Through booming crops, successful business transactions as well as through advantageous marriages, particular families began to exert great authority over the region and in the nation.

The Hampton family has long held a place of distinction in the state of South Carolina although its influences extended far beyond these borders. Like many others who established themselves in the Carolinas, the Hampton family had initially settled in the Virginia colony from England, where some genealogists traced the generations as far back as the eleventh century. William Hampton may have been the first of the family to arrive in the New World, followed by the establishment of his estate Hamptonfield. There are others that claim that the Reverend Thomas Hampton as the first Hampton to set foot on the American soil. No matter who first, the family was definitely in Virginia by the 1630s.[16] Thomas Hampton, Jr. was a clergyman in the Episcopal Church like his father; Thomas had a grandson also named John Hampton, Jr., who united the Hamptons to the Wade family by his marriage, thus the significance of the name Wade. Of their progeny, two, in their own manner, left distinctive marks on the colony of South Carolina. Daughter Rosamund Hampton married William Winn of the Winn brothers, who founded Winnsboro. However, it was John and Margaret Hampton, Jr.'s son Anthony who would truly

[15]Bremer, *Impressions*, 268.; Burton, *Father's*, 15.; Milling and Julien, *Beneath*, 1 and 2.; Rogers, Jr. "Transition," 87-88.; A. G. Smith, *Readjustment*, 1-2.; A. G. Smith, "Order," 95.; Stoney, *Low-Country*, 41.

[16]A. F. Hampton, "Family," 19, HFP, SCL, MD..; J. L. Miller, et al., "Partial History," HFP, SCL, MD, 2.

leave behind a more renowned legacy. Relocating to the region of Spartanburg before the American Revolutionary War, Anthony Hampton and his children would firmly establish the place of the Hamptons in South Carolina. Although he and his wife had seven children, his son Wade Hampton I would rise to the most notable distinction.[17]

In 1775, the family suffered a severe tragedy. With the open western lands still inhabited by Native American tribes and the White settlers continually encroaching upon their terrain, hostilities were frequent occurrences. To cultivate harmonious relations ahead of the war with the British, a contingency of Cherokees met with two of Anthony Hampton's sons. Although an amicable alliance had been reached, it had been concluded under false pretenses since the Native Americans had already agreed to act on behalf of the Crown to cause havoc among the colonists.[18] After the discussions had come to a close, the warriors burned the Hampton home and killed Anthony, his wife and two others. Those who survived the raid did so by hiding in the swamp while one youth was taken to reside with the tribe until returning to white civilization in 1777.[19] Colonial militia under Henry Hampton's leadership sought out these warriors and exacted vengeance. Meanwhile, others searched for various Cherokee communities and brought them to ruin.[20]

In the years that followed, Anthony Hampton's five surviving sons went on to serve the colonies in the Revolutionary War. One son, Wade Hampton I, earned distinction for his command of a cavalry regiment under the leadership of Brigadier General Thomas Sumter. The guerilla activities of these mounted soldiers were influential in the out-

---

[17]Letter, Dora E. Gunnerr to Commissioner of Pension, March 2, 1921, PHRPBLWAF.; A. F. Hampton, "Family," 19.; "Revolutionary Incidents," June 1843, HFP, SCL, MD.; Perry, *Vol. I*, 37.

[18]"Revolutionary," HFP, SCL MD.

[19]A. F. Hampton, "Family," 19.; "Revolutionary," HFC, SCL, MD.

[20]"Revolutionary," HFP, SCL, MD.

come of the war fought in South Carolina, and Hampton was thereafter lauded for his actions.[21] After the Revolutionary War, the young officer went on to pursue an agricultural career but later went on to serve in the War of 1812 as a one star general.[22] Even while serving his country on the field of battle, Wade Hampton still placed great emphasis on his home lands, leaving John Hopkins in charge of tending to the plantations.[23]

With cheap land readily available in the new state of South Carolina, Wade Hampton expanded his holdings. He purchased one thousand acres in 1789 that he added to land already owned. In addition, he possessed the Richland County plantation Hampton as a result of his marriage to his first wife Martha Epps Howell. It was upon these lands, near Mill Creek (Gill Creek), that Woodlands was constructed.[24] With direct access to the Congaree River, this plantation was optimally situated. The house itself was modest in structure and appearance. The plain Woodlands, although not powerful in appearance, was filled with uncommon luxuries. Through the front door, an individual walked directly to a stairwell which was properly positioned in the center hall. Each floor had four rooms total, with the stairs serving as a dividing point. An attached service room, which was not part of the original construction, was placed off the rear section of the home. Like many residences of the era, the detached kitchen was in its own structure.[25]

In September 1792, Wade Hampton I added an additional thousand acres to Woodlands, increasing his holdings to well over two

---

[21]Letter, Commissioner Earl D. Church to Mrs. J. D. Loudersilk, February 14, 1930, PHRPBLWAF.; A. F. Hampton, 'Family,' 19.; SSBHP, SCL, MD.; "Revolutionary," HFP, SCL, MD.; Triad, "Millwood," n.p.

[22]Letter, State of South Carolina. Richland District, Hampton, W10078, M-804, roll #1177.

[23]L. J. Hopkins, *Adams*, 13.

[24]Green, *Richland*, 40 and 41.; Hennig, *Great*, 9.; "Partial," HFP, SCL, MD, 15.; Moore, *Columbia*, 44.; Triad, "Millwood," n.p. The plantation name that Wade Hampton I became owner of through marriage was "Green Field."

[25]H. Hampton, "Hampton Houses," VGMP, SCL, MD.; Triad, "Millwood," n.p.

thousand acres.[26] Hampton grew indigo and food stuffs, but he was one the first to attempt to cultivate cotton. He saw great potential in cotton and hoped for a prosperous future, but the prospective for success was somewhat limited since it was so labor intensive to generate a propitious cotton crop. With Eli Whitney's patent of a functional cotton gin, cotton became economically feasible to grow, cultivate and market with a fair return.[27] Planters of the inland region of South Carolina, as well as Georgia and eventually North Carolina, saw a bright new future on the horizon with this crop. Accompanying this transition was an influx of more slaves.[28] In 1799, Hampton was not only among the forerunners in South Carolina who employed a gin and generated a substantial profit within the year but was also the initial South Carolinian to use hydro-sources to operate this gin at Woodlands.[29]

When the state capital transferred from Charleston to Columbia, Hampton sold primary land holdings at a profit. Many of the upcountry farmers deemed Charleston as not truly meeting their needs, nor serving their interests. Upcountry planters pushed for a centrally located capital, both geographically and culturally. In pursuit of a compromise solution, Revolutionary War veteran Senator John L. Gervais presented a bill in 1786 in which the capital would be moved to an undeveloped area located in the center of the state. Both houses passed a bill situating the new capital "...on a tract of land two square miles, near Friday's Ferry, on the Congaree River..." with the name Columbia to honor Christopher Columbus.[30] The new seat of government was formed in proximity to Wade Hampton I's plantation. Consequently, the land used to build this new city was purchased from him at a high cost. Hampton reinvested a majority these profits into equine

---

[26]Land survey dated July 7, 1789 and deed dated Sept. 5, 1791, WHP, SHC, MD.

[27]J.A. Turner, *Manual*, 287.; Whitney, *Patent Petition 1793*, NARA, RUSHR.

[28]Gates, *Farmer's*, 7-8. [Although this book title indicates later dates than the era being discussed, Gates refers to the 18th Century in this portion of the text.]; Ramsey, "Impact," 63.; Triad, "Millwood," n.p.; Wright, *Political Economy*, 19.

[29]Easterby, "Three.".; H. Hammond, "Agriculture," HHP, SCL, MD.; A. Hampton, "Family," 19.; HABS, MR, 1.; B. Taylor, "Commerce," 330.

[30]Lucas, *Burning*, 19.; Moore, *Columbia*, 43 and 45.; Salley, "Development," 2-3 and 6.

assets.[31] This commenced the Hampton family's pursuit of the purchase and racing of horses of great bloodlines.[32]

Wade Hampton I continued acquiring land holdings in South Carolina and in other states, setting the stage for long-term stability of the Hampton family. Gradually he became one of the largest property owners in the state and his holdings included cotton and sugar cane lands, city residences, slaves, and prize racehorses.[33] Following his second marriage to Harriet Flud, Wade Hampton I became a father. In 1791, Wade Hampton II, the first of eight children, was born.[34] Spending his early years at Woodlands along with his siblings, he grew accustomed to the life that was afforded those of the planter class. Wade II spent his time on the lands and among the fine thoroughbreds that raced on the family's private turf, gaining a great appreciation of both.[35] He also grew up in the lifestyle associated with a slave owning planter. Wade II and his youngest sister Susan Francis Hampton both carried on this legacy and built magnificent structures as their main residences in their native state of South Carolina.

Wade Hampton II was educated as was expected of the son of a respected planter. Though he opted not to finish his studies at South Carolina College, he turned his attention to the means that had made his father a wealthy man. Except when serving in the War of 1812, Wade Hampton II was a master of plantation lands.[36]All of his life's endeavors stood as a measure of his standing as a member of this elite aristocratic class. His land holdings, possessions and property earned

---

[31]Green, *Richland*, 41.; Hennig, *Great*, 9.

[32]Irving, *Jockey*, 169 and 177.

[33]A. Hampton, "Family," 19.; Irving, *Jockey*, 163, 165 and 169.; MNRHPHP.; *Richland District*, Equity Rolls 34 and 85.; Russell, "Description of Louisiana Plantation," HFP, SCL, MD.

[34]Bailey, et. al, *Biographical*, 654.; A. Hampton, "Family," 20.; W. H. Manning (?), "The Hampton Family of South Carolina," HAP, SCL, MD.; J. L. Miller, "The Hampton Family," VGMP, SCL, MD, 13.

[35]Easterby, "Three."; Meynard, *Venturers*, 145.

[36]Bailey, et. al., *Biographical*, 654.; Account-Wade II, HFP, SCL, MD.

him the reputation of "...a noble representative of the best school and class of Carolina planter."[37]

After the War of 1812, Wade Hampton II returned home and soon after married Ann Fitzsimons, the daughter of the wealthy Christopher Fitzsimons.[38] In celebration of their nuptials, the Fitzsimons gave Wade and Ann Hampton a plantation in Georgia.[39] As a gift to the newlywed couple, General Wade Hampton I also commissioned the construction of a home named Millwood adjacent to his Woodlands in Richland County.[40] Wade II and Ann hosted many social events at Millwood, which became known for its luxurious accommodations and fine food. Henry Junius Nott reveled in delight with his dinners with Wade Hampton II, stating "...it is not a bad country where one can...eat Scotch Salmon, pates foie gras,...not to mention the common things..."[41] On a visit to Millwood, George Tattersall wrote "the Champagne Corks are flying up to the ceiling and...there are 3 noisy fellows playing at 'vingt-un' [sic]..."[42]

As Wade II continued his social ascendancy, he modified his home accordingly. Impressed by the work done on the Charleston Hotel, Wade Hampton II employed one of these architects, Nathaniel Potter, who had worked with Charles F. Reinhart on the hotel. The

---

[37]Obituary, Wade Hampton II, *Charleston Daily Courier*, February 12, 1858.

[38]Wade Hampton II served under General Andrew Jackson at the Battle of New Orleans. [See Virginia Clay-Copton, *A Belle of the Fifties: Memoirs of Mrs. Clay, of Alabama, Covering Social and Political Life in Washington and the South, 1853-1866* (New York: Doubleday, Page & Company, 1905), 213.] As the story is told, he was then sent on to ride to Washington, DC to bring the news of the victory.

[39]Stroup, "Up-Country," p. Rsb—2.

[40]"Account –Wade Hampton II," HFP, SCL, MD.; H. Hampton, "Hampton," 1.; The bride's parents had also given a gift, that of a plantation called Goodale along with its slaves.

[41] Letter, Henry Junius Nott to Hugh S[winton] Legare, May 7, 1831, HJNP, SCL, MD.

[42]Letter, George Tattersall to J. Harvey, Esq. of N.Y., February 2, 1837, GTP, SCL, MD.; Vingt-en-um, which was mistakenly spelled as "vingt-un," is a card game.

façade of this hotel was adorned with a street-long row of Corinthian pillars, a testament to the architectural trends in the South employed by the planter class.[43] Thus Millwood was renovated in a similar fashion, and it became one of the most renowned and impressive structures in the South. With this vast transformation, the plantation became a true measure of its owner's standing.[44]

So taken by this transition of Millwood into a Greek Revival mansion, John B. Irving detailed his impression in his 27 September 1844 article for the *The News and Courier.*

> This mansion, only recently completed from designs by Potter, may be regarded as a fair specimen of the progress which architectural taste has been making of late years among us a fine effect is produced without any seeming effort to create it, unlike those labored production of false taste which too often disfigure the face of a country, reminding the classical observer of the pupil of Appelica, who not having the genius to represent Helen captivating, determined at all events to make her very fine.[45]

Millwood was an impressive structure with a majestic row of columns featured on the façade. After ascending up the stairway and passing through the colonnade across the porch, visitors enterd the house at the midpoint. Through the doorway, one stepped into an immense hallway that featured great works of art, such as original paintings like Edward Troye's *Bay Maria and Foal* as well as copies of famous Italian works such as *Christ Fed by Angels* painted by James DeVeaux. It was further embellished with the grand stairwell. The first floor was for entertainment and business while the second was used for the private chambers.[46] For social events, the eight rooms of the main floor could all be opened and, in conjunction with the two main hallways, created

---

[43]Irving, "Sporting." Irving mistakenly refers to Millwood as Woodlands in this article.; Meynard, *Venturers*, 159.; Ravenel, *Charleston*, 177.; Strong, "Hotel,", MSF, SCHS.; Morgan, "Proposed," MSF, SCHS, MD.

[44]R. L. Allen, "Letters," 20.; Heyward, "Glowing," WHP, SCHS, MD.; Irving, "Sporting."

[45]Irving, "Sporting."

[46]--, "Visit,.; Irving, "Sporting."; Stroup, "Up-Country," pp. Rsb-3 and Rsb-4.

the illusion of one gigantic space.[47] The Hamptons hosted many of the great social events of the day and became the location for the elite to gather.[48] However, the harsh realities by which this was all attained ultimately detracted from this beauty. The slaves, for the most part, were hidden from view. But they were the reason as to why Wade Hampton II owned these luxuries and was able to entertain as such.

Completed in 1844 and built upon a majestic plateau overlooking the Congaree River, Millwood dwarfed the surrounding structures. In the daytime, billowing trees shaded the long drive that led up to the main house; at night, rows of slaves bearing torches lit the way for evening visitors. Ornamental gardens encircled the home in ornamental patterns and eclipsed the view of the practical structures on the plantation. The first buildings seen were the kitchen as well as the barns for the horses, the animals of the greatest importance. With the finest thoroughbreds, the Hamptons were able to display their English noble background as well as enforce their American bloodline. In two distinct areas on the property were the slave quarters. Slave quarters for the fieldhands were on the edge of the cotton fields; slaves who were "skilled" resided nearer to the buildings that housed the machinery or equipment with which they worked.[49]

The aura projected by the Millwood plantation, with its stately oaks curving to guide and shade the entranceway to the majestic pillared mansion, helped foster the "moonlight and magnolia" mythology of the Old South among White Southerners. The sheer size of the property alone stood as a testament to the wealth, power and prestige of this planter family. Rising above the lands on a slight knoll, the Greek Revival house embodied all that was thought of the legendary antebellum South.[50] Millwood a symbol of the power of the upcountry cotton planter. Those who visited were awed by its impressive stature.

---

[47]Conjectural Diagram, MRCRF, SCDAH.; Irving, "Sporting."

[48]Cannaday, "Reconstruction's."

[49]L Allen, "Patronage," p. LA-5.; R. L. Allen, "Letters," 20.; -, 'Visit'.; Hennig, *Great*, 13.; Irving, "Sporting."; Wellman, *Giant*, 9, 37 and 38.; Both Hennig and Wellman were reliant upon R. L. Allen's visit and written text about Millwood.

[50]Irving, "Sporting."

The legacy of this home was to remain for generations as a symbol of the family's greatness.

These upcountry farmers and their plantations were used as the representations of the cotton plantation system, as shown to those traveling from abroad. Politician Henry Bailey wrote to John C. Calhoun on May 30, 1844 about the noted lawmaker Baron Von Raumer and his entourage's visit to South Carolina. Here he briefly mentioned the visit to Millwood: "They also were hospitably entertained at the plantations of Hampton and Tailors, which they examined very minutely, and they had a very full and fair opportunity of seeing something of the economy of a cotton plantation, and the treatment of slaves."[51] By 1850, Wade Hampton II, along with his three sons, all held the classification of planter in the Richland District census. Wade II's property value was assessed at around $90,000.[52]

Millwood was furnished with great precision, so noted in the press "...that it is not only remarkable for the taste, but also for the judgment with which it is finished."[53] The Hamptons carefully considered the placement of their belongs to demonstrate to a visitor that they had the means to spend lavishly. Since most visitors would only see the first floor of the home, the most impressive or expensive pieces of furniture were placed there. In the home, the splendor of the layout of the furnishings as well as the overall design engulfed the guests. The planter and mistress were intentional in what they wanted to portray to outsiders, as shown through these means.

The house, the family and the plantation as a whole were symbolic of the splendor of the cotton planter class. Through marriage, Sarah (Sally) Baxter of New York became a part of the Hampton family with her marriage to Wade II's son Frank. In letters to her parents and siblings, she seemed awestruck by the standard of living she was experiencing. "It is all such a new life, so different from anything we in the least know of at the north that until you see it you cannot form an idea of it." She continued on about the manner in which all aspects of life

---

[51]Letter, Henry Bailey to John C. Calhoun, May 30, 1844 in *Annual Report*, 236.

[52]Buff., *District*, 81.

[53]Irving, "Sporting."

were carried out that it "...makes it seem so natural that one forgets what is in reality great magnificence."[54] These accounts further demonstrate that the Greek Revival plantation house, its owner and possessions not only defined life in the South but also stood as symbols of the planter himself. All these elements combined to further differentiate the upcountry Southern planter from his low country counterparts as well as his Northern neighbors. The upcountry cotton planter used these possessions to define himself. They were the embodiment of the man.

To Wade Hampton II, however, this mansion was in fact his home, a place of solace and comfort. This was his plantation and Wade II was concerned about its successful operations while he was gone. At times, he expressed almost a sense of relief about his return to Millwood. Frequently Hampton expressed his happiness about being home in his letters. In one such note to his sister Mary, he wrote "Yesterday I reached this place & found all well."[55] James Henry Hammond, however, felt that Wade Hampton II's efforts to aggrandize his plantation home was done out of pure jealousy of Hammond's Silver Bluff plantation. He contended that Hampton was without the resources to enlarge Millwood but was so spurred on by his animosity as well as his desire to outdo Hammond.[56] Their bitterness towards each other stemmed from the founded allegations of Hammond's sexual assault of Hampton's daughters.[57] The opulence of Millwood was virtually unparalleled, with the exception of the Milford plantation and a few other families of equal stature of the Hampton wealth.[58] By the time of his

[54]Letter, Sally Baxter Hampton to George Baxter, December 29, 1859, in *A Divided Heart*, ed. A. F. Hampton, 29.

[55]Letter, Wade Hampton II to Mary, August 26, 1857, HFP, SCL, MD.

[56]James Henry Hammond diary entry, December 9, 1846, in *Secret*, ed. Bleser, 173-174.

[57]James Henry Hammond diary entry, December 9, 1846, in *Secret*, ed. Bleser, 174-176.

[58]R. L. Allen, "Letters," 20.; Clemens, *Marriage*, 98 and 114.; Irving, "Sporting."; Kennedy, *Men*, 346, 347, 349 and 352.; Meynard, *Venturers*, 172.; Triad, "Millwood," n.p.; Wellman, *Giant*, 9.; Little is known about Millwood, located on the outskirts of Columbia, South Carolina. Major General William Tecumseh Sherman's Union Army destroyed the home on February 17, 1865, leaving no

death Wade Hampton II had amassed over 1,079 acres of cotton growing land for the Millwood plantation alone, not including the Woodlands' 625 acres or any of his other vast land holdings.[59] Building a powerful house for such a great tract of land was only fitting. However, only the structure built by Wade Hampton II's sister and her husband, John Laurence Manning, rivaled this house's beauty.

For many years, the Richardson-Manning familial line dominated the gubernatorial ranks of South Carolina. Having arrived in America during the colonial era, the Manning family rapidly ascended into the upper hierarchy of governmental ranks. The young Laurence Manning, the initial family member in North America, had taken an active role in the northern campaigns of the Revolutionary War.[60] He later went on to serve his adopted home state of South Carolina by being appointed to handle administrative details but never rose above the office of adjutant general. Laurence Manning's descendants, however, were elected to the highest office in the state government.[61]

This colonist's grandson, John Laurence, was born in the early part of 1816 to the future governor, Richard Irvine Manning, and his wife Elizabeth Peyre Richardson Manning. The family resided at a plantation in Clarendon County, known as Hickory Hill.[62] John Laurence Manning went north to be educated at the College of New Jersey

---

more than the remnants of the columns. The similarity of Millwood to Milford has presented modern scholars with more details. Letitia Allen, in "Wade Hampton II's Patronage of Edward Troye" (p. LA-6) points out that there is only one painting that shows the plantation and that is Troye's "Argyle," which is of one of Hampton's prize racehorses. But Alexander Mackay-Smith, who states that the painting of "Pocahontas" also depicts the house and "Trifle" shows Woodlands, disputes this comment. (found in the Virginia Gurley Meynard Papers, box I, folder 97, South Caroliniana Library, Manuscripts Division.)

[59]Easterby, "Three."; Wade Hampton v. Catherine M. Hampton, et. al., Judgment Roll No 994, Office of the Clerk of the Court, Richland County, SCDAH.; Hampton also had 2,529 acres in Mississippi, 180 acres near Charleston, South Carolina and 8000 acres in Texas along with other vast tracts of land.

[60]W. Manning, "Sketch," MFPF, SCL, MD, p. 1.; T. Smith, "Living," 733.

[61]Meynard, Venturers, 517.

[62]Edmunds, Jr., "A Biographical Sketch," JLMP, SCL, MD, 1.; T. Smith, "Living," 733.

(Princeton University), but he did not graduate because he was required to return home when his father died in 1836. He finished his education in Columbia at South Carolina College, along with many of the other planters' sons.[63] His experience in New Jersey, however, had a profound impact upon him.

The importance of architectural style and decorating taste appealed to the young John L. Manning. While attending the College of New Jersey, he made the acquaintance of the gubernatorial family. In the realm of polite tradition, the governor invited Manning to his residence and treated him as a member of the family. He wrote home about the fine meals he shared with the family and described the décor of the Stockton home with great relish. Manning recounted that the dwelling's interior was like that "...of magnificence of descriptions of a palace." He went on, proclaiming "I have never seen such taste displayed in the adornment of a house, so simple yet so elegant."[64] Though the building of his Milford was many years in the future, perhaps he recalled these early observations when it came time to plan his own home, both structurally and decoratively.

Even though he didn't finish his education in New Jersey, the three years he spent in Princeton during the mid-1830s was not in vain.[65] John Manning came away with many great ideas what a home could represent as well as what it was capable of providing. Another attribute of the governor's residence that he would employ in his own home, one that actually helped it garnish the name "Manning's Folly," was the method of heating the rooms with stoves placed beneath the floorboards.[66]

John Laurence Manning married General Wade Hampton I's daughter Susan Francis Hampton, who had inherited a portion of her

---

[63]Meynard, *Venturers*, 517.; Family paperwork filed with Princeton University for John L. Manning, Class of Ex-1837, PUGBC, PUL,

[64]Letter, John L. Manning to Mother, January 6, 1835, JLMF, DRBSC.

[65]John L. Manning biographical information compilation for Class of Ex-1837, preparation material for the new edition of the General Catalogue of Alumni, OHGPU, DRBSC, PUL.

[66]Letter, John L. Manning to Mother, January 6, 1835, JLMF, DRBSC.

father's profitable Houmas plantation. During their first year of marriage, the couple hired Nathaniel Potter to design and build a residence that reflected their influence and prosperity.[67]

Nathaniel F. Potter had achieved a distinguished reputation as an architect of quality. Before John L. Manning hired Potter, the South Carolinian was advised "...that a Gentleman wishing to build a handsome house could not get into better hands..."[68] Although modifications were made to the initial house plan, the gentlemen entered into an agreement for construction of Milford on May 6, 1839. The "Articles of Agreement" provided for Nathaniel Potter "...to build & completely furnish A house 50 feet by 60 feet & A kitchen 50 feet by 20 feet...in the best Style & work manship [sic]..."[69] With this document, the project of constructing a grand plantation house and outer buildings for John L. Manning commenced.

John L. Manning never seemed to regret his choice of Nathaniel Potter as his architect. After receiving the architectural drawings from Potter, Manning wrote, "I can find no fault...[this portion of the letter was torn off] It suits my taste in every aspect."[70] Manning, delighted with the plans for his new home, quickly shared them with his acquaintances and reveled in their accolades. With such positive responses, Manning thought to share these expressions with his architect. In an afterthought in his letter to Nathaniel Potter, Manning proclaimed "the drawings have been very much admired by those...[torn] I have shown them. I only rec.d [sic] them yesterday."[71] It was through

---

[67]Letter, MO Miles (?) to E. G. R. Henry, May 13, 1838, BFP, SCL, MD.; A. Hampton, "Family," 20.; Jenrette, *Adventures*, 194.; Manning, "South," HFP, SCL, MD.; Meynard, *Venturers*, 140 and 517.; "Milford Plantation 1839-1969," MPSCRF, SCDAH.; T. Smith, "Living," 734.

[68]Letter, Mr. Gregg to John L. Manning, May 2, 1839, WCMFP, SCL, MD.

[69]"Articles of Agreement" signed by Jos. Fenney, C.L. Hampton, Nathaniel Potter and Jn. L. Manning, May 6, 1839, WCMFP, SCL, MD.

[70]Letter, John L. Manning to Nathaniel F. Potter, September 22, 1839, WCMFP, SCL, MD.

[71]Letter, John L. Manning to Nathaniel F. Potter, September 22, 1839, WCMFP, SCL, MD.

these plans that Manning saw the projection of his status in the plantation and policitical communities.

Construction of Milford and the outbuildings took place in the late 1830s and early 1840s and cost $45,300.00, an exorbitant figure for the time. However, it appeared that the expense was worthwhile as it was done to Manning's liking.[72] A monumental structure, Milford consisted of many novel features like the type of heating as well as the water system. Despite the fact that the residence was named Milford, it was frequently referred to as "Manning's Folly." This somewhat unflattering designation was due to the excesses of the house as well as the outlandish cost of construction.[73]

John and Susan Manning were both from families of the upper echelon of society. They constantly strove to maintain, if not elevate, their status and image and their upcountry Greek Revival mansion served as such a measure of their position. Nevertheless, this couple and their extravagant house did not impress all of South Carolina society. In May 1838, M. O. Miles (?) raised some doubts about Manning's character, writing "...I rather expect that his brilliant schemes will never be realized. An independently wealthy young man, with a wife fond of show...wealth is generally more worshipped then [sic] talent..."[74]

Trees draped in Spanish moss lined the path leading to the six Corinthian pillared main house and gave it an air of mystery. Externally, the structural setup of both Millwood and Milford were similar. One feature that made Milford so unusual was the entrance. The front of the home was "...dominated by the monumental portico of six stop [fluted] Corinthian columns modeled after the monument of Lysicrates at the floor of the Acropolis..."[75] The "...porch..." was

---

[72]Account Pages, John L. Manning, Esq. to NF Potter & C., November 1839—28 April 1841, WCMFP, SCL, MD.

[73]Edmunds, "A Biographical Sketch," 1 and 2.; Harmon, "Milford Mansion," JLMP, SCL, MD, 27.; HABS, "Milford."

[74]Letter, M. O. Miles (?) to E. G. R. Henry, May 13, 1838, BFP, SCL, MD.

[75]"Millford [sic] Plantation," Congaree Land Trust, November 9, 1997 in MRSCRF, SCDAH.

"...paved with black and white tiles..." which led to the "...mahogany door..." with silver-plated locks and hinges..."[76] Once inside the plantation home, however, it resembled other Southern styled architecture with its spacious center hall. The entrance incorporated Greek design adorning the entablature itself, resting above the pillars which graced the doorway.[77]

Historian E. T. H. Shaffer noted Milford as being a structure "...that linked the life of the Old South with a glory that was Greece..."[78] The house symbolized the ancient Greek temples and was a reminder of the power of slaveocracy. The interior design and decoration of Milford matched the exterior beauty. Each room had mahogany doors with silvers handles, and a centere stairwell circled up to the next levels of the house. Many of the designs were taken from the *Beauties of Modern Architecture* by Minard Lafever.[79] The ostentation of Milford was intentional. It showed all people Manning's power and wealth; he was able to spend lavishly without financial ruin. Milford was the definition of its owner.

The Calhoun family immigrated to America in the 1730s from Ireland and settled in South Carolina. Having migrated from Virginia to the Ninety-Sixth district in South Carolina, they encountered many of the familiar challenges such as surviving Native American attacks.[80] Patrick Calhoun was young when he made this move with his parents. He and "...his three brothers & his sister with her husband arrived in the district (Abbeville) February, 1756, & settled in a group in what is now known as Calhoun's Settlement..."[81] John C. Calhoun noted that

---

[76]Ibid.

[77]"Milford Plantation," MP, RS, SCHC, 3.

[78]Shaffer, *Gardens*, 184.

[79]Drawing/House Plans (Milford) by Nathaniel F. Potter, May 1839, WCMF, SCL, MD.; South Carolina Heritage Trust Advisory Board, Meeting, August 24, 1990, MPSCRF, SCDAH.; "Specifications for a House to be built in Sumpter [sic] district, South Carolina, for John L. Manning, Esq.," May 1839, WCMFP, SCL, MD.

[80]Letter, John C. Calhoun to Charles H. Allen, November 21, 1847, "Account," JCCP, SCL, MD..; Jenkins, *Life*, 19-20.

[81]Calhoun, "Account."

information about the move from Ireland was scarce, writing, "I am not certain who accompanied them, or who immediately followed them & settled in this neighborhood."[82] The family did, however, encounter violence during the course of the French and Indian War, which appeared to spur their movement to South Carolina.[83]

Once established in South Carolina, Patrick Calhoun began his life as a planter and a father, having married into the Caldwell family.[84] He and his wife Martha had five children. It was their fourth child that gained the most notoriety. John Caldwell Calhoun was born in 1782.[85] He grew up in modest accommodations but gained an "...independent mind..." from his father.[86] When his father died, Calhoun took over many of the duties of the farm until he left to study at Yale. He practiced law upon returning to South Carolina.[87] Soon after, Calhoun entered the world of politics with his election to the legislature.[88] Then "...in 1811, he married his second cousin Floride..."[89] Calhoun made his residence in the upcountry, a region where his wife's family owned property. His mother-in-law bought Clergy Hall (eventually Fort Hill) and its land, a location upon which John C. Calhoun and his wife resided.[90]

The Calhoun family established several large plantations in South Carolina. Bachelor James Edward Calhoun built an estate he named Millwood, which was along the Savannah River and the ship-shaped home served as a testament to his service in the Navy.[91] However, the grandest Calhoun property belonged to the well-known politician and

---

[82]Ibid.

[83]Ibid.; Jenkins, *Life*, 20.

[84]Jenkins, *Life*, 20-21.

[85]Coit, *Portrait*, 1.; Jenkins, *Life*, 24.

[86]Coit, *Portrait*, 5.

[87]Coit, *Portrait*, 9, 14, and 34.

[88]Coit, "Introduction," 3.

[89]Ibid, 2.

[90]"Fort Hill History," http://www.clemson.edu/about/history/properties/fort-hill/

[91]Letter, Granville Beal, manager of J. E. Calhoun Estate, to Gen. M. C. Butler, February 18, 1902, MCBP, SCL, MD.; E. Lander, Jr., *Patriarchy*, 11 and 12.

great statesman John C. Calhoun. On eleven hundred acres of land, a proportion of which was hereditary, Calhoun initially dwelled in the existing home until he modified it into a Greek Revival structure. Graced by four fluted pillars on three sides, the main portal to the interior was protected by a veranda. Massive oaks, creating a realm of mystique and elegance, graced the pathway leading to the entrance. The picturesque scenery, visible from all portions of the house, added to the forte of its overall beauty. Like many who opted to keep the professional aspects of their lives distinct from the personal, Calhoun's study was housed in an outer building.[92]

The seriousness of a familial medical condition spurred Calhoun to leave Washington in 1825. His son suffered from a lung condition, on that improved when they relocated.[93] John C. Calhoun wrote to his mother-in-law, Floride Bonneau Colhoun, about this decision to leave the Washington, D.C. home to move to South Carolina and outlined his plans for the transformation of the house. In this June 14, 1826 letter, he wrote that "...Floride, [Colhoun Calhoun] and myself have concluded, that we will best advance our interest by fixing our residence in the South instead of this place..." He also shared plans for the homestead, commenting that "...I have requested John [Ewing Colhoun] to have some improvements made in the house by repairing the piazza and enlarging the side, in which the stair case runs up, as you will see in my letter to him."[94]

Clergy Hall (Old Clergy Hall) was the name initially designated for the homestead that became the foundation of John C. Calhoun's Fort Hill plantation. When Calhoun relocated to the house in 1825, he began to renovate the home.[95] Calhoun recognized that the house was in dire need of repair, but he also saw a chance to adapt the resi-

---

[92]C.R.S. Horton, "Savannah," 25.; Mitchell, "Romance," 15.; Scoville, "A Visit," 527, 528 and 529.

[93]Wilson and Hemphill, eds., *Volume X*, xviii.

[94] Letter, John C. Calhoun to Floride Bonneau Colhoun, June 14, 1826, in *Volume X*, 130.

[95]--, "Beautiful Old Home," 14 and 15.; Fort Hill, National Register of Historic Places Inventory—Nomination Form, FHPCRF, SCAH.

dence to fit into the architectural style so enjoyed by his upcountry cotton planter class. John C. Calhoun immediately set to work transforming the appearance of both the interior but especially the exterior. From Washington, D.C., Calhoun wrote a letter to his brother-in-law, who was in the South Carolina upcountry. "I must request a favour [sic] of you, preparatory to our return, to have Clergy Hall repaired, so as to answer for a temporary residence. We wish the piazza to be repaired and such an enlargement of the space, through which the stair case passes, as will give a pantry of good size, and a comfortable bed chamber instead of the little room..."[96] Calhoun expressed great anticipation about the prospect of the potential this house: "Clergy Hall will be our future residence; and I have commenced improving by adding largely to the old establishment."[97] Thus the true transition of the house had begun. Altering the interior as well as the exterior of the structure signified not only the transference of ownership but the modification of the edifice to be a reflection of the owner's personality.

Not all Greek Revival homes originated in that architectural design. Calhoun opted to modify the house as well as the name. Determined to have the changes to the house and property made exactly to his specifications, Calhoun was compelled to stay in residence to oversee the alterations. He bound himself literally and figuratively to the estate, writing "...I cannot leave home without the greatest inconvenience. I may say, that I am setting a new place, and while at home, from publick [sic] business, my presence is continually necessary, with the workmen."[98] His presence had the intended effect; his home was dramatically transformed: "...the house will soon be completed; so remodelled [sic] you will not know it."[99] Clergy Hall was transformed into Fort Hill through the expansion of the colonnade and veranda, thus

---

[96]Letter, John C. Calhoun to John Ewing Colhoun, June 14, 1826 in *Volume X*, 131.

[97]Letter, John C. Calhoun to Lt. Edward Colhoun, December 24, 1826 in *Volume X*, 239.

[98]Letter, John C. Calhoun to Rev. Moses Waddel, July 23, 1827, in *Volume X*, 296.

[99]Letter, John E. Colhoun to James E. Colhoun, May 4, 1827, quoted in the editor's preface of the 1827 chapter of *Volume X*.

allowing it to truly become a Greek Revival house.[100] From the entranceway looking out, the panorama of the countryside was impressive.[101]

The name of the plantation was in fact significant to the owner. For example, John C. Calhoun called his upcountry plantation by its old name, Clergy Hall, upon its acquisition and for a few years thereafter.[102] It was not until 1830 that he referred to the plantation by the name Fort Hill. This was after the renovations were completed. Most importantly, the personality of the home had melded with that of John Calhoun.[103] This was also at a time when Calhoun and President Andrew Jackson had verbally sparred at the Jefferson Day Banquet and their professional relationship had begun to decline. It also coincided with the start of the nullification crisis.[104]

John C. Calhoun welcomed visitors, calling upon friends, colleagues, associates, and acquaintances alike to find their way to his plantation whenever they were near.[105] Visitors accounted for this, as the house was an insightful look into the owner's character and caliber. During the course of one of his trips through the United States, George W. Featherstonhaugh was a guest at Calhoun's plantation. He wrote of his feelings about both the planter and the plantation home, ascertaining that "...here I found myself in a charming house, amidst all the refinement and comfort that was inseparable from the condition of

---

[100]Letter, John C. Calhoun to John E. Calhoun, June 14, 1826, JCCP, SCL, MD.

[101]Scoville, "A Visit," 529.

[102]See letters: John C. Calhoun to John Edward Colhoun, June 14, 1826 on pp. 130-131, John C. Calhoun to Lt. James Edward Colhoun, December 24, 1826 on pp. 238-240 and John C. Calhoun to John Edward Colhoun, January 15, 1827 on p. 254 in *Volume X*.

[103] Letter, John C. Calhoun to John Branch, August 6, 1830 in *Volume XI*, 213-214.; Letter, John C. Calhoun to Virgil Maxcy, August 6, 1830 in *Volume XI*, 214-215.; As the editor Clyde Wilson states after the letter to John Branch, "this is on of the two earliest extant letters datelined "Fort Hill" by Calhoun."

[104]"VP John Calhoun," http://www.senate.gov/artandhistory/history/common/generic/VP_John_Calhoun.htm

[105]Letter, John C. Calhoun to Honorable Ingersoll, August 14, 1847, JCCP, SCL, MD.

well-bred and honourable [sic] persons."[106] Calhoun was the master of this world, his world of Fort Hill. On these lands and in these buildings, he lived up to his reputation that "he was born and educated a ruler."[107] It was on Fort Hill that Calhoun was his own man. In the political world, no matter the position he held, he was always technically dominated by another, whether it was the President or the wishes of Congress as a whole. Fort Hill was, however, his domain and his alone. He was able to conform and mold this entire plantation to reflect who he was as an individual and a man. It was a retreat, a place of solace; but also, his power was absolute here, something that he lacked in the nation's capital. Here, he controlled his slaves, their labor and their production, all of which furnished his wealth.

Calhoun had been intentional about his choice to live in the upcountry of the state. He knew this area presented less competition; masters of great cotton plantations were fewer in number in the upcountry region. He also knew the area was relatively unaffected by disease; planters of the low country were plagued with threats of sickness, especially "fever," hence the upcountry was optimal for more salubrious conditions. In writing to Martin van Buren in 1826, John C. Calhoun attested to the benefits of residing in this area. "Our residence in [South] Carolina is near the mountains in a delightful and healthy climate." He followed this sentiment up a little more just a few months later, reporting that "we find the mountains in a delightful and healthy climate."[108] In September of 1826, he shared with another acquaintance almost the exact same information, that "we find the climate here under our little mountain delightful. We are all well..."[109] Calhoun even went on to proclaim in another latter that "this [is] the best climates in the country, being almost except from bilious cases as any part of New

---

[106]Featherstonhaugh, *Canoe*, 267.

[107]Maury, "This Great Statesman," 74.

[108]Letter, John C. Calhoun to Martin Van Buren, July 7, 1826, in *Volume X*, 156.

[109]Letter, John C. Calhoun to Micah Sterling, September 21, 1826, in *Volume X*, 205.

England and much more so from other diseases."[110] For this planter, the upcountry was the idyllic locale in which to live, to prosper and in which to cultivate a flourishing cotton crop, relatively immune from the pestilence and diseases that plagued the low country plantations.

It was from Fort Hill in 1831 that Calhoun composed his "Address To The People Of South Carolina," in which he espoused his theories of states' rights in regard to the tariff issue that was plaguing the American South, specifically South Carolina.[111] It appears as though there was a connection between these sentiments and those which were embodied in his plantation house. The elitism expressed in this address was tied to the tradition of the ancient-based architectural design of his home. Power was a commonality. The essence of Aristotle's support of slavery was often apparent in Calhoun's staunch support of slavey. He referenced this specifically in his correspondence, encouraging this person "...to read the best elementary treatise on Government, including Aristotle's, which I regard as among the best..."[112] Nevertheless, it seems that Calhoun received the greatest gratification from his plantation lands. He immersed himself in all the activities of Fort Hill whenever he was in residence.[113] When Calhoun took a brief break from public service in 1843, he found great comfort and solace in Fort Hill. Calhoun had left Washington because "his private affairs had become considerably embarrassed, in consequence of his protracted absences from home, and his inability to supervise and direct their management except during brief intervals."[114] Although he appears to have wanted to stay out of the political forum, he did ultimately return. However, biographer John S. Jenkins wrote in 1852 about Calhoun: "Retired to the privacy of his beautiful home at Fort Hill...he was far

---

[110]Letter, John C. Calhoun to Christopher Vandeventer, July 23, 1827, in *Volume X*, 296.

[111]Jenkins, *Life*, 161.

[112]Quoted in S. Sara Morrison, "Recollecting Artistotle," 248.

[113]Letter, John C. Calhoun to Mrs. A[nna] M[aria Calhoun] Clemson, April 6, 1839, in *Volume XIV*, 600.

[114]Jenkins, *Life*, 400.

happier, in the enjoyment of domestic happiness, and in the occupations and pursuits of a planter, than while mingling in the bustle and turmoil of party politics..."[115]

It was at Fort Hill that Calhoun was truly in his essence, embodying all of the characterization of a proper gentleman as well as being at ease within his own element.[116] In a letter he wrote from Fort Hill to Secretary of State James Buchanan, Calhoun expressed the happiness he felt in being at his Greek Revival cotton plantation: "As to my going again into the Senate, I do not contemplate to return ever again to publick [sic] life. I am entirely content with the portion of the publick [sic] honors, which have fallen to my share, and expect to spend the rest of my days in retirement, in my quiet retreat near the foot of the mountains. I find ample & agreeable occupation both of mind & body."[117]

Even while in Washington, D.C., Calhoun cared for the productive operations of Fort Hill. Success on the plantation meant money, power and continued mastery of the slaves. The more acreage that was accrued facilitated Calhoun with the lands necessary to grow cotton and other crops. Fort Hill eventually had "...400 improved acres and 950 unimproved acres of land..." on which, among other crops, "...64 bales of cotton at 400 pounds per bale..." were cultivated. Over the years, Calhoun really bonded with his daughter Anna Maria through their elaborate political discussions and written correspondence. In addition, she spent time aiding her father in his work in the capital. Calhoun relied heavily upon her insight as to the ongoing affairs of the plantation.[118] Her marriage to Thomas Green Clemson drew Anna Marie's husband into this special bond that was shared between Anna Marie and her father, granting him much favor with Calhoun. During

---

[115]Ibid, 401.

[116]Perry, *Reminiscences*, 45.

[117]Letter, John C. Calhoun to James Buchanan, August 30, 1845 in *Volume XXII*, 98.

[118] Letter Anna Calhoun to Patrick Calhoun, August 27, 1837, JCCP, SC, RMCL in Sublette, "The Letters of Anna Calhoun Clemson," SCL, MD.; *American Historical Association Report*, 1899, Volume II, 309 and 316.

time of absence from Fort Hill, Calhoun accorded Clemson with managerial tasks in his stead.[119] Clemson took his supervisory duties very seriously. He oversaw operations and meticulously sought payments for materials and goods from those who purchased from Calhoun without extending any special concessions.[120] This ensured smooth operations as well as a more efficient cotton production without Calhoun's presence. The property eventually came under Clemson's tutelage after John C. Calhoun's passing.

Biographer Margaret L. Coit acknowledged in her Pulitzer Prize work *John C. Calhoun: American Portrait* that it was his plantation house that really had the greatest meaning to Calhoun writing "Fort Hill was the symbol of all in life that he prized."[121] It was his homestead, the location where his power was definite and absolute. Calhoun served America in various elected positions as prominent as vice president. Despite having held high national political office, Calhoun found his greatest satisfaction in being a planter, writing, "I am a planter—a cotton planter."[122] W.J. Megginson contended in his book *African American Life in South Carolina's Upper Piedmont 1780-1900* that "although employing an overseer Calhoun thrived on personal involvement."[123] Regardless of how much he wanted to be involved in the operations, the overseer was a matter of necessity while he was absent from Fort Hill. Calhoun embraced the life of the politician and the planter, in which he attained success in both.

John C. Calhoun's infrequent breaks from Washington, D.C. were spent at Fort Hill, where he further embraced and relished his life as a planter. He wrote to his daughter on April 6, 1839 from Fort Hill proclaiming "I have been more engaged about the plantation & garden,

---

[119]Letter, Anna Calhoun Clemson to John C. Calhoun, December 21, 1840, JCCP, SC, RMCL in Sublette, "The Letters of Anna Calhoun Clemson," SCL, MD.; Holmes, *Thomas Green Clemson*, 16-17.

[120]Letter, Thomas Green Clemson to James E. Calhoun, January 8, 1843, TGCP, SCL, MD.; Letter, Thomas Green Clemson to James E. Calhoun, March 25, 1843, TGCP, SCL, MD.

[121]Coit, *Portrait*, 385.

[122]J. Calhoun, "Resolution On The Slave Question" in *Calhoun*, ed. Coit, 51.

[123]Megginson, *Upper*, 48.

than you have ever seen me. With the exception of meal time, I am scarcely ever in the House." Calhoun continued, voicing his enthusiasm about his actions at the plantation. "...I frequently am out, with the exception of a half hour at dinner from breakfast till [sic] nearly dark; so anxious am I to seize on the breif [sic] interval of leisure, from other vocations, to put the place in good order."[124]

The upcountry cotton planter created the illusion of an idealistic world in which he thought those of a lower station of life would want to emulate. The Greek Revival plantation home to which he attached himself did differentiate him from the previous generation of planter. However, it was just a means of beautifying the exterior of a world that's interior was harsh and brutal. Operation and maintenance of a cotton plantation was based on the labor of slaves. Cotton planters were responsible for this. Not all were born into this station in life; many worked, through various means, to make it to the planter ranks. At times, one ascended to this position through marriage. Many prominent South Carolina families were united through marriage. Some, in fact, used their marital relations to such powerful families to aid in their rise to power. James Henry Hammond was one who initially benefited from his extended relations to the Hamptons as well as through his own marriage into the Fitzsimons family. From a reasonably modest background, James Henry Hammond's father Elisha had migrated from the North to South Carolina intent on establishing an academic institution there. It was the elder Hammond's pursuit to set up an academic institution upon his arrival in the southern state.[125] It was here that Elisha Hammond met his wife, who had aspirations of an inheritance she did not receive until late in life, and where their progeny were

---

[124]Letter, John C. Calhoun to Mrs. A. M. Clemson, April 6, 1839 in *Volume XIV*, 600.

[125]"The Hammonds," HBCFP, SCL, MD, 7.; Meynard, *Venturers*, 155.; Elisha Hammond's initial purpose of relocating to South Carolina is not specifically clear, for there are dissenting opinions as to why he relocated. In *Secret And Sacred: The Diaries of James Henry Hammond, a Southern Slaveholder*, editor Carol Bleser notes that Hammond "...went, for reasons unknown..." but later became a teacher, professor and principal. (pp. 3 and 4)

born and raised.[126] The Hammonds had several children, but it was their eldest son who achieved the lifestyle that had eluded his parents. James Henry Hammond was born on November 15, 1807, the sixth generation of the family name born in the United States.[127]

Driven from an early age to attain success and wealth, James Henry Hammond truly began his pursuit of a planter class life following his graduation from South Carolina College. Continuing his studies in law, Hammond then started his legal practice in 1828. Although he was steadily gaining notoriety in this field, his intentions swayed towards the political arena. Hammond then began working as an editor of a newspaper published in the state capital, through which he was able to promote his political theories.[128] His position as editor increased his name recognition, but it did not bring him the desired wealth or status. Ultimately though, he lacked the familial ties to the South Carolina elite and was determined to attain them through marriage.

Wade Hampton II, active himself in government, frequently entertained the great political minds of the day at his lavish Millwood plantation. At one such event, James Henry Hammond met a plain, yet exceptionally wealthy young woman who conveniently was the sister of Hampton's wife, Catherine Fitzsimons. Hammond courted her, and she, against her family's wishes, eventually became his wife.[129] With this marriage, the "outsider" began climbing his way to the ranks of the top of the social hierarchy. The realm of the planter class no longer stood out of his reach, for Hammond acquired his wife's inheritance, an extensive plantation complete with enough slaves to classify him as a large property holder.[130] The newlyweds moved to Silver Bluff in the

---

[126]Bleser, *Secret*, 3-4 and 15.

[127]Ibid, 4.; H. Hammond, "Sketch of James Henry Hammond," JHHP, SCL, MD.

[128]Bleser, ed., *The Hammonds of Redcliffe*, 4.; Bleser, *Secret*, 6.; Meynard, *Venturers*, 155.

[129]Bailey, et. al., *Directory*, 655.; Faust, *Mastery*, 58 and 61.; Meynard, *Venturers*, 155.; Perry, *Writings*, 326.

[130]Clay-Copton, *Belle*, p89.; Faust, *Mastery*, 64.; James Henry Hammond, "Hammond's Letters on Slavery" in *Voices*, ed. Gallay: 387-404, 387.

western portion of South Carolina to begin their lives together.[131] Upon this Beech Island land, Hammond began his ascent in to the life of a planter. He used these lands to cultivate healthy cotton crops, thus allowing him to truly become a master of the lands and the slaves.[132]

As he gained wealth and status, James Henry Hammond participated in many activities of this planter class. Active in the growing of profitable crops as well as in the politics of both his state and nation, he also turned his attention to various forms of livestock. In addition to the animals necessary for the operations of a farm, Hammond invested in the planters' sport of horse racing. Taking full and partial ownership of some of the great turf equine bloodlines, he was able to join the planter ranks and participate in the popular race season.[133]

During the 1850s, Hammond sought to build a testament to his status and constructed a new home designated as Redcliffe a few miles away from his other plantations. In Hammond's mind, it was a house to rival all others and to be worthy of someone of his stature.[134] There was nothing discernibly different about the plantation houses at Silverton and Silver Bluff, drawing no accolades from Hammond's peers; therefore, he was motivated to have Redcliffe built to show his standing in the planter ranks.[135] Not surprisingly though, the Redcliffe plantation was built on the foundations of these other plantations, both financially and geographically. Redcliffe provided "...an extensive view of the surrounding country, reaching even Silverton, the great Cotton and corn plantation..." which usually sent "...500 bales of Cotton and 30,000 or 40,000 bushels of corn to the Savannah market."[136]

---

[131]H. Hammond, "Sketch."; Perry, *Reminiscences*, 105.

[132]Letter, James Henry Hammond to Mrs. C.E. Hammond, April 6, 1842, JHHP, SHC.; Perry, *Reminiscences*, 105.

[133]Harry Hammond, "The Estate of James H. Hammond Deceased in Account with Harry Hammond Executor," Account Book 1886-1893, HHP, SCL, MD.; James Henry Hammond, Stud Book, 1833-1839, JHHP, SCL, MD.; James Henry Hammond, Stud Book, 1833-1840, JHHP, SCL, MD.; Mooney, *Race*, 32.

[134]"Hammonds," HBCFP, SCL, MD, 7 and 25.; Letter, L. Berkman to Hon J. H. Hammond, April 16, 1859, JHHP, SCL, MD.

[135]Billings, "Notes," RACRF, SCDAH.

[136]"Editorial Correspondence," *Charleston Courier.*

In 1855, when Hammond acquired the property where he built Redcliffe, there was already an existing structure upon it. Having determined that this house did not meet his needs, coupled with his aspiration to construct the grandest homestead in the state, Hammond opted to have a larger and more prominent home erected on these lands. He named the plantation estate and house Redcliffe after the terrain. Hammond lamented that he would have rather built the home he had in Columbia on this land, but he put his future in the hands of Redcliffe. This was to be his enduring legacy.[137]

Throughout the entire building process, Hammond was filled with great anxiety and anticipation. He wanted the house erected and bemoaned to his son Harry Hammond, who at the time was abroad, that he feared it would be quite some time before it was built and ready for use. Construction seemed to come to a relative standstill, according to Hammond, as he waited for the lumber to be prepared for the building process.[138] Eventually, the plantation home was completed and Hammond had his enduring structure that was yet another symbolic testament to the legacy of his life and actions.

As a recognized member of this social class, he was seen as both "...an opulent planter..." and "...an accomplished gentleman..."[139] Hammond now had another residence, one that reflected his status. The house, Redcliffe, a Greek Revival structure that stood upon hundreds of acres, was finished before the close of the 1850s.[140] Hammond filled the house with fine furnishings and magnificent pieces of art, acquired on various visits overseas.[141] Redcliffe, although located adjacent

---

[137]James Henry Hammond diary entry, May 12, 1855, in Bleser, *Secret*, 266.

[138]Letter, James Henry Hammond to Harry Hammond, JHHP, SCL, MD.

[139]Letter, G. W. Featherstonhaugh to Sir Tho. Dyke Acland, June 2, 1836, JHHP, SCL, MD.; Letter, Dr. H. Hunth to Mons. Hyde Nouville, June 6, 1836, JHHP, SCL, MD.

[140]Ballard, et. al., "Slave Quarters," 4.; "Editorial Correspondence," *Charleston Courier.*; Letter, James Henry Hammond to Col. M. C. M. Hammond, June 24, 1859, JHHP, SCL, MD.; "The Hammonds," HBCFP, SCL, MD, 25 and 27.

[141]Shaw, "Some Notes," RACRF, SCDAH, 8.; "Paintings," JHHP, SCL, MD.; Though many paintings had been commissioned for use in Silver Bluff, some were relocated to Redcliffe.

to the plantation lands proper, stood as a testament to the legacy Hammond aspired to leave behind.

This house embodied all the components of the patrician lifestyle James Henry Hammond had striven to attain. Redcliffe was meticulously laid out and each room was properly furnished and adorned.[142] Each piece of furniture, every fireplace mantle, and all artwork were selected as a means to display Hammond's wealth. It served as a means for Hammond to show his status. James Chesnut gave Hammond his greatest accolade in a letter he wrote him in 1859 proclaiming "your classic taste, & love of antiquity have, it seems, carried you beyond the Classic Era-even to the time & example of the patriarchs."[143]

It was said of James Henry Hammond that "...his desire..." was "to develop what was, in fact, one of the most productive plantations in South Carolina...Redcliffe..."[144] In contrast though, Hammond asserted that the building and move to Redcliffe was done in an attempt to ease his ill health fostered by an ulcer. He reinforced this idea in a letter to his son, stating that from the initial evening there he found "...the air better & sleep better..." Regarding his health, Hammond continued on stating [I] "...altogether am better", but his motivation was rooted much deeper.[145] Hammond sought to build the greatest house in the Palmetto state, hoping to usurp that honor from Governor Manning's plantation home, Milford.[146] As Hammond ascended into the rank of the planter elite, he was determined to prove that he belonged in that place. Maintenance of a grand, if not the best plantation home, was one such means. People do not agree that Redcliffe was a grander structure. Regarding Redcliffe and Milford as projections of the men who had them built, Roger G. Kennedy, in his *Architecture, Men, Women And Money In America 1600-1860* (1985), proclaimed that James Henry Hammond's Redcliffe "...is a graceless barn of a place, as

[142]"Editorial Correspondence," *Charleston Courier*.

[143] Letter, James Chesnut to James Henry Hammond, 1859, JHHP, SCL, MD.

[144]Clay-Copton, *Belle*, 213.

[145]Letter, James Henry Hammond to "Major" (Col. M.C.M. Hammond), June 24, 1859, JHHP, SCL, MD.

[146] Billings, "Notes," RACRF, SCDAH.; Shaffer, *Gardens*, 184.

a representative of the harsh, unapologetic, egocentric and querulous man who built it as is Milford of the stately and fastidious Manning."[147] The elegance and beauty of Milford in fact surpasses that of Redcliffe.

Hammond opted to use Redcliffe as more of a haven of recreation and investigation into new agricultural techniques instead of his main area of operations for his cultivation of cotton. The Greek Revival homestead he built here also served as a testament of his planter standing "as well as a servant of S.C."[148] He used this land for a variety of agricultural pursuits. Hammond's affinity for fine wine probably helped spur his decision to try his hand a cultivating his own vintage, as he was a self-proclaimed connoisseur. In fact while he traveled abroad in the 1830s, Hammond duly noted his pleasure in viewing where the grapes were cultivated and the wine produced, as well as his acquisition of a variety of vintages.[149] Over the years he purchased wines both at home and abroad. He also took the time to pursue means to cultivate the grapes before setting his sights on trying this venture at Redcliffe.[150] Though he was no longer making his grand trips to Europe, he remained intrigued by wine, hence his desire to produce it at Redcliffe and "...dug a wine cellar to support his vineyard experiments."[151]

Redcliffe held a special place to James Henry Hammond. It was with great pride and enthusiasm that he penned his "...first letter..." from the plantation to William Gilmore Simms, unable to conceal his excitement in being at his new residence.[152] In fact within a few years of taking up residence there, Hammond reflected upon giving up his

---

[147]Kennedy, Revival, 361.

[148]Ballard, et. al., "Slave Quarters," 4.; Painting of Redcliffe, 1858, in "James H. Hammond," HBCFP, SCL, MD, 26.

[149]James Henry Hammond, Diary of European Trip, April 8, 1837—November 18, 1837, entry April 8, 1837 from Paris, JHHP, SCL, MD.

[150]James Henry Hammond, Diary of European Trip, April 8, 1837 - November 18, 1837, entry

April 8,1837 from Paris, JHHP, SCL, MD.; Letter, C. M. Grant to James Henry Hammond, 6 February 1832, JHHP, SCL, MD.; Letter, Higham Fife (?) to James Henry Hammond, August 7, 183_, JHHP, SCL, MD.

[151]Ballard, et. al, "Quarters," 4.

[152]Letter, James Henry Hammond to William G. Simms, May 13, 1855, JHHP, LOC, MD.

prominent role as master of so many lands and devoting himself completely to the actions being undertaken at Redcliffe.[153]

Hammond's passion and enthusiasm for his new estate were beyond the basic appeal of another plantation. There was a great sense of accomplishment in the development of this new venture. Admittedly, Redcliffe had deeper meaning as well. Amid great scandal that involved his sexual assault of his young nieces, Hammond decided to abandon his residence in the state capital. He felt that "...the Columbia clique" had denied him his "...moral character and ...were determined to destroy whatever reputation..." that he had made for himself.[154] With the problems at hand, Hammond found a great escape from his actions and persecution in Redcliffe. Through this plantation, Hammond achieved one of the goals he sought with great zest; he created a permanent legacy to be viewed by future generations.

These nineteenth century upcountry cotton planters were trying to distinguish themselves from the past precedents established by the previous generation's planter class. However, some elements still remained. Just as Thomas Jefferson positioned his Monticello facing west, as to look to the future, James Henry Hammond technically followed suit. Hammond geographically situated Redcliffe westward to match his vision of expansion. He was adamant "...that it must face South or SW."[155] Although the aspect of positioning the house in a specific direction might have been overlooked by the average person, its message was clear to the planter class. They looked upon their present and their future.

Many plantations graced the lands of the Palmetto state. Although the state's reputation for planter wealth originated with the low country, the upcountry cotton planters facilitated its continuance. Since the great plantation wealth originated in the low country, these planters

---

[153]Letter, James Henry Hammond to Major, July 8, 1859, JHHP, SCL, MD.

[154]Letter, James Henry Hammond to William G. Simms, February 27, 1856, JHHP, LOC, MD.

[155]Letter, James Henry Hammond to Harry Hammond, September 21, 1855, JHHP, SCL, MD.

had set the architectural. Those in the upcountry initially did not receive the same recognition. This notion stemmed particularly from the fact that upcountry plantation homes were initially not as grand as those of the low country. However, in time, this changed.[156] The Hamptons, Hammonds, Calhouns and Mannings brought these attributes to the upcountry region through their construction and modification of their plantation houses. Their Greek Revival homes served as representations of the grandeur of life that was attained through slave ownership and the cultivation of cotton. James Henry Hammond attested to the power of cotton before Congress when he made his grand declaration that "cotton is king."[157]

Antebellum South Carolina appeared to offer much to the cotton planter elite. Those who journeyed to this state frequently found the people hospitable though perhaps some customs and institutions were foreign. Reality was camouflaged because it was in fact a cruel environment, one forged by the labor of the enslaved. The splendor of the Greek Revival mansions masked the horrors that enabled them to be built. Planters of upcountry South Carolina desired to be recognized among the upper echelons of society. It was a process which took time, many slaves, successful crops and their plantation homes. Though Charleston and the surrounding vicinity held the reputation for being the area for the elite, the upcountry cotton planters established a society that tried to rival the one of the low country. These upcountry planter families helped South Carolina maintain the rights to the notion that it was in fact "...the oldest cotton state..."[158]

---

[156]Cunningham, "South Carolina Architecture," MVWP, SCL, MD.

[157]Hammond, "Mud-Sill" Speech," in *Defended*, ed. McKitrick: 121-125, 121.

[158]Olmsted, *Kingdom*, 528.

CHAPTER 4

GREEK REVIVAL PLANTATION HOMES IN UPCOUNTRY GEORGIA AND NORTH CAROLINA

South Carolina was not alone in featuring cotton planters and their Greek Revival plantation homes. Georgia was home to both plantation and town houses of this chosen architectural style. Though North Carolina was never renowned for its cotton cultivation, those who did take the risk to grow this crop there and were successful also embraced Greek Revival architecture. The planters of these states were not unlike those of South Carolina. Each man sought to display his power and wealth through possessions. Every slave, horse, piece of art and building was a testament to this. However, it was the ownership of a Greek Revival plantation house that was symbolic of the power generated through a slave driven market of production and sale of cotton.

Georgia slaveholders, as in many Southern states of similar socio-economic structure, had great influence on the government. Political leaders gave audience to the influential landowners as well as to those who traded the resources. On all levels of the government, those who owned chattel property and the extensive plantations upon which they toiled had a powerful voice.[1] However, there were in fact a relative few who had vast holdings. In the decades that preceded the Civil War, there were fewer than three thousand individuals in the entire South who counted at least one hundred slaves on their rosters.

Although not all lands within the state were fertile enough for cotton production, there were regions of Georgia that allowed these planters to produce the bountiful crops that would propel them into positions of wealth and power. This crop proved to be one of the dominant goods produced within the state.[2] J. T. Trowbridge wrote in his 1866 book *The South* that "the southwestern part of Georgia is one of

---

[1] Collins, *White*, 2.; Dodd, *Kingdom*, 121.; Flanders, *Plantation*, 280.
[2] J. Stuart, *Three Years*, 85.

the most fertile sections of the South; it is the region of larges plantations and rich planters. The northern half of the State is practically unproductive: it is the region of small planters…"[3] This is not entirely true however. Planters were prosperous in the upcountry region where they grew cotton and built their Greek Revival homes. They challenged Trowbridge's assessments and proved him wrong.

It was from the successful production of the cotton crop that certain planters began to build testaments to their slave generated power and lasting legacies via the Greek Revival house. During the 1820s through the 1850s, Greek Revival plantation homes began springing up throughout Georgia. Though Georgia planters tended to maintain a more humble lifestyle, those who embarked on building in the grand manner stood out. Greek Revival held a special meaning to these men of power, for it was symbolic of the majestic mien of Periclean Athens. Whereas architectural styling in the North evolved earlier out of Greek Revival, the antebellum South held to the features of this design for a lengthier period.[4]

Georgia's population changed in 1790 when people left the state.[5] In time, this changed and more individuals relocated to the state. Few, however, cultivated cotton and thus it was claimed that Georgia "…had ceased to be the "First Cotton State in the Union."[6] Lands taken from the Cherokee allowed planters to expand their plantation assets.[7] It was the terrain in the central region of the state that was the most conducive to the cultivation of the cotton crop. Here the men who held these lands enjoyed the benefits of their slaves' labor and gained wealth from the production of cotton.[8] It was in the antebellum time that the piedmont cotton planters built their Greek Revival homes, making a mark of permanency.

---

[3]Trowbridge, *The South*, 464.

[4]Flanders, *Plantation Slavery*, 126.; Linley, *Catalog*, 96 and 97.; Perkerson, *Columns*, 5-6.

[5]Jones, *First*, IX.

[6]--, *Memorial Of The Cotton Planters' Convention*, GDAH, RB.

[7]A. G. Cook, *Baldwin*, 15-16.; J. W. Smith, *Georgia's Legacy*, 151.

[8]Jones, *First*, XIII.

Georgia had plantations of many varieties. However, like most Southern states, those who maintained the vast estates with the pillared mansions were among a select few. In his noted work, *Plantation Slavery in Georgia* (1933), Ralph Betts Flanders emphasized that though there was an adequate number of people living in this high standard, "...they were the exception rather than the rule."[9]

Those who had the wealth and status in the upcountry built or remodeled their homes accordingly to use the Greek Revival architectural style. Samuel Lowther was one of these men. With his marriage to the wealthy, twice widowed Elisabeth Slatter Bunkley Billingslea,[10] attorney and planter Samuel Lowther brought changes to his home in Clinton, Georgia in multiple ways.[11] Not only did he introduce a new wife to the homestead but he also made modifications to the structure itself to conform it into the popular upcountry cotton planter's style. Lowther Hall, built by Samuel Lowther between 1822 and 1823, became a Greek Revival home with the addition of a portico and columns. The house featured a wide center hall that was highlighted by free-standing, gradual-spiral staircase. This grand stairwell completed the hall. Curving to the second floor, each step was carved with elegant detail.[12] The staircase accentuated the room. Upon entering the house, one was drawn to the dominating structure. The plantation owners, Samuel and Elisabeth Lowther, descended the curvature of the stairs to welcome guests to their home. Visitors were immersed this moment. As the first glimpse into the life of the planter and his house, it left a powerful impression.

Samuel Lowther was not alone in making additions to transform the architectural style of his house. The Oaks was built on the plantation lands just on the outskirts of the town of Madison. The date of construction and original owner are in question, but it is assumed that William Jones financed the building of the house somewhere between

---

[9]Flanders, *Plantation Slavery*, 94.

[10]White, *Historical Collections*, 506.

[11]Marriages, *The Macon Georgia Telegraph*, February 4, 1832.

[12]Photographs of the Historic American Buildings Survey, Interiors-Lowther Hall, Georgia Tech online catalog—http://www.library.gatech.edu/archives/habs/HABS_PG_13_61.htm

1808 and 1840. The Oaks was initially more of a Federal style home to which a piazza was added in order to transform it into a Greek Revival structure.[13] It was most likely modified into a Greek Revival structure in 1832. The simple addition of a pillared porch transformed the style of the house. This was not an uncommon occurrence at the time. At its peak, the plantation swelled to a staggering 12,500 acres.[14]

Although it is not known who the original owners of this house were, it is recognized that William Jones was in possession of this planation when the alterations took place. Cotton was a primary crop grown on the property surrounding the big house.[15] Jones eventually sold The Oaks although apparently he maintained a portion of land.[16] Once William Cousins took ownership in 1840, he proceeded to add more land, which in turn required more slave labor.[17] More lands and slaves equated to more production and income, which allowed Cousins to purchase more furnishings and decorations for the home.

Some of the upcountry Georgia cotton planters opted not to build their Greek Revival mansions on their actual plantation lands. Judge John Harris owned fertile acreage just beyond the outskirts of Atlanta's marketplace. After careful contemplation, he had a six-columned mansion built to serve as a home. Resting on his plantation grounds adjacent to the Ulcofauhachee River near Covington, the home stood as a testament to his wealth. The building was later given the name of White Hall, which was the same title bestowed upon an older estate in the same vicinity.[18] In certain instances the geographic positioning of some of the plantation homes was altered by the changing landscape.

---

[13]M. Williams, "The Oaks," 3. (Marshall Williams was the Morgan County Records Archivist). With the growing trend of Greek Revival architecture, houses were frequently converted from one type to the Greek Revival style.

[14]Gleason, Homes, 44.

[15]Gleason, *Homes*, 44.; M. Williams, "The Oaks."

[16]Baldwin County, BCDBJ, 502.

[17]"A Summary of the Tax Records for The Oaks Plantation For the Years 1838 through 1883" in Williams, "The Oaks."

[18]Gleason, *Homes*, 37. Also of note, this classical Greek Revival home inspired Margaret Mitchell, author of *Gone With the Wind*, to inform David O. Selznick's historical staff to use this house for 'Twelve Oaks,' home of Ashley Wilkes' family.

The further development of the town of Covington is one such instance, and it transformed the setting of Judge John Harris' Greek Revival home, which once stood in the midst of cotton fields. Gradually these lands were built upon, transitioning this plantation home into a town house.[19] According to records, "...Harris owned 32 slaves and close to 2300 acres of land in Newton County."[20]

White Hall, as the plantation house came to be known, rivaled the beauty of the other pillared mansions of the state.[21] The name White Hall, however, seemed to be a popular name among the planter class in Georgia. One such plantation was also of the Greek Revival architectural style and actually located not all that far from Harris' home.[22] Another noted plantation bearing the same name was constructed in the vicinity of the Savannah River. However, the master of the Savannah River property opted never to reside there but instead use it during the course of his journeys.[23] The significance and symbolism of the name White Hall, however, is shrouded in mystery left solely to speculation.

Another six-columned home that rested slightly off the plantation lands proper was Rose Hill (Tucker-Hatcher House), now known as Lockerly Hall. It is one of the state's most prominent representations of temple-like architecture, was constructed in 1839. Commonly referred to as "Daniel Tucker's house...", Richard J. Nicholls initially owned the Greek Revival home, as well as the surrounding twenty-one hundred acres. Six pillars of the Doric order and floor-to-ceiling windows highlighted the front portico, approximately fifty-nine feet by eleven feet in diameter. Rose Hill followed along fairly standard architectural plans for its layout. On the first floor, the windows are floor to ceiling, which offer air flow. Each room was separated by pocket doors.

---

[19]Howard, ed., *Landmarks*, 94.

[20]Newton County Historical Society, *History of NEWTON COUNTY Georgia*, 59.

[21]Gleason, *Homes*, 37.

[22]Linley, *Catalog*, 102.

[23]Savannah Unit, Georgia Writers' Project, "Whitehall Plantation, Part I," *The Georgia Historical Quarterly* XXV (1941): 341-464, pp. 341 and 342.; Savannah Unit, Georgia Writers' Project, "Whitehall Plantation, Part II," *The Georgia Historical Quarterly* XXVI (1942): 40-62, p. 60.

When they were opened, it enabled the planter to create a great open aired ballroom. Mahogany was used extensively for the woodworking throughout the house. This majestic Greek Revival home stood slightly off the cotton lands that were just two miles away.[24] Rose Hill is situated near the antebellum Georgia capital of Milledgeville. The house contains mahogany handrails and lighting fixtures of the finest crystal.[25] All details of the home indicated that the builder and owner was of great wealth and carefully considered what the structure and furnishings told the outside world. Judge Daniel R. Tucker, the next owner of this house and property, originated from Richland County in South Carolina, which was home to the Wade Hampton family. He moved when he was in his late twenties to try his fortunes in Georgia whereupon he commenced his life as a cotton planter there.[26] In the 1860 census, Daniel Tucker was categorized as a planter with property valued between $52,000 and $95,000.[27]

James C. Bonner contended in his *Milledgeville: Georgia's Antebellum Capitol* (1978) that Rose Hill would be "...considered to be a perfect example of the plantation house..."[28] Other historians have echoed this sentiment as well. (Of note, the name of the house was changed to Lockerly in the 20th Century.) For example, David King Gleason proclaimed in *Antebellum Homes Of Georgia* that "...Lockerly remains one of the most outstanding examples of the classic Greek Revival plantation home."[29] Frederick Doveton Nichols echoed this analysis in *The Early Architecture of Georgia* (1957). Nichols' research led him to the conclusion of "in the development of the temple form, the next step

---

[24]HABS, MV, BC, Survey No. GA-1151, Data Sheet #2.; Bonner, *Milledgeville*, 123.; Gleason, *Homes*, 50.; Linley, *Middle*, 79-80.; personal observations of Lockerly, August 2003, as well as discussions with Lockerly/local historian Murali Thirumal and Rick Mayfield.

[25]Bonner, "Lockerly."; Bonner, *Milledgeville*, 123.; Gleason, *Homes*, 50.; Linley, *Middle*, 79-80.; personal observations of Lockerly, August 2003 as well as discussions with Lockerly/local historians Murali Thirumal and Rick Mayfield. Lockerly Hall is a 20th Century name.

[26]A. G. Cook, *Baldwin*, 457.

[27]Ingmire, "Citizens," 32. This work is merely a copy of the 1860 census.

[28]Bonner, *Milledgeville*, 123.

[29]Gleason, *Homes*, 50.

was taken at Lockerly, 1839, near Milledgeville, which has academic plan and an heroic Doric portico without a pediment."[30] Although this plantation house geographically pushed the lower borders of the upcountry, it highlighted the ambiance and the potency of this architectural design.

Daniel Tucker was clearly a planter of means, as indicated not only by his plantation earnings but also by the grandeur of this house.[31] Designs featured in Rose Hill were taken from Minard Lafever's *Beauties of Modern Architecture* (1835).[32] Lafever had written this book as well as others to help builders create or transition homes into Greek Revival. Daniel D. Reiff claimed in *Houses from Books: Treatises, Pattern Books, and Catalogs in American Architecture, 1738-1950: A History and Guide* (2000) that Lafever's books, along with others like Asher Benjamin's *The Practical House Carpenter: Being a Complete Development of the Grecian Order of Architecture* (1830) "...were of immense importance for the spread of Greek Revival."[33]

In addition to the Greek Revival plantations found in the upcountry of Georgia, there were also ones located further north in North Carolina. The agricultural practices of North Carolina revolved around timber and tobacco. Cotton was grown in the state, however, it was never cultivated in the same proportions as it was in South Carolina and Georgia. At times, North Carolina was viewed in a derogatory manner. This was reflected when Frederick Law Olmsted journeyed throughout the state and made the dubious comment that "North Carolina has a proverbial reputation for the ignorance and torpidity of her people..."[34]

North Carolina planters as a whole did not appear to accumulate the vast wealth of those of South Carolina or the other surrounding cotton states. Viewed as "a valley of humiliation between two mountains of conceit," the state lagged behind economically.[35] To some,

---

[30]Nichols, *Early*, 127.
[31]Ingmire, "Citizens," 32.
[32]Nichols, *Early*, 139.
[33]Reiff, *Houses from Books*, 46.
[34]Olmsted, *Kingdom*, 190.
[35]Draper, "Southern Plantations," 2.

North Carolina was merely a region to be passed through en route between South Carolina and Virginia.[36] Few of the plantations in North Carolina matched the grandeur found in South Carolina and Georgia. Farmers of the state had concentrated their efforts more on the production of crops like tobacco and corn, with climatic conditions not always suited for the cultivation of cotton. Profits generated from coastal rice production and piedmont cotton and tobacco did, however, push some planters into the upper echelons of the planter ranks.[37] Most in North Carolina, though, were seen as never to meet the same prestige as the planters in their neighboring states.

Exceptions, however, were found. Warren County, North Carolina was prosperous due to the thriving town of Warrenton as well as the plantation culture.[38] It geographically borders Virginia, thus inheriting some of that states' traditions as well.[39] It was in this county that planter William Williams had Montmorenci constructed, a plantation that was heralded for its beauty and presentation that other local planters imitated. Catherine W. Bishir, in her *Southern Built*, wrote that "a half dozen major houses bespeak Montmorenci connections clearly and abundantly; as many more houses employ some of the same motifs. All are within thirty miles of Montmorenci..."[40] Others sought to emulate Williams' home, which added to the aura of this planter's image and power.

Warren County was created in 1779, having been assembled from the northern portion of the larger Bute County.[41] Soon after its founding, this county held the distinction of being one with more slaves than whites.[42] In fact in 1820, there were 6,754 slaves out of a total population of 11,158. Of the 4,404 whites, 3,265 of them were involved in

---

[36]G. G. Johnson, *A Social History*, 115.

[37]Censer, *Children*, 1 and 4.

[38]Bishir and Southern, *Guide*, 146.

[39]*State Records of North Carolina*, XXIV, 227.

[40]Bishir, *Southern*, 171.

[41]"North Carolina County Development," Genealogical Services Branch, State Library of North Carolina, Raleigh, North Carolina.

[42]Bishir and Southern, *Guide*, 146.; Bishir, "Montmorenci," 86.; These sources differ slightly as to if it was the only county or one of three North Carolina

cultivation and crop raising.[43] Referred to as "...that well establishment..." which resided near to Shocco Springs, Montmorenci had a land holding of approximately seventeen hundred acres.[44]

Wealthier than many planters in the region, Williams was a preeminent North Carolina planter. His decision to build Montmorenci on his lands helped affirm his status and place.[45] His family had long resided in this area of North Carolina and Montmorenci was to be a testament to them, to their power, as well as their overall ranking at the top of the planter elite.

Building Montmorenci was an enterprising undertaking. Although records do not indicate which architects built the home, historians assume that they were most likely from Philadelphia. He also purchased furnishings from Philadelphia for his masterpiece home.[46] Montmorenci was actually just one of many plantations owned by Williams, some of which came from inheritance. It was of great importance to him was the fact that he owned over ninety slaves.[47] But it was on the Montmorenci lands that he chose to build his great house.

Montmorenci was one of the greatest examples of this renaissance in architecture that began in the early nineteenth century. Although constructed slightly before the heightened demands for changes in home building occurred, this plantation set the tone for North Carolina. One of the most prosperous of North Carolina planters, William Williams had this home constructed on one of his numerous properties which was near the border of Virginia. Filled with extravagant contents

---

counties that had more African-Americans than whites. In *The County of Warren North Carolina 1586-1917* (Chapel Hill: The University of North Carolina Press, 1959), Manly Wade Wellman supports the notion that Warren was the only one in the state with these population proportions. (67)

[43]*1820 Federal Census of North Carolina, Volume LII, Warren County*, 32-33.

[44]*Roanoke Advocate*, November 8, 1832; *Roanoke Advocate*, November 22, 1832.

[45]Bishir, "Montmorenci," 85.

[46] Bishir, "Montmorenci," 85 and 88.; Bishir, *Built*, 166.; Kennedy, *Men*, 271.; "Land And Negroes For Sale," *Roanoke Advocate*, November 8, 1832, November 15, 1832 and November 22, 1832.

[47]William Williams, Warren County Record of Taxable Property, 1824-1828, North Carolina Division of Archives and History.

virtually unheard of to most North Carolinians, Montmorenci defined the decadence of this era of building. In Catherine Bishir's contribution to the compendium edited by Doug Swain, *Carolina Dwellings* (1978), Bishir states that Montmorenci provided impetus for the distinctive and "...highly personalized..." designed for the few prosperous planters of that vicinity.[48]

The façade of Montmorenci was graced with eight slim columns, paired into four separate entities.[49] Throughout the house were "...rich cornices, mantels, and moldings" that provided a dominant air of elegance and refinement.[50] Certain features of the interior made this house memorable. One was the fireplace mantle that was found in the main drawing room. The detail of the work on this piece includes a representation of the famous Battle of Lake Erie in the War of 1812.[51] This was most likely in recognition to Williams' service in this war.

Undoubtedly, it was the staircase which held the greatest place of prominence in the plantation house. It was a free supporting grand staircase which spiraled up to the second floor.[52]

---

[48]Bishir, "Montmorenci," 85.

[49]Artistic rendering of Montmorenci (1J-10), Winterthur Library, Winterthur Archives.; Photographs, Montmorenci, Winterthur Library, Winterthur Archives.

[50]Cantor, *Winterthur*, 189.

[51]Denmark Raleigh photographs, fireplace—Montmorenci (1J-14), (1J-15) and (1J-16), Winterthur Library, Winterthur Archives.; Figure 3, Bishir, "Montmorenci," 88.; McFarland, Warren, 114.; It is not clear who the designer of the mantle was, although Robert Wellford has been credited. The mantle appears to follow one of Owen Biddle's plates in his *Young Carpenter's Assistant* (1805), which was designated to be sold in cities like Philadelphia, where Williams obtained much of his workers and furniture.

[52]Bishir, "Montmorenci," 85, 88 and 90.; Lane, *North Carolina*, 137, 138 and 139.; Denmark Raleigh photographs, staircase—Montmorenci (1J-11), DRPM, WL, WA..; *Roanoke Advocate*, November 8,1832; *Roanoke Advocate*, November 22, 1832. Montmorenci was razed in 1940. Henry du Pont purchased the staircase, as well as the façade and pieces of molding of Montmorenci at the time of its demolition. During the course of transporting the staircase to Delaware, it fell off the truck and was destroyed. It has been reproduced with just a slight variation in the curve and it is a central feature of Winterthur in Delaware.

What was especially unique was the free standing design, detailed with elaborate motifs on the side.[53] The staircase was the first thing seen upon entering the home, a location from which the family descended in order to receive their guests.

In 1825, the Marquis de Lafayette visited Montmorenci during his tour of the United States. Williams was one of the representatives who reported to the state government on the overall conditions and activities of Lafayette's visit.[54] Montmorenci was the grandest plantation of the region, symbolic of the powerful elite in America. Williams' importance was evidenced by the fact that Lafayette took the time to go to his plantation.

The Cameron family also held a place of distinction in North Carolina. In the late 18th century when Richard Bennehan left his Virginia home behind to commence his life as a North Carolina planter, the Bennehan-Cameron families began their rise to power.[55] With the acquisition of lands from a variety of sources, inclusive of ones forcibly taken from the local Native Americans, Bennehan rapidly moved into the planter ranks.[56] Meanwhile, Duncan Cameron had come to North Carolina and met with great success as a lawyer.[57] It was then he began courting Rebecca Bennehan, an act that led him to a victorious duel with another one of her suitors.[58] In the end, Duncan Cameron married the young lady whose family was actively engaged in the plantation culture.[59] Cameron successfully built up his land holdings to become one

---

[53]Denmark Raleigh photograph, staircase—Montmorenci (1J-11), DRPM, WL, WA.; Bishir, "Montmorenci," 90.; McFarland, Warren, 119.

[54]*Raleigh Register And North Carolina State Gazette*, March 13, 1825, NCDAH.

[55]Anderson, *Piedmont*, 1.

[56]Letter, William Johnston to Richard Bennehan, November 5, 1778, RBLM, NCDAH.

[57]Wheeler, *Traditional Statements*, 417.

[58]Letter, Duncan Cameron to Thomas Dudley Bennhan, April 21, 1803, CFP, SHC.

[59]Letter, Mary Bennehan to Duncan Cameron, December 5, 1802, CFP, SHC.

of the greatest landowners in the state, aided by his affiliation and collaborations with the Bennehans.[60]

It was Cameron's son Paul, however, who truly embraced the life of the planter. Although he attempted to make his living in other pursuits, he found his way back to being a planter.[61] Paul and Anne Ruffin Cameron took up residence at one of the family's plantations, Fairntosh.[62] Although he had inherited plantations and would continue to do so with the demise of various family members, Fairntosh did not officially come into his possession until the passing of his father.[63] During the course of his residence there, Paul Cameron made many alterations to both the land and to the overall appearance of the house.

While Duncan Cameron resided in this house that he had built, "he...made Fairntosh a little city..."[64] The plantation, first under Duncan Cameron's leadership then under his son Paul, became a self-contained world with the main house and various outer structures operating collectively. Initially built in the Federal style, Fairntosh was transformed into the upcountry cotton planters' favored architectural style, that of Greek Revival, after Paul Cameron took possession.[65] The renovations began in 1827.[66] The front of the house was marked by its six pillars, all in the most simplistic and oldest column order.[67] The money generated from the cultivation of the crops on the property enabled Cameron to make these renovations. As the slaves toiled in the fields to get these crops to market, the profits fostered their master with

---

[60]"Table Showing Some Land Purchases of The Bennehans and Camerons" in Sanders, *Cameron*, 70.

[61]Letter, William E. Anderson to Paul C. Cameron with notes written on by Paul Cameron, November 1837, CFP, SHC.

[62]Letter, Thomas Bennehan to Anne Cameron, May 14, 1836, CFP, SHC.

[63]Duncan Cameron Will, DCW, DC, NCDAH.; Duncan Cameron Will, 1853, DCW, WC, NCDAH, 224-229.; Orange County, North Carolina Deeds, Book 28, p. 100, OCDB, NCDAH.; Orange County Wills, OCWBF, NCDAH, 375.; Person County, North Carolina Deeds, PCNCD, NCDAH, 294.

[64]Letter, Paul Cameron to his sister, February 17, 1829, CFP, SHC.

[65]Letter, Jean Cameron Syme to Mary Anderson, May 31, 1827, CFP, SHC.; Sanders, *Cameron Plantation, 50.*

[66]Ibid.

[67]Fairntosh Plantation, FPNRHPI, NCDAH.; Fairntosh Plantation photograph, NCDAH.

the necessary resources in which to create his modified Greek Revival mansion. Although cotton was a major crop grown on the plantation lands, other commodities like tobacco and foodstuffs were cultivated as well by at least one thousand slaves. It was estimated that this was "...the largest landed estate in the Carolinas..."[68] Cameron grew cotton in North Carolina as well as on his deep South lands. He was, however, cognizant of the fact that it was a risky venture to grow cotton in North Carolina.[69] By the early part of the nineteenth century, there were "...over 8,000..." acres on Fairntosh plantation.[70] Statistics show that Paul Cameron had 470 people enslaved on this property in 1860 as he had moved many slaves to other plantations.[71] It is unclear, however, how much cotton was cultivated. Paul C. Cameron was recognized by his fellow North Carolinians as being "...the best practical farmer and the best manager of servants..."[72] This statement must of course be viewed in the context of the time in which it was written. Cameron had many slaves. Abner Jordan, who was one of his slaves, estimated that he held "...five thousan' [sic]" people in bondage.[73] Having such a vast force of free laborers enabled Paul Cameron to maintain the upkeep of his properties. His plantations were all renowned for their landscape designs and appearances as well as their productive capacities.[74]

Paul C. Cameron affirmed that it was his intent to keep the home in the family. Though the house had been built under the guidance of his father and then was inherited and modified by the younger Cameron, he specified his desire to keep all the plantations in the family's custody. He wrote that "...Fairntosh...I hope," will "long be held and

---

[68]Lossing, *Pictorial Field-Book*, 351.

[69]Letter, Paul Cameron to Joseph Roulhac, May 1854, BCP, SHC.

[70]Mattison, "History And Architecture Of Orange County, North Carolina," http://www.hpo.ncdcr.gov/surveyreports/orangecountysurveypubmanuscript-1996.pdf., 12.

[71]Ibid.

[72]T J Swain, "Petition for Amnesty," PCCPCW, NCDAH.

[73]Wailey, "Abner Jordan Ex-Slave, 95 years" in *North Carolina Narratives Part 2*, 35.

[74]Obituary of Hon. Paul Carrington Cameron, "The Death Of Mr. Cameron," January 7, 1891, *The News and Courier*.

owned by the heirs of Richard Bennehan and Duncan Cameron."[75] The name of the plantation manor house was of significance to the planter and his family. Although there were not records for all of the homes, the Cameron family named their house Fairntosh "...after the ancestral manor of..." their "...Scottish forebearers [sic]."[76]

The Cameron family of North Carolina also found their place among the greatest of property holders in the state. Through the growing of various crops, the family continued its pursuit of prosperity, which peaked with the production of cotton. Further construction of homes coincided with the successful crops and a high market. Paul Cameron had the most prominent of these structures built in Hillsborough, North Carolina, the plantation house he named Burnside.[77] However, Fairntosh was the main family structure. This modified Greek Revival plantation house reflected the power and legacy of the Cameron family. Paul Cameron later defended Fairntosh and his family's possessions when Union soldiers raided the home during the Civil War.

Through the Greek Revival plantation house, these upcountry planters were truly able to reflect their status. The house symbolized all that these men were—planter, master and leader. Built by slave labor and the profits they generated, the big house was a vivid representation of the world of slavery. Though the household pediment did not have slaves carved into it, the essence of slave ownership was projected through the imposing pillars and the majestic pediment. This was the world of the upcountry cotton slave owner. The planter's power and wealth were displayed through his home, its contents and his property. The Greek Revival plantation house filled with its furnishings and art were all possible because of the slaves who toiled in the fields. Although the house was emblematic of the planter himself, a man who was a pillar in the community as well as in the nation, it was also a reflection of the institution of slavery.

---

[75]Will of Paul C. Cameron, 1881, NCW, CC, NCDAH.

[76]Nathans, *Free*, 17.

[77]Sanders, *Cameron*, 60.

Parthenon, Greece.

Courtesy Heidi Amelia-Anne Weber

First Baptist Church, Columbia, South Carolina.

Courtesy Heidi Amelia-Anne Weber

Charleston Hotel, South Carolina, ca. 1861–1865.

Courtesy Library of Congress

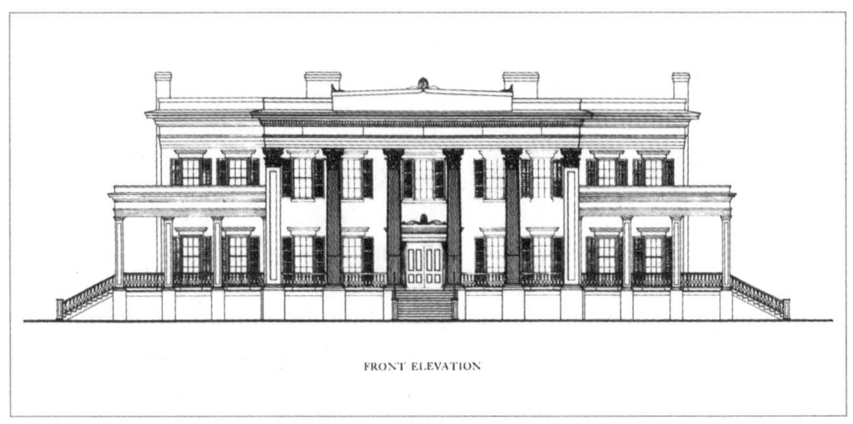

Millwood Plantation, Architect's Rendering.

Millwood, Architect's Rendering, Courtesy Historic Columbia

Millwood, Main House Ruins, South Carolina.

Courtesy Library of Congress

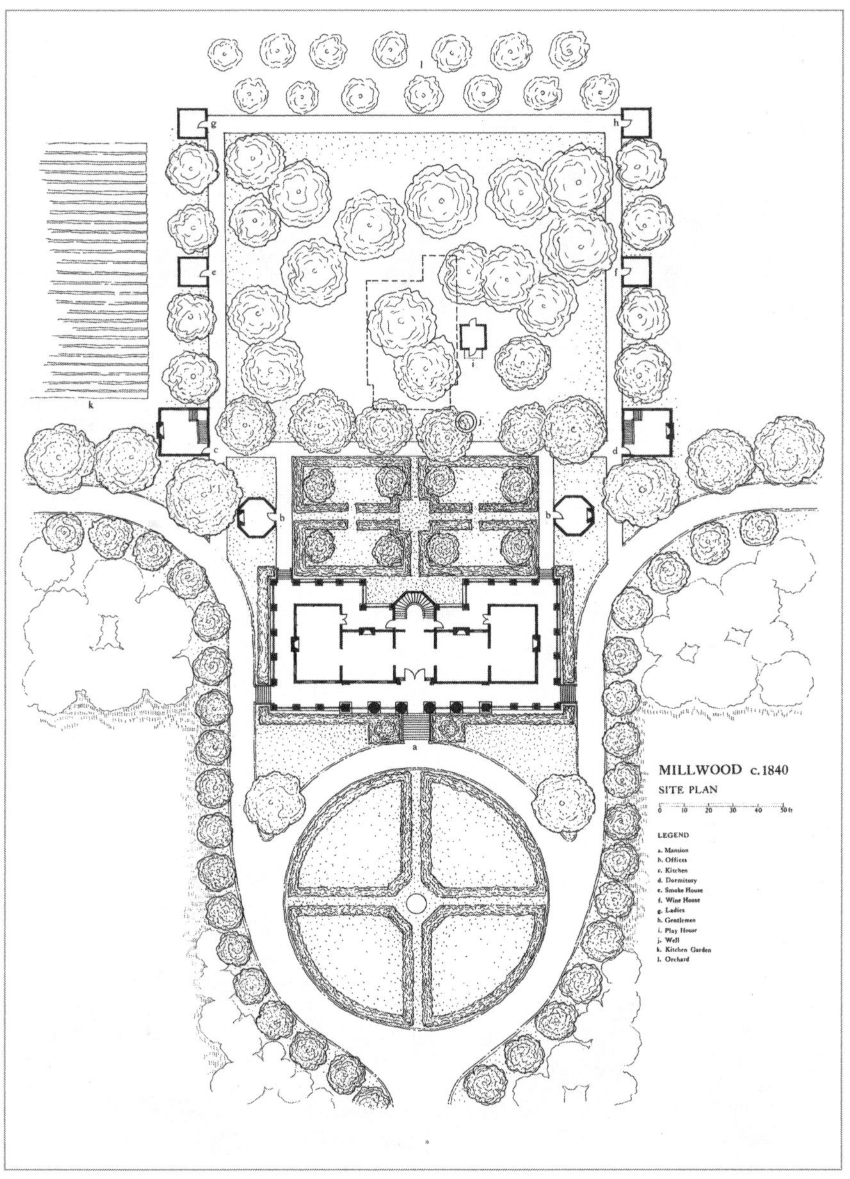

Millwood Site Plan by John C. Califf, ca. 1840.

Courtesy South Caroliniana Library

Milford Plantation, Façade Details, Sumter County, South Carolina.

Courtesy Library of Congress

Milford Plantation, Right Elevation with Kitchen,
Sumter County, South Carolina.

Courtesy Library of Congress

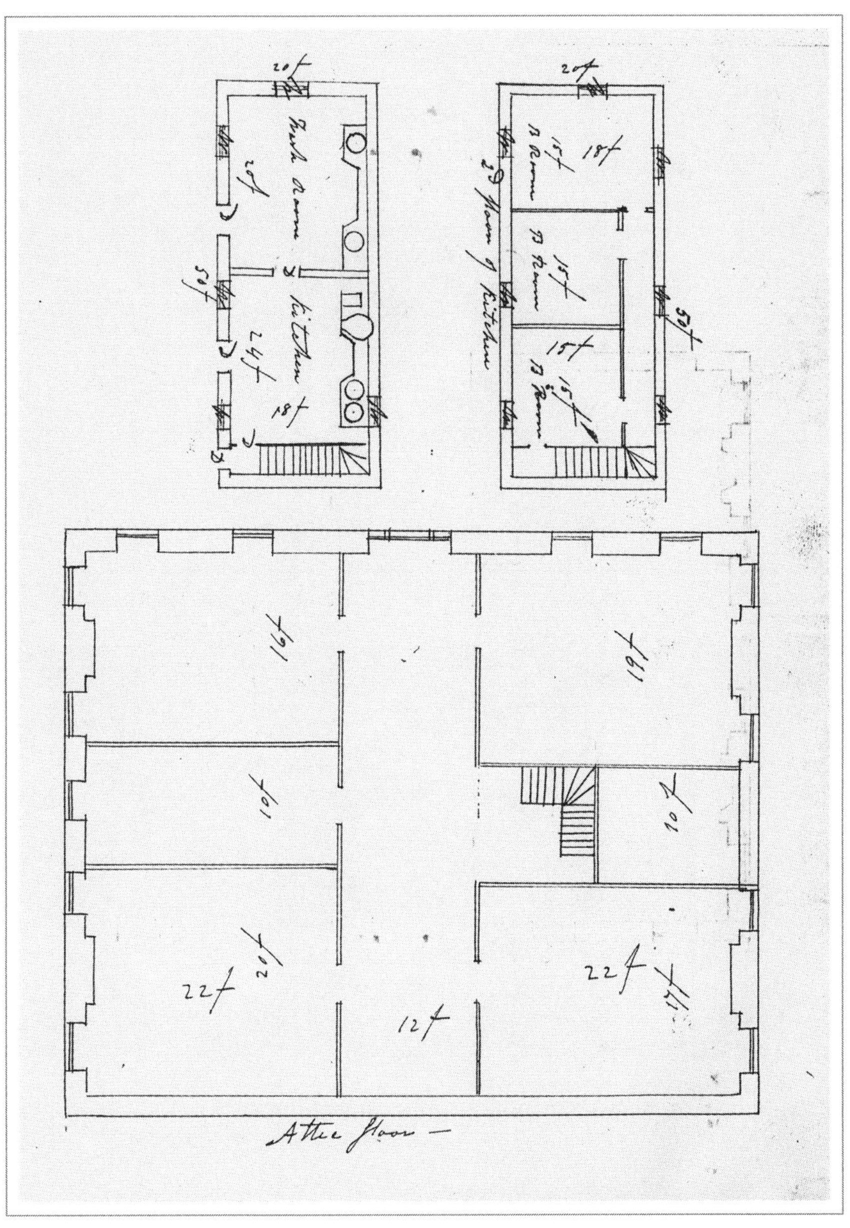

Architectural Design of Milford showing separate kitchen,
May 1839, Nathaniel F. Potter.

Courtesy Williams-Chesnut-Manning Families Papers, South Caroliniana Library, Manuscripts Division

Milford Plantation, Interior-Dining Room Doors,
Sumter County, South Carolina

Courtesy Library of Congress

Milford Plantation, Interior, Central Hall,
Sumter County, South Carolina.

Courtesy Library of Congress

Redcliffe painting by George Hammond (1858).

Courtesy Hammond, Bryan & Cumming Families Papers, South Caroliniana Library, Manuscripts Division

Redcliffe, Beech Island, South Carolina.

Courtesy Heidi Amelia-Anne Weber

Fort Hill, Clemson University campus, South Carolina.

Courtesy Heidi Amelia-Anne Weber

Fort Hill Library, Clemson University campus, South Carolina.

Courtesy Heidi Amelia-Anne Weber

Lowther Hall, Front View, Clinton, Jones County, Georgia.

Courtesy Library of Congress

Lowther Hall, Interior Stairs, Clinton, Jones County, Georgia.

Courtesy Library of Congress

The Oaks, Morgan County, Georgia.

Courtesy Morgan County Records Archives, Madison, Georgia

Montmorenci, Artist Drawing of House.

Courtesy Winterthur Library, Winterthur Archives

Montmorenci ruins.

Courtesy University of Chicago Press

Montmorenci, Fireplace (taken before house was torn down), Warrenton, Warren County, North Carolina. Photo by Denmark Raleigh.

Courtesy Winterthur Library, Winterthur Archives

Montmorenci staircase, 1938.

Courtesy Library of Congress

Rose Hill, Milledgeville, Baldwin County, Georgia.

Courtesy Lockerly Arboretum

Fairntosh, Durham vicinity, Durham County, North Carolina.

Courtesy Library of Congress

Ruins of Mr. Clarkson's House, formerly the home of Governor Hammond, Columbia, South Carolina, 1865.

Courtesy South Caroliniana Library, Manuscripts Division

CHAPTER 5

THE UPCOUNTRY COTTON PLANTER AND THE PLANTATION DESIGN

Antebellum residences were expressions of stature as well as functional, convivial and livable quarters.[1] The upcountry dwelling represented the family and embodied all that was "genteel" about the South. The planter's family also was reflective of his character. Their actions were indicators of his moral fiber. The plantation manor represented its owner and his family, standing as a testament to their owner's gentility and refinement.[2] Nevertheless, the upcountry cotton plantation was composed of various buildings that helped to define the operations of the plantation. Landscape design and the variety of exterior structures also helped display the status of the planter in addition to being functional. A variety of exterior structures which displayed the diversity of the plantation's operations, complemented by the decorative adornment of trees and flowers, presented a precise image of who the planter was as a man to outsiders who caught a glimpse of this magnificent display.

Even though the house was but one feature of the plantation unit, the greatest efforts were concentrated on its construction. Most could not afford to erect mansions of legendary status. However the main house, regardless of its appearance, was a central feature of this self-contained community. Richard Malcolm Johnston reflected upon growing up on a plantation, commenting that "some of the very best and greatest men of the South were planters, who were fonder of their homes then [sic] the most ambitious could possibly be in public office."[3] The house was in fact a symbol of wealth, power and control maintained by this class; it was the embodiment of the planter and his life. As was proclaimed about the Cameron's Fairntosh plantation,

---

[1]Andrews, *Ambition*, 103.; Bushman, *Refinement*, 446.

[2]Johnston, "Planter," 39.; Stowe, *Intimacy*, 122.

[3]Johnston, "Planter," 38.

"…*this House* was built on 'Honor!'"[4] The house and the lands upon which it stood were a source of great pride to these cotton planters.

Cotton was the nineteenth century's primary crop. James Henry Hammond proclaimed, "Cotton is king."[5] The consummate politician John C. Calhoun expressed the pride he felt in his cotton lands and the outcome of those who toiled to produce these crops. His proclamation of "I am a planter-a cotton planter" was telling for it emphasized the importance of this world to an individual who had many roles in the political arena.[6] Calhoun found great satisfaction in his plantation home as well. He extended invitations to those he held in fond regard to visit his home. Calhoun wrote to Charles Lanman, author/editor of the *Dictionary of the United States Congress* [I] "…will expect you to make my residence a resting place in your tour. There is not part of the chain, which I have ever seen more wild and picturesque than that in my vicinity."[7]

Calhoun was even insistent to some that they lodge at Fort Hill. He vigorously proclaimed to the Honorable C. J. Ingersoll that "…you must not pass without calling me & spending with me, what time you can. I will take no excuse."[8] It was evident that Calhoun wished to show Fort Hill and all of its amenities to both his friends and acquaintance. By allowing a select few into this world, these individuals took a glimpse of a life that many people longed for. The realities of these planters' lives as slave masters and farmers were rarely ever seen.

The outlying region of the property was carefully set up in accordance with the owner's desires. Gardens filled with flowering bushes,

---

[4]Comment by William Lougee, quoted in Letter, Paul Cameron to Duncan Cameron, October 3, 1850, CFP, SHC.

[5]Hammond, "Speech on the Admission of Kansas." / "Mud-Sill." in *Defended*, ed. McKitrick: 121-125.

[6]Calhoun, "Resolutions On The Slave Question" in *Calhoun*, ed. Coit: 50-51, p. 51.

[7]Letter, John C. Calhoun to Charles Lanman, April 1, 1848, JCCP, SCL, MD.; Letter of Introduction for Mr. Charles Lanman, Hon. Thompson to John C. Calhoun, April 1, 1848, JCCP, SCL, MD.

[8]Letter, John C. Calhoun to Honorable Ingersoll, August 14, 1847, JCCP, SCL, MD.

shrubbery, and majestic trees, traditionally surrounded the main house, and the paths leading to the home were meticulously cultivated.[9] Many of the large plantation houses and their cultivated grounds evoked responses such as "...Southern beauty reposing upon a luxurious bed of flowers in a nectarine grove...who...bring to her the most precious fruits and ornaments."[10]

Common among the great Georgia and South Carolina plantations was the entranceway. Plantations contained pathways described as "...broad and lengthy avenues leading to the house..." centered amidst "...the trees."[11] The driveway, which created the path for anyone approaching the main house, was carefully laid out. It was a statement, a means to impress. A lengthy promenade, slightly curved, took the visitor to the steps where the planter would await. At Millwood, for example, slaves held torches while standing along the borders of the trail to illuminate the night traveler's route to the home.[12] Large and imposing oaks were common on Georgia and Carolina plantations; sometimes draped with Spanish moss, the exuded the splendor of this Southern world. The mighty oak trees provided shade from the potent sun, masked portions of the property and created an ornamental presentation leading to the magnificent structure.[13] Londoner Charles

---

[9]--, "Visit."; Draper, "Southern Plantations," 2.; Draper, "Southern Plantations II," 121.; "Editorial Correspondence," *Charleston Courier*.; Hall, "Hospitable," 98.; Irving, "Sporting."; Whipple, *Bishop Whipple's*, 12.

[10]Bremer, *Impressions*, 268. Frederika Bremer, of Stockholm, Sweden, visited the United States on a 'Grand Tour,' traveling throughout both North and South. She detested the institution of slavery but was fond of the South and her plantations.

[11]Thomas, *Secret*, 94.; Ella Thomas' description of plantation entranceways was about Georgia.

[12]—, "Visit."; R. L. Allen, "Letters," 20.; Thomas, *Secret*, 94.; DeSaussure, *Old*, 30.; Irving, "Sporting."; Perry, *Volume II*, 335.

[13]Riley, "Sycamore," 370. Mrs. Riley reflected upon the gardens and tree lined entranceways of her family's South Carolina plantations.; R. Taylor, *Antebellum South Carolina*, 9.; Personal observations made of plantation entrances at Redcliffe and Millwood (although I have never been able to gain permission to walk on the property where Millwood once stood, even though I have made many attempts.)

Mackay noted that the "...melancholy trees form the most conspicuous feature of the landscape of the two Carolinas and Georgia."[14] Massive oaks, with their branches drooping from the weight of the "...tyllindria...", almost masked the slave cabins from the sight of the main grounds.[15]

Wade Hampton II placed great consideration in the overall design of the property as well as the house itself at Millwood. The pathway leading to the plantation house was lined by the towering evergreen trees that shaded the trail, opening into an exposed green. Here the vegetation was more sporadic, but the area was filled with grass and strategically positioned bushes. The colors of the variety of plants gradually deepened in the approach to the summit of the house itself.[16] Newspaper reporter John B. Irving described the entranceway and landscape of Millwood in his 1844 article, "Sporting Epistle From South Carolina," expounding that it gave "...the place an appearance of eternal summer."[17] He wrote that the house "...stands on a ground of which every advantage has been taken."[18] Irving furthered his description, incorporating that "the carriage road bordered by ever greens [sic], traces its way thro' [sic] an open lawn with here and there a shrub, or tree, contrasting agreeably with the dark verdue [sic] of the thicker groups of foliage immediately above the mansion."[19] Flanking the house were the dwellings for those who handled the horses in addition to the facilities for exercising and conditioning the animals.

On the opposite side stood many of the other structures necessary for the operation of the plantation, along with areas for food cultivation. Additional stables for the working and general use horses were placed in this vicinity as well.[20]

---

[14]C. Mackay, "General James Gadsden's," 209.; Charles Mackay was a newspaper editor for *The Illustrated London News*, who took a lengthy vacation traveling the United States in the late 1850s.

[15]Olmsted, *Journeys, vol. I*, 234.

[16]Irving, "Sporting."

[17]--, "Visit."

[18]Irving, "Sporting."

[19]Irving, "Sporting."

[20]Ibid.

Most of these plantations featured detailed landscape architecture leading up to and surrounding the big house. Interestingly, James Henry Hammond was somewhat in a quandary as to what landscape best suited Redcliffe. Since Hammond was "...not much inclined to go to the trouble of an extensive pleasure ground...," he sought advice; T. Berkman told Hammond to plant a minimal variety of decorative vegetation if only to enhance the structure.[21]

Though the fruits of his efforts were not entirely seen until later years, perhaps not until even modern day, the plan that James Henry Hammond made for the entranceway to Redcliffe provided an air of mystique. Massive trees line the entranceway, tucking the mansion house away from the mere passerby's observation, and created a sense of anticipation in what great structure lay ahead.[22] Seeking to have Redcliffe's landscaping perfectly manicured, Hammond asked friends for suggestions as to enhance the property's appearance. After designing his own proposal, he forwarded it on to friends and acquaintances for their input. One response gave Hammond the accolades he desired: "Your splendid <u>house</u>, is a Lordly residence, and requires...a <u>park</u>."[23] Upon visiting Redcliffe, a reporter for the *Charleston Daily Courier* described the layout and design of the property in terms of Roman mythology: "The grounds about the mansion of Redcliffe, are handsomely laid out and adorned with floral charm; and are also enriched with the treasures of Ceres and Pomona, the vegetable garden and the orchard, yielding a wealth of luscious fruits and marrowy esculents.[24]

Hammond was not alone in paying careful attention to the landscape design at Redcliffe. The same was true for Fort Hill. The abundant vegetation that filled the surrounding yard almost completely obscured Fort Hill from sight. But Calhoun did not plant these massive trees.[25] He, however, oversaw a good deal of the landscaping that took

---

[21]Letter, T. (or L.) Berkman to James Henry Hammond, April 16, 1859, JHHP, SCL, MD.

[22]Personal observations of Redcliffe.

[23]Letter, T. (or L.) Berkman to James Henry Hammond, April 16, 1859, JHHP, SCL, MD.

[24]"Editorial Correspondence," *Charleston Courier.*

[25]Pendleton Correspondent, "Home Life."

place on Fort Hill. Though trees were already plentiful on the property, Calhoun designed the layout and placement of the more decorative trees and various bushes. Among the favorites were the fruit trees, most likely because they had beautiful flowers and because they also provided food.[26] He called upon the initial owner of the property, his mother-in-law Floride Bonneau Colhoun, for some of her low country vegetation. He asked that she "...bring up a few small orange plants...as I feel confident that with a little attention and care they will succeed on the south side of our house..." Calhoun also requested "some blue grass seed for the yard in the fall, two or three pomgenet [sic] plants in a box, and a few real yam potatoes to obtain seed from another year..."[27]

Among the scores of trees at Fort Hill were ones that had been gifts from the other two members of the "Great Triumvirate," Daniel Webster and Henry Clay. Though much of the landscape design of Fort Hill reflected John C. Calhoun's persona, other portions were symbolic of his absences. His wife Floride modified the landscape of the plantation as well, particularly during her times of loneliness as an almost therapeutic manner while her husband was away.[28] Though Calhoun was the master statesman, some friends and acquaintances thought it was his wife who was the domineering force in his life. Upon her visit to Fort Hill years after John C. Calhoun's death, Clara Walton Alger recorded in her travel journal her thoughts regarding Mrs. Calhoun, that she "...is said to have ruled her husband."[29] This statement, in essence, helps to indicate that her efforts in designing the landscape of Fort Hill were certainly made of her own accord, not to be challenged or altered at the whims of John C. Calhoun.

These upcountry cotton planters placed emphasis on the landscape design of their plantations. When Paul and Anne Cameron took up permanent residence at Fairntosh, they were determined to alter the appearance of the land as well as that of the house and acquired plants

---

[26]Pendleton Correspondent, "John C. Calhoun's Home Life," *Anderson Daily Mail*, October 23, 1929.

[27]Letter, John C. Calhoun to Mother (Floride Bonneau Colhoun), April 9, 1827, JCCP, SCL, MD.

[28]National Register of Historic Places Inventory, NFFH, SCDAH, 1, 2 and 4.

[29]Clara Walton Adger Journal, entry March 26, 1854, ABFP, SCL, MD.

from their acquaintances to enhance the grounds. Though Paul Cameron's parents had done some planting on the property previously, it was rather sparse; they had spent most of their time clearing away the unruly brush.[30] In turn, this left Paul Cameron to modify the land to his own accord. A "...cedar hedge..." was laid out from "...the piazza down to the enclosure around the grove..."[31] A variety of flowering fruit trees as well as other flora were artistically arranged throughout the property, many of which were gifted from Anne's family, the Ruffins. The Camerons also built a greenhouse in order to cultivate various forms of vegetation.[32] Though it took years to plant and cultivate all the trees, bushes and flowers, the Camerons designed an aesthetically appealing setting for their home.

Each planter had his own ideas as to the landscaping for his property. Every plant, flower and tree was carefully selected and placement was done with precision. Judge John Harris's home Whitehall was framed by a variety of different trees. The entranceway and surrounding lawn were carefully designed and decorated with "...spruce pines; deodars and cedars..." along with the native "...boxwood..."[33] Though these trees were beautiful, they were also functional, providing cover from sun.

Of all the ornamental plants as well as those used for foodstuffs, at Redcliffe it was the plethora of grape vines that took precedence.[34] Hammond hoped this homestead would not be one of extensive laborious efforts, but more for pleasurable enterprises, which included cultivating grapes for wine production. The vines grew across the property where they prospered from the ideal soil. An acquaintance of James

[30]Accounts, dated February 11, 1811, November 25, 1811, April 17, 1817 and April 10, 1816, CFP, SHC.

[31]Letter, Margaret B. Cameron to Paul C. Cameron, June 18, 1845, CFC, SHC.

[32]Accounts, dated January 22, 1854 and March 9, 1854, CFP, SHC.; Letter, Annie Cameron to Paul C. Cameron, April 12, 1854, CFP, SHC.

[33]Howard, ed., *Landmarks*, 94.

[34]"Editorial Correspondence," *Charleston Courier.*

Henry Hammond's noted "...that he had never seen any thing to compare with it in Europe or America."[35]

While the landscape designs were beautiful, they were not the sources of a planter's wealth. The cotton that surrounded the plantation home was the most important plant on these properties. At some of the plantations, the cotton was even a part of the landscape design. For example, when cotton was in bloom at Milford, the fields next to the home "...became white."[36] At Fort Hill, those cotton and corn lands were deemed as having been "...grand beyond description."[37]

Trees on the plantation usually served multiple purposes. Aside from being decorative, they were functional. The land on which Paul Cameron's Fairntosh was built also provided building wood for construction as well as the incendiary material used to fire the kiln. Though not always in use, the kiln produced the much needed brick on the plantation. When the major renovations were undertaken at Fairntosh, inclusive of the construction of new buildings as well as alterations to the house itself, the bricks that were used were made on the plantation.[38] Since labor was abundant from the slaves, Cameron was able to produce much of the needed building materials on the property.

Fairntosh was not the only plantation with the capacity to create its own building materials. In the "Articles of Agreement" signed for the building of Milford, it was clearly specified that John Manning was responsible for providing all of the materials necessary for the construction of his house. It can be assessed that "...the bricks..." were forged either on the property or nearby and "...the yellow pine lumber..." was felled there, since the region was renowned for these type of tree.[39] It made financial sense for the planter to manufacture most of the building materials himself in order to avoid the cost of the transportation

---

[35]Letter, James Henry Hammond to Major (Col. M. C. Hammond), June 24, 1859, JHHP, SCL, MD.

[36]Kennedy, *Revival*, 12.

[37]Scoville, "A Visit," 530.

[38]Paul C. Cameron, Journal entry, September 19, 1850, CFP, SHC.

[39]"Articles of Agreement," signed by Jos. Fenney, C. L. Hampton, Nathaniel Potter and Jn. L. Manning, May 6, 1839, WCMFP, SCL, MD.; Milford Plantation 1839-1969, Sumter County File.

them. In addition, this reduced the overall expenditure for the construction of the plantation house especially since the work was done by his own slaves. Using their own resources and labor sources enabled the planters to be more liberal with their spending as they purchased furnishings for their homes.

There were many buildings necessary in the creation of the plantation community. Outbuildings likes barns, forges, stables and others all supported the wide range of plantation work. Since chattel slaves were most significant to the successful operation of the plantation, their residences were located within range of the main house. Various types of bungalows housed the slaves. Typically whitewashed wooden structures, these buildings were aligned in rows to the rear of the master's house and usually in close proximity to the fields. The tendency was to build these cabins to the rear of the master's house but on certain properties they were placed in the forefront, as a means to impress outsiders. The planter's estate also contained the appropriate facilities that accommodated successful working operations and self-reliance.[40]

There were many buildings necessary in the creation the plantation community—outbuildings such as barns, forges, stables, and others which all supported the wide range of plantation work. Slaves performed nearly all of this work, so their residences were located within range of the big house and the fields. Typically whitewashed wooden structures, these cabins were necessary yet were not as attractive. They were often aligned in rows to the rear of the master's house and typically close to the fields. The positioning of the slave cabins was done in accordance to the planter's desires. However, it was standard to have the fields where the crops were cultivated immediately adjacent to all structures on the plantation, so that the time would not be wasted in moving

[40] --, "A Few Facts Of Slavery" As Told by Celeste Avery-Ex-Slave" in *Georgia Narrative Parts 1 and 2*, 22.; Ballard, et. al., "Slave Quarters," 4.; Bishir, "Spirit," 135-136.; Bremer, *Impressions*, 288.; Flanders, *Plantation Slavery*, 94.; Grootkerk, "Artistic," 33.; C. R. S. Horton, "Savannah," 18.; Triad, "Millwood," n.p.; Vlach, *Back*, 21 and 34.

the laborers to their work.[41] Efficiency and time management were what mattered to the planter.

Constructed of various materials, the slave cabins ranged in level of adequacy and comfort from plantation to plantation. Stone was used for the construction of the slaves' housing at Fort Hill. These structures were made "...of stone of superior masonry, two hundred and ten feet in length, divided into apartments, with separate fire-places, sufficiently large for all the purposes of comfort and healthiful [sic] ventilation."[42] Fort Hill's slave residences were also strategically positioned near all the fields, much like they were at other plantations. Although slave quarters were far from comfortable, they were simply shelter.[43] The cabins were minimal, set up in accordance to what the planter wished to afford his property. A medical doctor pointed out "...that the slave, who built our mansions, buys our fine clothes, and supplies our tables with delicacies, has a right to a comfortable house, and sufficient food and clothing."[44] In many ways this is ironic. This doctor recognized that these slaves were the reason why the men of means maintained their status. However, he asserted "rights" entitled to slaves. Slaves lacked any real privileges. It was not clear as to whom this doctor was, but his words were idealistic in nature.

It was the slave who toiled in the other outer buildings, making this self-contained world a prosperous one. Planters associated the growth of these staple crops with the laborious efforts of the chattel. The institution of holding men and women in bondage was the key to prosperity that was found in the cultivation of cotton as well as other agricultural goods, thus allowing these planters to build their Greek Revival homes.[45] As Edward E. Baptist attested in his *The Half Has Never Been Told* that "cotton was the most important raw material of

---

[41]Easterby, "Three."; Orser and Nekola, "Slavery to Tenancy," in *The Architecture of Slavery*, ed. Singleton, 69.; Scoville, "A Visit," 529.

[42]Pendleton Agricultural Society, *Southern Cultivator*, 98.

[43]Vlach, *Back*, 153, 155 and 158.

[44]--, "Ga., 1860, physician," in *Advice*, ed. Breeden: 135-139, p. 136.

[45]Calhoun, "Domestic Slavery" in *Defended*, 17.; Letter, James Henry Hammond to William W. Wightman, June 7,1840, WMWP, SCHS, MD.

the industrial revolution that created our modern world economy."[46] He furthered this idea, pointing out that "enslaved African Americans were the world's most efficient producers of cotton."[47] The market economy, cotton and slavery were interwoven together.

At Fairntosh, there were two homes just on the outskirts of the main portion of the property. These two were the closest in proximity to the main house. Although there are no specific records, it is possible that the "...cook and...male attendants" lived there.[48] At Redcliffe, the slaves' crude cabins were hidden, eclipsed by Hammond's beautiful home.[49] Though these slaves gave him his wealth, they were unworthy of being conspicuous, yet were accessible enough when it suited him.

Separate from the slave cabins was a house for the White overseer. However, not all planters employed an overseer; some found them more troublesome than useful, like James Henry Hammond, who believed "if there were no overseers at all planters would get on far better."[50] The upcountry planters varied as to their opinions about the necessity and use of these men. Many were adamantly against letting others manage their slaves. In contrast, Paul C. Cameron trusted and relied upon his overseer Samuel Piper. He was such a trustworthy employee that Cameron relocated him to Fairntosh and built a home there for him.[51] John Manning had individual homes erected for the gardeners as well as the porter. The same was done for those Manning considered were on the staff, who held a different classification than those who were slaves.[52] These individuals were viewed more like servants as they were more visible on the property since they were not in the fields.

Slave cabins were important structures on the upcountry cotton plantations. They were essential because they housed the sources of the

---

[46]Baptist, *Half*, 113.

[47]Ibid.

[48]Nathans, *Free*, 17.

[49]E. W. Sweet, "The House that Cotton Built," 20.

[50]Letter, James Henry Hammond to My Dear Wife (Catherine), August 8, 1845, JHHP, SHC.

[51]Letter, Anne R. Cameron to Paul Cameron, December 1850, CFP, SHC.

[52]John L. Manning Account Book, Cost of Construction of Milford, WCMFP, SCL, MD.

planter's wealth. Ultimately, they were among the most important buildings on the property. However, to ensure successful operations as well as a comfortable life for the planter and his family, various other edifices were necessary as well. Another important outbuilding on the Southern plantation was the kitchen. Heated solely by fireplaces and illuminated by candlelight, the big house was always exposed to the potential for fire; an attached kitchen with a fireplace or crude oven would have amplified this risk. To help mitigate of cooking fires, kitchens were commonly built in separate structures. Usually in proximity to the main house, particularly to the dining room, kitchens were situated far enough away for some added safety, but they also served to separate the master's family from the slaves preparing the food.

The contract between John L. Manning and his architect, Nathaniel F. Potter, signed May 6, 1839, provided for the construction of both Milford as well as a separate kitchen facility.[53] In his initial designs for Milford's kitchen, Nathaniel Potter planned the structure to be "twenty feet by fifty feet two stories high the first story 10 feet."[54] What Potter erected matched the modernism found in this plantation house, for it included not only the sizeable fireplace but an apparatus that cooked the food through the use of "...fire boxes underneath..."[55] Calhoun's Fort Hill had a separate kitchen as well. The area used for the readying and cooking of the family meals was built from trees felled on the property. The wooden structure was kept partially masked from plain sight by an avenue of coniferous cedars.[56]

Other outbuildings were less utilitarian and reflected the affluence of the property owners. In addition to the detached kitchen, Redcliffe

[53]"Articles of Agreement," between John L. Manning and Nathaniel F. Potter, May 6, 1839, WCMFP, SCL, MD.; Harmon, "Milford Plantation," MP, RS, SCHC, 1.

[54]Nathaniel F. Potter, "Specifications for the Kitchen for John L. Manning's house," May 1839, WCMFP, SCL, MD.

[55]---, "Milford," 4.

[56]Ingersoll, "Summer," 894.

also had a variety of other structures necessary for the favorable operations of a plantation.[57] One other distinctive building found on the grounds of Redcliffe that was the "...subterranean wine cellar..." built separately from the house and was "...excavated twenty feet below the surface and covered by a wooden building, is admirably constructed, and all necessary machinery and preparations are ready for the manufacture of wine on an extensive scale." This was "...covered by a wooden building..."[58] Although the building was obscured from sight and protected by another structure, it was a prominent and well known feature. Wade Hampton II's Millwood featured a "winehouse" [sic]. This structure differed greatly from Hammond's wine cellar. Not only was it constructed above ground but also because it was built as a Greek Revival structure, thus symbolically further tying these men to this architectural style.[59]

Ensuring the effective operations of a vast upcountry cotton plantation required great cooperation, a tremendous amount of work and a variety of buildings to help it be relatively self-sufficient. It was a delicate balance that was never easily attained. John Townsend Trowbridge astutely assessed this during the course of his visit to the South, stating that "the life of the planter is one of care and uncertainty."[60]

Other important buildings common on plantations related directly to the production and marketing of cotton and other crops. Most of these upcountry planters included mills as well as cotton presses and cotton gins on their plantations.[61] Other buildings housed equipment or animals. Redcliffe, for example, was in many ways a self-contained world. "On the plantation was a large grist-mill,..." as well as "...the sawmill, which had turned out all the lumber used in the building of "Redcliffe."[62] In addition to these structures, "...the blacksmith was to be found at his forge, the wheelwright in his shop, and the stock-minder guarding the

---

[57]Ballard, et. al., "Slave Quarters," 4 and 5.; James Henry Hammond, James Henry Hammond Plantation Records #2, January 6, 1857, JHHP, SCL, MD.

[58]"Editorial Correspondence," *Charleston Courier.*

[59]Triad, "Millwood," n.p.

[60]Trowbridge, *The South*, 329.

[61]--, "Home Life," *The Anderson Daily Mail.*; Triad, "Millwood," n.p.

[62]Clay-Copton, *Belle_*, 214.

welfare of his charges."[63] At Fort Hill, there were barns, stables, milk houses, chicken coops and carriage houses, that all supported the daily operations of the plantation. The buildings were constructed with a sense of permanency in mind and were accommodating for the work which was to be conducted within them.[64] The variety of structures at Fort Hill served functional purposes. During his many absences from the plantation, John Calhoun kept abreast of the conditions of the property by his wife Floride. In one such letter, in attempt to provide him with imagery of his property, she wrote "...we went by the mill and returned by the millpond."[65] Meanwhile, his son-in-law wrote more of the business aspects. Calhoun, even in absentia, wanted all aspects of his property to be under constant surveillance, as to ensure its productivity.

For the Milford plantation, Potter designed an animal barn that was done in the same architectural style as the main house.[66] Designing and constructing additional buildings in Greek Revival, which followed the architectural plan of the main house, was very symbolic. It certainly was an indicator of the planter who owned this property. This showed how precise his attention to detail was as well as his concern for how the overall presentation of the property reflected him. Among other pleasures that life afforded them, a horse of fine breeding was a favorite of the planter. Though farm animals were usually plentiful, among them the draft horse, an exquisitely bred equine held a place of distinction on the plantation.[67] Many planters maintained "...strong stables..." recognizing

---

[63]Ibid.

[64]Pendleton Agricultural Society, *Southern Cultivator*, 98.

[65]Letter, Floride Calhoun to John C. Calhoun, May 22, 1844, in *Vol. XVIII: 1844*, 580.

[66]Nathaniel F. Potter, "Specifications for a Barn for John L. Manning, Esq. to be Erected on his Plantation in Claredon S.C.," WCMFP, SCL, MD.

[67] -, "The South Carolina Turf," *The News and Courier*, September 27, 1844.; Account Book, The Estate of James Henry Hammond Deceased, HHP, SCL, MD.; Irving, "Sporting."; Mackay-Smith, *Race*, 68 and 70.; Stud Book 1833-1839, "Pedigrees, Purchases, Sales & Raves of Blood Horses Belonging Wholly or in Part to James Henry Hammond, Silver Bluff, Barnwell, S.C. 1833," JHHP, SCL, MD.; Stud Book 1833-1840, "Journals, Recipees [sic], Expenses & c of Blood Horses Belonging Wholly or in part to James H. Hammond, Silver Bluff, Barnwell, S.C. 1833," JHHP, SCL, MD.; In Irving's "Sporting" article, he refers

the lineage of the horse.[68] Horses were brought to the American South from all over the world with planters desiring the highest quality stock, particularly those that were English.[69] John C. Calhoun was noted for his fine line of horses, which were offspring of the greatest racing studs found in Great Britain and America.[70] Thomas Greene Clemson, John C. Calhoun's son-in-law, upheld the tradition of maintaining these finely bred horses at Fort Hill.[71]

These prize animals held a prominent place in the world of the planter. Bertram Wyatt-Brown contended in his *Southern Honor: Ethics & Behavior in the Old South* (1983) that familial pedigree was essential for both people and their equines. "Like horses, human beings were supposed to exhibit traits of lineage."[72]

Not all planters readily embraced the horse race, though overall they did seem to be the greatest patrons. North Carolina planter Richard Bennehan regularly attended the races and made many purchases of fine blood horses, especially in a joint venture with his partner Duncan Cameron.[73] Although Duncan's son Paul followed in his father's footsteps and was engaged in planting, held a drastically different view on the sport. "For myself" he proclaimed in a letter to his father "I want nothing to do with the race horse..."[74] Though he held the preeminent equine in high regard, his loyalty did not lay with the pageantry of the sport. In ways, this seemed ironic. One can only speculate as to the reason, but it appeared as though he viewed it as an unnecessary and pompous display

---

to Wade Hampton II's property as Woodlands. Wade I owned Woodlands, which Wade II absorbed into his Millwood plantation. The correct name of the property was Millwood.

[68]Irving, "Sporting."

[69]R. L. Allen, "Letters," 20.; Irving, *Jockey*, 178.; Perry, *Volume II*, 336.; *The Raleigh Register*, July 28, 1806, obituary of Launcelot Thorpe, North Carolina Division of Archives and History, microfilm.

[70] Pendleton Agricultural Society, "Report Of The Committee," 99.

[71]Holmes, *Thomas Greene Clemson*, 37.

[72]Wyatt-Brown, *Southern Honor*, 119.

[73]Tax lists (1791, 1796, 1797, 1798, 1802 and 1824), Richard Bennehan, CFP, SHC.

[74]Letter, Paul C. Cameron to Duncan Cameron, August 28, 1847, CFP, SHC.

of one's status. Paul Cameron seemed more concerned with the practical aspects of planting rather than constant elevation of his social standing.

Stables were carefully constructed and maintained. Paul Cameron took great pains in composing the architectural design for the elaborate barn, that served mostly as a stable, which graced one of his other plantation properties. Its immense space was further complemented by the overall beauty of its planning.[75] In certain instances, like that on the grounds of Governor John Laurence Manning's Milford plantation, the structures for the horses as well as their equipment matched the architectural style of the house itself.[76] Architect Nathaniel F. Potter's designs for the plantation house, its interior structures and the barn carefully included colonnade. In the "Specifications for a Barn for John L. Manning," it was detailed that "...columns..." were to be "...fluted in the most approved manner."[77] The pairing of the Greek Revival format of house and stable seemed to symbolize the symmetry of the entire operation.

Since blood horses were an important component of the planter's life as well as another measure of definition of his character, stables were carefully positioned on the property. At Millwood, the horses were kept in proximity to the great house as to be readily accessible and visible to the planter himself yet hidden from the public eye. This was also done for the benefit of guests who were granted their choice of steed by Wade Hampton II during the course of their stay.[78] Having visited Millwood and enjoying the hospitality of his host, John B. Irving wrote that "...for no man can be fonder of fine horses than Col. Hampton."[79] This planter was known for many things in his life, but

---

[75]Anderson, *Piedmont*, 57-58.

[76]Nathaniel F. Potter, "Specifications for a Barn for John L. Manning Esq. to be Erected on his Plantation in Claredon So Ca [sic]," WCMFP, SCL, MD.; Jenrette, *Adventures*, 208. Mr. Jenrette had purchased and restored many historic houses, one of which is Milford (Millford).

[77]Nathaniel F. Potter, "Specifications for a Barn for John L. Manning, Esq to be Erected on his Plantation in Claredon So Ca [sic]," WCMFP, SCL, MD.

[78]Irving, *Jockey*, 177.; Irving, "Sporting."; Mackay-Smith, *Portraits*, 68-69.; Meynard, *Venturers*, 172.; Wellman, *Giant*, 38.

[79]Irving, *Jockey*, 177.

many knew him for his active participation in the import, breeding, racing and stud services of his pedigreed horses.[80] It served as a measure of control as well as a display of status.

Wade II so esteemed his exquisite pedigreed horses, inclusive of Monarch, Pocahontas, and Argyle, at Millwood that he provided them with luxurious quarters.[81] Those for breeding as well as those used for racing were placed in "…the eastern stable…" which was positioned next to the housing for the jockeys and those who tended to them.[82] Racing was a popular pastime for the planter class, especially in South Carolina. When the races were taking place, the city of Charleston was filled with the planter elite in addition to the many locals.[83]

Horse racing has deep roots in America. The first official race occurred at the Newmarket track in Nassau County, New York, in 1665. Racing gained attention all over and quickly found popularity in the South.[84] Turf races gave the planter elite an opportunity to display their wealth apart from their lavish homes. Though participation in this pastime had dwindled greatly in the post-Revolutionary era in South Carolina, as well as in other regions, affluent landowners and high-ranking military officers sought to infuse new life into the sport.[85] This activity gained interest as planters purchased and readied their horses. These

---

[80]Account, "Wade II," HFP, SCL, MD.; Hampton, ed., *Divided*, 31.; Harry R. E. Hampton, "The Second Wade," VGMP, SCL, MD.; Millwood, MNRHPHP.; Perry, *Reminiscences*, 336.

[81]*American Turf Register and Sporting Magazine*, 244.; Hampton, *Divided*, 31.; Irving, *Jockey*, 178-180.; Irving, "Sporting.".; Letter, Wade Hampton II to James Henry Hammond, March 13, 1840 in *Family Letters*, 30.; Mackay-Smith, *Race*, 75, 416 and 421.; Meynard, "Portraits Of Horses," VGMP, SCL, MD, 1 and 4.

[82]Triad, "Millwood," n.p.

[83]Letter, Wade Hampton II to John L. Skinner, December 8, 1845, HFP, SCL, MD..; Letter, Robert M. Cahusac to William Porcher, February 17, 1822, RMCP, SCHS, MD.

[84]C. Collins, *Sporting Gallery*, n.p.; Eisenberg, "Off to the Races," 101.; Lero, "The History of Horse Racing In North America," http://ezinearticles.com/?The-History-of-Horse-Racing-In-North-America&id=1075530

[85]Irving, *Jockey*, 163.; Letter, February 17, 1822, Robert M. Cahusac to William Porcher, RMCP, SCHS, MD.

animals became common possessions among this social class.[86] A horse of fine breeding was symbolic of victory and power. With their financial support and continued backing, horse racing again became the popular gentlemen's recreation. Much like the style of architecture they selected for their plantation homes, their main pastime, the race, had its roots firmly based in Greek tradition.[87] Racing was a featured event in the ancient Greek Olympics.[88] Horse racing of ancient times held a common tie with the antebellum era regarding the status of the owners. Waldo E. Sweet noted in his *Sport And Recreation In Ancient Greece: A Sourcebook with Translations* (1987) that "Greek horse racing…participation was confined to those of great wealth."[89] Horse racing, whether in ancient or antebellum times, is a sport for the affluent.

As Southern plantation owners gravitated towards horse racing, they needed skilled riders. Planters found that in their slaves, who were forcibly tailored into premier jockeys. As Katherine C. Mooney writes in *Race Horse Men,* "from the beginning of American racing, some of nature's most prominent turfmen were Southerners, and at the track they practiced sophisticated and complex forms of human bondage…"[90] There were many political and social aspects of the racetrack, as it was tied to the institution of slavery. Mooney contended that "the racetrack was…an institution open to the conflicts of the outside world, to debates over how a true democracy should allocate authority, how a slave society could both preserve itself and thrive. At the track Southerners…justified the immunity it should enjoy from Northern interference…"[91] There was a complex relationship between the plantation owner and his jockeys. Often, the planter deferred to the judgment and skill of the proficient jockey. In a way, the complex dynamics associated with horseracing helped to weaken the institution of slavery because jockeys had a modicum of control in this arena as it effectivey separated

---

[86]W. W. Dixon, "Eli Harrison: Ex-Slave 87 Years" in *South Carolina Narratives Parts 1 and 2*, 245.; Dodd, *Statesmen Of The Old South*, 98.

[87]Easterby, "Three."

[88]Perrottet, *Olympics*, 93 and 194.; W. Sweet, *Sport*, 89.

[89]W. Sweet, *Sport*, 89.

[90]Mooney, *Race*, 6.

[91]Ibid, 27.

Blackness fron slavery. These planters owned both the horse who raced as well as the slave who was the jockey, so while the jockey might have had short-term control over the horse, the plantations owner still controlled them both. An efficacious turfman and a fast-moving horse displayed power and most importantly control.

Prize money and racing glory were certainly welcomed by antebellum planters, but they mostly aspired to own a great horse. Mooney writes that "the nineteenth-century track became a proving ground for the powerful and aspiring..."[92] Racehorses and their proficient riders' successes defined the planter. Turf races all over the South sported high stakes, some of which were even provided by the planter entrants themselves.[93] In his historical account *The South Carolina Jockey Club* (1857), J. B. Irving assessed the planters' affinity for their beasts, writing "The gentlemen of the Turf...never ran their horses for the pecuniary value of the prize to be won, but solely for the honor that a horse of their own breeding and training should distinguish himself."[94]

There were many planters who owned thoroughbreds who did not participate in the well-regarded races or commission paintings. The mere ownership of the animal was adequate enough. James Henry Hammond went to great pains to take possession, or in some instances partial ownership, of some fine blood horses. In 1835, for example, he purchased "3/5ths of Argyle."[95] Horses were treasured possessions that enhanced the status of the planter. They symbolized money and power.

South Carolina and her planters were not alone in their affinity for the great bloodlines of these masterful beasts. The state of North Carolina was home to many of the revered equines as well who competed in the contests of speed. The noted planter William Williams of Warrenton, North Carolina, maintained a track on his estate, which drew

---

[92]Mooney, *Race*, 5.

[93]Irving, *Jockey*, 181.; Irving, "Sporting."; In the "Sporting," author J. B. Irving mentions that "...the winner of the Great Peyton Stakes of $34,000 at Nashville..." would be at the next major South Carolina race—an example of the size of the purses available.

[94]Irving, *Jockey*, 11-12.

[96]*Raleigh Register And North Carolina State Gazette*, February 18, 1825.; Montgomery, *Warrenton*, 32.

some of the best horses for competition.[96] Impressive horses also stood stud within Warren and the nearby Chatham counties, as well as in some other parts of the state. Legendary equines like Hambletonian, Washington, Escape, and Uncle Sam were offered for their stud at various plantations. These services were placed for sale in newsprint alongside advertisements for the opportunities to purchase commodities in *The American Race Turf Register, Sportsman's Herald and General Stud Book*, like slaves, medicines and estates.[97] It should be noted that both the sale of stud horses' services and human slaves were incorporated in these particular sources. Slaves technically were put on equal priority of the sperm of prize horses. This is very telling of the vantage point of the priorities of these men, what was significant regarding possession and ownership; in essence, the ultimate value of life. The relevance of the great horse was of high priority to members of the planter class. They were representations of class and fine breeding and were recognized by their lineage. In many ways, the horse was defined like the planter was, not only through his familial line, also his ability to take the lead and dominate.

Accommodations for and the articles used in the ownership and significance of a horse also found a special place in the domain of the planter. Necessaries, such as that as the bridle or saddle were common items presented for purchase.[98] The carriage, though a familiar item, could also foretell the nature of the individual in whose possession it was maintained. William Williams indulged in the commissioning of a somewhat extravagant and flashy carriage. It was "...Cromic [sic] yellow and when varnished a light orange."[99] The extraordinary quality of the appearance of Williams' carriage helped evince his status, wealth and power. Concern over the welfare of the carriages as well as the fine

---

[96]*Raleigh Register And North Carolina State Gazette*, February 18, 1825.; Montgomery, *Warrenton*, 32.

[97]*Raleigh Register And North Carolina State Gazette*, February 18, 1825 and March 25, 1825.; *Warrenton (North-Carolina) Reporter*, March 2, 1827 and May 9, 1835.

[98]*The Raleigh Register*, July 28, 1806, NCDAH.

[99]Letter, S. H. Williams to Melissa T. Williams, April 13, 1819, PP, NCDAH.

steeds were of interest to the planter, for he wanted them to be properly maintained following his passing. Williams carefully specified into whose custody they were remanded in his will.[100] This gentleman was not alone in performing this action, for many placed great consideration as to where their prized possession would find their homes after the days of those particular men had ended.

Fine thoroughbreds on the turf represented the planter and his ability to dominate in yet another realm. Upcountry planters once again found themselves in the upper echelons of the social ladder. he luxury of owning these animals, providing elaborate structures for their stables as well as the ability to have their likenesses painted and displayed on their walls added another dimension of the master's power. Having a slave who was a victorious jockey added another component. As much as these great horses, their beautiful stables and the paintings that represented their images found places of honor in the world of the southern planter, art in general held a position of prominence as well.

Each plantation was built to represent both the needs of the planter as well as the image he was trying to portray. Though many plantations featured some commonalities, each one was inherently a representation of the man who owned the individual property. These upcountry Georgia, South Carolina, and North Carolina cotton planters took great pains to modify their plantations to fit their needs, their operations, and their personalities. So much of their lifestyle as slave masters was found in their Greek Revival homes, as well as the entire operations and structures of the plantation. Every aspect, from the tree lined entranceways to the overall layout of the outer buildings, was done with great precision. As important as the furnishings and décor of the plantation house were to the upcountry cotton planter, the outside of the home was equally significant. Most would only get a glimpse of his world through a visual contact of the surrounding grounds of the big house. For those not permitted into the inner sanctuary of the upcountry cotton planter, this had to be a lasting impression. It was a reminder of why this man was dominant in society and politics. One was to be

[100]William Williams Will 1832, WCW, NCDAH.; William Williams Will 1838, WCW, NCDAH.

overawed by the magnitude of this impressive architectural structure. Every facet of the Greek Revival as well as its overall appearance represented these upcountry slaveholding cotton planters.

CHAPTER 6

A VIEW INSIDE THE HOME

Expressions of gentility and refinement were carefully revealed within the structure and furnishings of the big house. Along with the massive trees and flowers that decorated the property, displays of wealth and power were evident through the diversity of outer plantation buildings. Rooms within the big house also helped to foster the image of power that the planter was striving to project. A proper gentleman who prided himself on his honor displayed his power and status with his home. The house was a tangible entity, one that the planter could nurture and reflect upon with great pride.[1] The beauty of the homestead came at great cost as it was founded on the labors of whose lives had been stolen from them.

Steadily increasing, albeit sometimes fluctuating, cotton prices afforded those who prospered the opportunity to indulge in finer quality possessions for the interior of the home. The planter relied on even minor details of interior décor to demonstrate his status. Within the interior of the big house, the careful placement of fresh floral arrangements in artisan crafted vases, the availability of great works of literature, Greek texts, as well as a lexicon and a Christian Bible indicated to others that he was cultured, educated, and Christian.[2] But in reality, he owned human lives.

The role of women as plantation mistresses should not be overlooked here. Her various duties on the plantation were inclusive of maintenance of the household. As Elizabeth Fox-Genovese assessed in *Within the Plantation Household,* "the mistress of the household...assumed the mantle of ruling lady..." overseeing the house and its natural

---

[1]Irving, "Sporting."; Johnston, "Planter," 38.; Kasson, *Rudeness*, 169 and 170.

[2]Thomas, *Secret*, ed. Burr, 100.; "Editorial Correspondence," *Charleston Courier*.; Kennedy, *Men*, 347.; Perry, *Reminiscences*, 108.; Personal observations of James Henry Hammond's library contents at Redcliffe, August 2003.

extensions, notable flower and vegetable gardens…" among other domestic duties.[3] In essence, the woman of the house was responsible for its overall appearance and upkeep. Although these planters often did not mention their wives' influence in the décor and design of the home, it is clear they had an influential role.

The interior design of the Greek Revival plantation house was planned to incorporate necessary rooms but also to provide for circulation of air in the warm climate. Many of these homes shared somewhat similar patterns although were modified in accordance with the specific desires of each individual. The layout of Lowther Hall entailed a standard pairing of rooms on each side of the wide center hall, capped by the grand spiral stairwell in the rear. The parlor was placed on the immediate left, which connected with the sitting room. On the right side of the first floor was the formal dinner area as well as the planter's sleeping quarters. The four rooms on the second floor were designated as bedrooms, and occasionally were used for other multipurpose functions.[4]

Rose Hill's (Lockerly) interior design was that of the standard two by two room pattern. The dual parlors on the right side of the house could be kept separate by the closing of the mahogany pocket doors or expanded into one large ballroom setting. Immediately to the left of the center hall was the dining room, which was backed by the master bedroom. All four rooms of the second floor were used as sleeping quarters. Italian marble had been incorporated for the fireplaces, but was used on the first floor only, where it could be seen. What was placed in the private quarters on the next level of the house was merely a facsimile.[5] Visitors normally did not set foot on the second floor, therefore the planter was able to reduce some of his expenditures for the overall design on this level.

Though in Rose Hill (Lockerly) reproductions were used on the second floor in the areas that would be out of sight of the passing visitor, the same was not true for Millwood. No expense was spared in the

---

[3]Fox-Genovese, *Within*, 109 and 116.

[4]HABS, JC, LH, HRBML, pp. 1 and 2.

[5]Personal observations of Lockerly Hall and discussion with Lockerly's historian Murali Thirumal.

decoration and furnishings of the bedrooms found on the second level of Millwood.[6]

Millwood underwent dramatic transformations and renovations. Initially the house was simple in design with a large center hall flanked by twenty by twenty feet rooms on each side.[7] With Nathaniel F. Potter's renovations, the house was enlarged so that the first floor contained eight rooms, four on each side of the wide center hall.[8] Among the rooms featured on the entrance level were "the drawing room…the dining room…a business room…" and "…a music room."[9] "The second floor contained sleeping apartments of various sizes, also handsomely furnished."[10] John B. Irving shared the details of these extensive renovations in his 1844 article "Sporting Epistle From South Carolina."[11] The people of South Carolina were interested in the actions and lifestyle of the elite, much like people of the modern era. This brought insight into a world that most never saw or attained.

There was an openness in the design and structure of Millwood that created a sense of space. Sally Baxter Hampton, who had but recently married into the Hampton family, wrote to her sister back home in New York detailing her new life in South Carolina, especially her time at Millwood. "We sat on the piazza all the afternoon & evening & dined with windows wide open…"[12] This account set the tone of the encompassing capaciousness of the house which was magnified with the opening of the windows to extend the floorplan on to the porch.

Milford had two main floors as well as an attic floor. The main level of the house featured a wide center hall with two large rooms on each side. In the rear portion of the first floor, the grand spiral staircase

---

[6]Irving, "Sporting."

[7]House design, Millwood c. 1817, MRCRF, SCDAH.

[8]Seale, "Diagram of Interior Sketch," MRCRF, SCDAH.

[9]Irving, "Sporting."

[10]Ibid.

[11]Ibid.

[12]Letter, Sally Baxter Hampton to Lucy Baxter, December 23 and 24, 1855, in *Divided*, ed. Hampton: 26-29, 28.

began its climb to the next level. There were four rooms on each side of the second floor while the "attic floor" had six rooms in all.[13]

James Henry Hammond's Redcliffe followed the four rooms to a floor plan, with a grand center hall dividing the rooms.[14] Unique to this mansion was the stairwell. Instead of the typical stairway which ascends facing the hall, the stairs faced the back entrance, which helped for better movement of the air.[15] Faced with the intense heat and humidity of the region, Hammond attempted to alleviate these conditions with this alternate architectural plan.

Although each planter had his home constructed to his individual specifications, there was a tendency toward certain commonalities. Each home contained an area for receiving guests on the first floor. This locale was important for it would grant the first impression of the homestead to the outsider.[16] A formal dining room was usually found on this floor as well. Frequently the plantation owners selected the finest china and silver place settings. Paul C. Cameron carefully selected his silver purchases from the most exclusive stores like Bailey & Co. in Philadelphia. Sitting rooms or a study was another universal component of a planter's household.[17] This was an area for conducting business; it was also a location for social receptions.

The foyer and the parlor were the two most important rooms within the plantation home and by far the most impressive. Upon walking through the main entrance, one would be awestruck by the stairwell, found either in the center or to the right of the vestibule. Common among the Greek Revival plantations were the freestanding spiral wooden staircases. Parts that supported the handrails tended to be sturdier that those found in earlier stairwells. Owners descended these stairs to receive their guests in a scene that created a lasting impression.

---

[13]Nathaniel F. Potter, House plans for Milford, May 1839, WCMFP, SCL, MD.

[14]"Editorial Correspondence," *Charleston Courier.*

[15]Personal observations of Redcliffe Plantation.

[16]Thomas, *Secret*, ed. Burr, 95.

[17]Bailey & Co. Receipt, Paul C. Cameron, October 18, 1860 and October 19, 1860, CFP, SHC.; May, "Advice," 19.; Stanley's China Ledger, Estate of Wade Hampton, Stanley's China Hall, Columbia, LP, SCL, MD.

More detail was etched in the wood, providing for a more curvilinear form.[18] The entranceway granted one the first impression of the home and its contents. It was to present a "sense of quality of the house."[19]

Since all guests passed through the parlor, hence the greatest efforts were placed into its furnishing and decoration. It was also the locale for entertainment and displays of proper social graces, such as the European tradition of high tea.[20] A small table with matching chairs was central to the room to accommodate such events. The entertainment value of the room was critical since plantations were self-sufficient units, located far from the city. Musical instruments such as the harp or a piano, and books were often kept in the paror, especially if there was not a separate library.[21] The Camerons placed their multiple pianos, violins, and flutes in the parlor at Fairntosh.[22] In addition to the parlor, Millwood had "…a music room."[23] These components all designated wealth, status and culture.

Upon occupying the house, Paul and Anne Cameron took great pains and many years to furnish Fairntosh to their liking. Seeking to use styles that reflected the popular trends of the day, like the ornate Rococo Revival with its curvilinear designs,[24] the Camerons carefully positioned these pieces of furniture in the parlor where they would have

---

[18]Gaines, *Development*, 167.; Gleason, *Homes*, 50.; Linley, *Catalog*, p80 and 113.; Kennedy, *Men*, 355-356.; Montmorenci Staircase (at Winterthur) Photographs, IJ-4, IJ-5, IJ-23, IJ-24, MWLWA.; Nathaniel F. Potter, House Plans for Milford Prints, WCMFP, SCL, MD.; Wellman, *Giant*, 9 (relies upon R. L. Allen's 1800's accounts).

[19] May, "Advice," 21.

[20]Thomas, *Secret*, 95.; Letter, Margaret to Elizabeth S. W. Chanler, January 5, 1831, ESWCP, SCL, MD.; Jones and Williams, *Beautiful*, 110.

[21]Hundley, *Social Relations*, 57.; Jones and Williams, *Beautiful*, 111.; Mayhew and Myers, *Documentary*, 100 and 104.

[22]Anderson, *Piedmont*, 54.

[23]Irving, "Sporting."

[24]Joseph T. Butler, on page 69 of his *Field Guide to American Antique Furniture: A Unique Visual System for Identifying the Style of Virtually Any Piece of American Antique Furniture* (New York: Holt Paperbacks, 1986), stated that "from the 1840s through the end of the century, Rococo was the most popular furniture style in the United States."

the greatest visibility. In addition to being stylish, many of the furnishings were reflective of the family's dynamic. As a token of affection for his daughter-in-law Anne, Duncan Cameron obtained a variety of seating "...for her parlour [sic]."[25]

Furniture was placed prominently within the parlor. Frequently, the mistress was responsible for the task of properly placing and arranging the furnishings.[26] Each plantation home was distinct, for there was no set standard for the interiors. However, furniture pieces were usually family heirlooms, in addition to those of Empire and Greek Revival styles. There was a strong trend towards classical themes. With the numerous intermarriages of plantation families, many furnishings had been passed down through generations.[27] Although this generation of upcountry cotton planter sought to distinguish himself from his predecessors, he in fact embraced his legacy through means as simple as incorporating familial furniture into his Greek Revival plantation home.

Chairs placed in the parlor were neither bulky nor cumbersome, so as to allow for arrangement to accommodate more guests. The Empire style chair was most commonly found in this room. Charleston furniture makers did produce many of these particular pieces. Acanthus leaves were commonly found etched into the chair backs.[28] In addition to the armchairs, there were sofas or settees as well as a matching set of seating pieces. Grandfather clocks, étagères, and gaming tables were also used to furnish the parlor.[29]

Windows were a powerful expression of prestige. Most early homes, including plantation houses in Georgia, South Carolina and North Carolina, did not have glass panes and only had gaps between

---

[25]Letter, Duncan Cameron to Paul and Anne Cameron, May 13, 1845, CFP, SHC.

[26]"Editorial Correspondence," *Charleston Courier*.; Hale, "Domestic Economy No. 1," 42.

[27]---, "American Classic," 23.; Bremer, *Impressions,* 286.; Mayhew and Myers, *Documentary*, 100 and 104.

[28]---, "Classic," 44.; Horton, *Museum*, n. p.; Mayhew and Myers, *Documentary*, 108.

[29]Horton, *Museum*, n. p.; Jones and Williams, *Beautiful*, 111.

the wooden logs to serve as a means of light and air circulation.[30] With the construction of these permanent residences, windows became more common. Windows in the parlor were frequently floor to ceiling, thus permitting a greater flow of air on the milder days. They also served a secondary purpose as doors, providing an exit to the front portico. Embroidered curtains were selected in color combinations to complement the color of the walls.[31]

John L. Manning carefully approved of the windows selected for Milford. In order to affect the best possible illumination for the second level of the home, particularly for "...the dresssing [sic] rooms," he opted to place "...fine windows on each side..."[32] Manning made it clear his preference for the type of glass, particularly the tint, for the household windows. He carefully altered the original selection as to best illuminate his home. "As regards the window Mirror glass I prefer [torn section—missing] to the green. I think that all the glass was to be the [torn section—missing] brown glass except some small portio [sic] [torn section—missing]..."[33]

Wade Hampton II added an even more elaborate touch in Millwood by having stained glass windows placed on the wall behind the stairwell, illuminating the stairs in a graceful and delicate manner.[34] The entrance hall thus was elegantly complemented by "...a staircase of much beauty of proportion, lighted from above by richly stained glass, producing a mellow and most agreeable tone of light."[35] These windows conjured up the imagery of a church or temple.

In keeping with the theme of Greek Revival architecture, the classics were revived through both art and furniture. People deemed ancient Athens as the zenith of beauty in the arts, styles and structures.

---

[30]E. Burke, *Pleasure*, 32.; Parsons, *Inside*, 109.; Olmsted, *Kingdom*, 160, 161 and 165.

[31]Horton, *Museum*, n. p.; Hall, "Hospitable," 98.

[32]Letter, Nathaniel F. Potter to John L. Manning, May 12, 1839, WCMFP, SCL, MD.

[33]Letter, John Manning to Nathaniel F. Potter [partial—letter is torn], September 22, 1839, WCMFP, SCL, MD.

[34]Irving, "Sporting."

[35]Ibid.

By copying or creating an American version of the works, the planters paid homage to this ancient era and its poignant legacy of architectural styling and slavery.[36] In turn, they were making these works their own and equating themselves to the ancient rulers, or perhaps even gods.

Specific details of some homes, though, remain unknown, whether it is due to a lack of adequate record keeping, document obscurity, or loss and destruction of familial papers. For example, specifics of the contents and furnishings of Millwood are relatively unknown, for most possessions and some familial papers were destroyed in a fire during the Union Army's occupation of Columbia, South Carolina, in February 1865. There is, however, one noteworthy chair that survived, a"…wicker, semi-arm chair…" where Wade Hampton II was sitting when drew his last breath in 1858.[37] The list of items sold from William Williams estate shows that there were many pieces of furniture. However, the inventory is relatively vague; for example, a "dozen chairs" were specified without further detail. The most detailed account was for items like the "writing desk" and the "candlestick snuffers." Since the list did not specify in which rooms he had placed these objects, historians can only speculate as to the design and placement of these furnishing.[38]

These upcountry cotton planters sought to differentiate themselves from their predecessors or ancestors by building more permanent homes in the Greek Revival style, as opposed to the previously dominant Federal form. Although they were distinguishing themselves from their antecedents, many of these men did retain various components of the past. For example at Fort Hill, John C. Calhoun embraced America's revolutionary history through his possession of a specific chair. General George Washington used this piece of furniture at his headquarters during the battle of Trenton, New Jersey, in 1776. This prized chair was featured on the first floor in Calhoun's sitting room.[39] This

---

[36]Greenough, "American," 206 and 209.; Letter, James Chesnut to James Henry Hammond, 1859, JHHP, SCL, MD.; Morse, "The Fine Arts," 70.; Signourney, "The Perception of the Beautiful," 9.; Tucker, "On," 559.

[37]H. R. E. Hampton, "The Second Wade," VGMP, SCL, MD.

[38]The Estate of Genl. William Williams, Court 1835, WCER, NCDAH.

[39]Ingersoll, "Summer,": 892-895, p. 894.

bond with the past represented the planter's acknowledgement of his, or at least his nation's, traditions. In many ways it was perhaps fitting that Calhoun, the so-called "Father of Secession," held on to an article that was used by the military leader of the American revolutionary cause. This chair was symbolic of the bond he held with Washington, who was a fellow southern planter.

Certain types of wood were particularly suited for southern plantation parlors. Mahogany was commonly used in seating furniture and tables. A reasonably sturdy wood, it generated the best-polished finish.[40] The pocket doors which sectioned off the rooms at Rose Hill (Lockerly) were made of mahogany.[41] These elegant mahogany doors, when drawn from their pockets, blended with the adorned, covered walls. Throughout Manning's Milford, mahogany was the chosen wood for the doors. It was specified that the doors would follow the patterns drawn by Minard Lafever in his *Modern Architecture*; the favored plates were seven, fourteen and nineteen.[42] Pine was native to the Carolinas, hence it was used in furniture making as well as in the overall construction of the house. Yellow pine, specifically, was used to build many of the household furnishings.[43] In fact, the "Articles of Agreement" that was signed between John L. Manning and architect Nathaniel F. Potter explicitly included that the timber to be used in the construction of Milford was to be "...yellow pine..."[44] At Redcliffe, the wood from the indigenous sycamore trees was used extensively in the decorative framing and railings of the household as well as the shelving that held Hammond's extensive book collection.[45]

---

[40]Horton, *Museum*, n. p.; Parkes, *Domestic Duties*.

[41]Discussions with Lockerly's historian Murali Thirumal as well as personal observations made at Lockerly.

[42]Nathaniel F. Potter, "Specifications for a House to be built in Sumpter [sic] district, South Carolina, for John L. Manning, Esq.," May 1839, WCMFP, SCL, MD.

[43]Ellett, "The Noble Wife," 121.; Horton, *Museum*, n. p.; Olmstead, *Kingdom* (1984 version), 134 and 135.; Triad, "Millwood," n.p.

[44]"Articles of Agreement," between John L. Manning and Nathaniel F. Potter, May 6, 1839, WCMFP, SCL, MD.

[45]"Editorial Correspondence," *Charleston Courier*.

The use of color on the walls themselves added depth, warmth, and a sense of quality, whether the walls were covered with fine papers or painted to complement the hues of the artwork and draperies.[46] Contrary to his stance on the tariffs on foreign goods, John C. Calhoun adorned his walls at Fort Hill with trendy wallpapers designed in France.[47] This, in turn, reflected his desire to maintain a home that kept with the current trends in both architectural and interior designs as well as setting standards among his upcountry peers. As Candace M. Volz explains, the "…high style wallpaper selections for their time periods…" are "…further evidence of the Calhoun's "stylish" household."[48] White paint, however, was not commonly used on the walls. Plantation owners generally avoided painting the walls white because they thought it deficient of character, distinction, and dignity. This color had been used prominently during the colonial years due to its minimal cost; in the antebellum period, slave cabins and residences of poor Whites tended to be whitewashed, and it was common to find the same for the interiors since it was readily affordable. Plantation owners sought to distinguish themselves from the masses, so while it was acceptable to have the exterior of their homes painted white, they tended to not use white in the interior. Despite the trend away from using white for the shading of their walls, not everyone followed suit. Nathaniel F. Potter detailed clearly in his "Specifications for a House to be built in Sumpter [sic] district, South Carolina, for John L. Manning, Esq." that "all the wood work…except, the floors…" was "…to be painted…white…"[49]

Paintings by both American and European artists hung on the walls—near the windowns and over the mantels - of the Greek Revival

---

Beecher, 390.; Haweis, *American Decoration*, 217.; Lounsbury, ed., *An Illustrated Glossary*, 404-405.; May, "Advice," 20. [46]

[47] Candace M. Volz, "An Analysis of the Interiors of Fort Hill, The John C. Calhoun House," http://www.volzassociates.com/Calhoun_House_files/JohnC Calhoun_Excerpt.pdf, pp. I-2—I-3.

[48] Volz, "Analysis," p. I-2.

[49] Nathaniel F. Potter, "Specifications for a House to be built in Sumpter district, South Carolina, for John L. Manning, Esq.," May 1839, WCMFP, SCL, MD.

parlor and entrance halls. Typically, paintings were of family members, landscape scenes, prize animals, their magnificent estates, and sometimes reproductions of the great classics.[50] Fort Hill's parlor walls were filled with paintings of various Calhouns, three specifically of the statesman. In the dining room hung a painting of Calhoun, that had been commissioned in his early career.[51]

Art was very important in the décor of the Greek Revival upcountry cotton plantation. Their racehorses were such treasured assets that some planters commissioned formal paintings to be hung in their homes. In the antebellum era, many artists specialized in landscape and portrait paintings but relatively few who stood out in the painting of animals. Edward Troye was one who excelled at painting animals, an art form that had gained much popularity during this time period.[52] Troye's budding reputation brought him to the South, where many commissioned him to paint their prize steeds. Often these oil paintings showed the horse prominently in the foreground, with the estate and main house in the background. Yet the representation of the horse served multiple purposes. The painting of the horse served multiple purposes—it showed off the magnificent hose, chronicled its bloodline, and captured the affluence and beauty of the planter's estate. Edward Troye's works, though at times done with artistic liberty and enhancement, served as solid representations to suit those multiple needs.[53]

On his first lengthy visit to the South, Troye made the acquaintance of Colonel Wade Hampton II, who contracted him to paint some of his prize steeds. Having been commissioned to paint one of the greatest fillies found on the turf, Trifle, Edward Troye gained a notable

---

[50]L. Allen, "Patronage," pp. LA1 and LA6.; Downing, *Country*, p. 319.; "Editorial Correspondence," *Charleston Courier*.; Gaines, *Development*, 167.; Grootkerk, "Artistic," 34.; "List of Paintings Collected by James Henry Hammond," JHHP, SCL, MD.; Mayhew and Myers, *Documentary*, 112.; Sigourney, "Perceptions," 10.; Mackay-Smith, *Race*, 69 and 70.

[51]Clara Walton Adger Journal, March 26, 1854, ABFP, SCL, MD.

[52]L. Allen, "Patronage," p. LA-2.; Hollingsworth, "Equine," 3948 and 3949.; Vosburgh, "Horse Portraiture in America."

[53]L. Allen, "Patronage," pp. LA-1 and LA-2.; Hollingsworth, "Equine," 3948 and 3949.; H. W. Smith, "Best," 41.

reputation for himself.[54] This was to be the first of many stays at Millwood, for Hampton would commission Troye to capture the likenesses of his prominent bloodline horses.[55] This planter was a great patron of the arts and frequently commissioned painters as well as sculptors for various pieces over the years. Troye was but one of many who visited Millwood as a commissioned artist.[56] Troye's Trifle painting, however, found very special and prominent places of display in the big house.[57]

Among the paintings that Troye composed at Millwood were of two of the colonel's finest bred horses, Argyle and Pocahontas. Both were of great racing bloodlines that had proven themselves on the turf. In the paintings, the horses were majestically situated in the forefront of the house that had been built as a wedding present for Wade II and his bride.[58] When Troye finished these paintings, Hampton displayed them in vestibule so that all visitors could appreciate the beauty and elegance of his prize animals.[59] This further exemplified the planter's power and served as representations of the fine breeding of both the man and the animals.

Many other members of the South Carolina Jockey Club as well as planters all over the South employed Troye to paint their horses, as well as other animals. But it was really the horse that was the desired

---

[54]Hollingsworth, "Equine Art," 41.

[55]Stroup, "Up-Country," p. Rsb-3.

[56]"Wade Hampton II and Artists," VGMP, SCL, MD.; Stroup, "Up-Country," p. Rsb-3.

[57]Irving, "Sporting."; Meynard, "Portraits," 1.; Triad, "Millwood," n.p.

[58]Mackay-Smith, "Comments on Letitia Adams," VGMP, SCL, MD.; Mackay-Smith, *Race*, 69, 70 and 416.; Meynard, "Portraits," 3.; Meynard, *Venturers*, 158.; Edward Troye's paintings of Argyle, Pocahontas, Sovereign and Trifle that had been commissioned by Wade Hampton II are owned by the Yale University Art Gallery. On contacting them, I was told that they did not know the location of *Sovereign* and that the other three paintings were in storage and are not available to be viewed by the public. *The American Sporting Gallery* contains a collection of engravings of famous racehorses done in the early 19th century for *The American Sporting Gallery* newspaper, among them is the engraving of Monarch with Millwood in the background, which was based mostly on Troye's painting, as well as others.

[59]Irving, "Sporting."; Meynard, "Portraits," 1.; Meynard, *Venturers*, 158.

subject.[60] The homestead, the occasional jockey astride or alongside his mount, the stable attendant or valet were always overshadowed by the presence of the equine in the painting. But it is significant to note that slaves were included in these paintings. This was especially important to the upcountry cotton planters because it drew attention to their social ranking.

Between 1836, when Troye painted Argyle and Pocahontas, and 1840, when he returned to Millwood, he had traveled throughout the South to plantations and turf racing yard to perform his art.[61] In those four years, Wade II had renovated Millwood and transformed the house into a masterpiece of the Greek Revival design.

Few houses could rival its magnificence and beauty.[62] Though the plantation was truly "a social center for notables of the day," Hampton opted for Troye not to include it in the background of the next series of paintings.[63] When Troye painted the renowned horse Argyle, Hampton included his father's home The Woodlands in the background. The artist then painted Monarch, Bay Maria and Foal, and Maria West and Foal during that visit. In subsequent visits, Troye also painted other horses such as American Eclipse, a forefather of the racing legend Man O'War.[64]

Edward Troye, though having gained the reputation as the greatest horse painter of his day, was not the only artist brought to Hampton's attention.[65] French painter Henri de Lattre captured the images of another mare and her offspring at the Millwood breeding farm and

---

[60]Hollingsworth, "Equine," 3949 and 3950.; H. W. Smith, "Best," 41 and 47.; H. W. Smith, "Edward Troye," 96-97. The last section in Mackay-Smith's *Race Horses* book, he has an index of the known Troye paintings and for whom they were painted. The list is rife with the names of planters. Many of his paintings were not signed, so the total number is not known.

[61]Mackay-Smith, Race, 416-421.; H. W. Smith, "Best," 41 and 47.; H. W. Smith, "Edward Troye," 96.

[62]-, "Visit."; R. L. Allen, "Letters," 20.; Easterby, "Three."; Irving, "Sporting."

[63]Cannaday, "Reconstruction's."

[64]L. Allen, "Patronage," pp. LA-7 and LA-8.; Mackay-Smith, "Commentary."; Meynard, "Portraits," 2-6.

[65]H. W. Smith, "Edward Troye," 41.; Meynard, "Portraits," 2-6.

Charleston artist James De Veaux, whose career had been aided in various means by the Colonel Hampton and his brother-in-law John L. Manning, painted Monarch.[66] Ownership of this horse, much like so many of the other truly greats, was the source of tremendous pride for his owner.[67] Monarch received attention both on and off the track; when it came time for him to again be the subject of a painting for his owner's homestead, the news reported, "Monarch is 'sitting' for his portrait at Columbia."[68] The paintings of these horses were of great importance to Wade Hampton II. Their speed, beauty, and laurels added a different dimension of definition of their owner's character as well as to the house, with their images hanging in proud display upon the oft-viewed walls. John B. Irving clearly noted in his 1844 article that on the first floor of Millwood, "...the walls...are adorned by highly finished colored portraits taken from life of some of the favorite horses of the proprietor..."[69]

Artwork was essential to the definition of the cotton planter and while portraits of his noble steeds were relevant, the planter was also a patron of other types of art. James Henry Hammond was a great collector and he used these pieces to adorn his Beech Island plantation.[70] During the course of his European travels, Hammond commissioned notable artists to paint their original works as well as many of the classic pieces. Many of these works of art were initially used to adorn his other properties but they eventually made their way to Redcliffe. Paintings like Raffaello's (Raphael's) *Fornarina* and Leonardo da Vinci's *Vanity And Modesty* were flawlessly reproduced and prominently hanged in his dining room. While he was in Rome on a grand European tour, Hammond added to his collection. One such purchase was that of the fa-

[66]Mackay-Smith, *Race*, 71.; Meynard, "Portraits," 4 and 6.; Stroup, "Up-Country," p. Rsb-4.

[67]Letter, Wade Hampton II to James Henry Hammond, March 13, 1840, in *Family*, 30.

[68]*Spirit of the Times*, March 23, 1839, 309.

[69]Irving, "Sporting."

[70]"Editorial Correspondence," *Charleston Courier*.

mous *Transfiguration*, which was painted by Italian artist August Temmel.[71] Hammond commissioned copies of other Raffaello and Domenichino paintings, like the *Hunt Of Diana*, for his parlor but also purchased original pieces like Anyder's *Game Piece* and Verstappen's *Falls Of Tivoli* for this room as well.[72] Many of these paintings embodied the rich historical tradition of the glorious ancient empires. Drew Gilpin Faust assessed in her *James Henry Hammond and the Old South: A Design for Mastery* (1985) that Hammond "…as connoisseur and collector, he could achieve the more practical and worldly advantages accruing to the upward mobile from profitable investment and tasteful conspicuous consumption."[73] Hammond was trying to cement his place in high society. Displaying fine art helped him justify, if only to himself, that he was familiar with the finer things in life.

In addition to all of the portraits of his esteemed steeds, Wade Hampton II sponsored the works of artists such as Hiram Powers and William H. Scarborough. Powers sculpted various pieces, inclusive of a bust of the planter himself, and Scarborough painted Wade Hampton II. The Hampton-Preston-Manning families sent artist James DeVeaux to Europe on a few occasions to recreate some of the old classic paintings.[74] Other artists were also commissioned to paint various scenes from abroad as well.[75] Many of the works that graced Hampton's walls represented various aspects of the planter's life.[76]

Along with masterpieces, original or copied, and the paintings of the prize animals, planters commissioned family portraits and paintings of the property. The William Williams family commissioned noted

[71]Hammond Traveling Account, May 1836 - November 1837, February 12, 1837, JHHP. SCL, MD.

[72]"Editorial Correspondence," *Charleston Courier*.; List of Paintings Collected By James Henry Hammond 1807-1864, JHHP. SCL. MD.; Prices in Rome of Art, February 21, 1837, JHHP, SCL, MD.

[73] Faust, *Mastery*, 195.

[74]*Charleston Courier*, May 20, 1841.; "Wade II Hampton and artists," VMP, SCL, MD.; Painting of Wade Hampton II by William H. Scarborough, Historic Columbia Foundation.

[75]Letter, Chapman to Madam, May 22, 1858, HFP, SCL, MD.

[76]*Charleston Courier*, September 27, 1844.

painter Charles Wilson Peale to paint of a likeness of one of the female family members.[77] The parlor walls of Fort Hill were filled with various paintings of each Calhoun at all stages of their lives. Of note were the mountings and edging which encased the images.[78]

Paul Cameron acquired the painting of his father that was the commissioned work of William Garl Browne and hung it in one of the most prominent areas of the plantation home.[79] Cameron carefully designated that the "...furniture...books, portraits..." were to stay with his spouse and then passed on to his daughter following her mother's demise.[80]

The big house was a common feature in paintings that adorned the household walls, particularly those of the entrance hall and the parlor. Other paintings, however, featured the homesteads as mere background subjects. In the famed Edwin Troye paintings of Wade Hampton II's racehorses, three of the works of art integrated plantation homes in the background; one has his father's homestead while the other two show Millwood before its renovations. In all of the paintings, the horse is the primary subject and the house is merely a secondary image.[81] Many times when the planters commissioned paintings, the intent was to show the homestead in all its glory. However, that was not always the case.

Not all historians agree that the planter's commissioning of an artistic rendering of his plantation house was done for posterity. John Michael Vlach contends in *The Planter's Prospect:* that the planters desired the painting be a source of reflection upon which he could gaze. It was to be for him to look upon his homestead, not to be a documentary account; the paintings were to be a record that revealed the landscape more than the homestead.[82] The paintings serve as a glimpse into

---

[77]Kennedy, *Men*, 271.

[78]Ingersoll, "Summer," 894.

[79]Letter, Paul C. Cameron to Duncan Cameron, January 1, 1852, CFP, SHC.

[80]Will of Paul C. Cameron, 1881, NCW, CC, NCDAH, 5.

[81]Mackay-Smith, "Comments," VGMP. SCL, MD.; Mackay-Smith, *Race,* 416 and 421..

[82]Vlach, *Privilege*, 20 and 23.

the life of the planter. They show what these men valued and what they deemed as important.

While the walls were elaborately decorated with paintings, the ceiling were plain. Ceilings frequently had little adornment. The most elaborate of ceiling decorations was inclusive of a foliage derived center medallion.[83]

Part of the décor of Milford was left to the fancies of John L. Manning's wife Susan Frances Hampton Manning. He clearly specified that she was more adept to select "...the mantle mirrors..." for two of the main rooms of the first level of the house.[84] Manning did clarify to the architect though that they were to be made from "...the richest gilt for the drawing room and bronze for the dining room."[85] Manning expected his home to meet or exeed the expectations of the ladies of high society who were privileged to see them. These women were also the ones who made comments about the home and furnishings to others, generating a great source of information that spread to people who would never set foot in the plantation house.

Many other essential interior features were used as displays of wealth. Fireplaces were necessary within the household, serving as the principal mode of heating, but they served an aesthetic role as well. The fireplace mantels of Montmorenci were unique. In the two foremost rooms on the first floor, where the mantels would have been seen by all who entered the residence, the fireplaces featured designs honoring the War of 1812.[86] Though these mantles incorporated Americana themes, the doorway moldings reflected a classical Greek element.[87] A fireplace mantle on the main floor of Lowther Hall featured a detailed center

---

[83]---, "Classic," 44.; Downing, *Country*, 319 [reprint of 1850 edition].; Hall. "Hospital," 95.; Jones and Williams, *Beautiful*, 111.; May, "Advice," 19 and 21.

[84]Letter, John Manning to Nathaniel F. Potter [partial letter—portions torn], September 22, 1839, WCMFP, SCL, MD.

[85]Ibid.

[86]McFarland, *Warren*, 23.; Photograph, Montmorenci parlor mantle, MWLWA.

[87]Photographs, Montmorenci doorway mantles, MWLWA.

emblem. The mantle was white, which stood in sharp contrast to the brick interior.[88]

Milford's fireplace mantels were made of marble much like those in Millwood. They were chosen by John L. Manning as per the "Articles of Agreement" he signed with his architect.[89] By selecting his own mantels, Manning not only had a greater input into the overall design of the furnishings of the house but also personally ensured the highest quality for what was being placed in the plantation house.

Behind all of these elaborate decorations, furnishing, structures and interior designs were the slaves. It was the slave who was emblematic of the planter's prosperity. They cultivated his cotton, which enabled him to have all these possessions. The planters used the slaves as symbols of status. As Thavolia Glymph noted in her *Out Of The House Of Bondage* that, "slaves, like English china, conveyed household wealth and standing in the community; the greater number of slaves on display, the greater the household's wealth and reputation. Slaveholders themselves were generally eager to give this impression...[90]

Slaves were visible measurers of social standing. Continuing in this similar ideology, Walter Johnson asserted in his *Soul By Soul* that "the outward face of a slaveholding household-the driver of the carriage, the greeting given at the door, the supervision of the child, the service at the table-was often a slave."[91] Ownership of slaves was the most poignant means for planters to display their power and authority.

In addition to the decorative elements, there were also certain features critical to its overall operation. One important aspect of the plantation was the master's library. Though not always found within the big house itself, for it frequently was a completely separate structure, the library was a place for business but also for reflection. The library was

---

[88]Photographs of the Historic American Buildings Survey, Interiors-Lowther Hall, online Georgia Tech catalog, http://www.library.gatech.edu/archives/habs/HABS_PH_046.htm

[89]"Articles of Agreement," signed by Jos. Fenney, C. L. Hampton, Nathaniel Potter and Jno. L. Manning, May 6, 1839, WCMFP, SCL, MD.; Irving, "Sporting."

[90]Glymph, *Bondage*, 151.

[91]Johnson, *Soul*, 89.

also a place of family activity. Wade Hampton II used this room to bring his children together to recount great tales of the past.[92]

The libraries of plantation owners often held legal and historical tomes, but the "...Greek and Latin classics" were common as well, perhaps enhancing their appreciation and understanding of the ancient societies which they found themselves so entwined.[93] Regarding planters and their tendency to embrace the classics, Joseph P. Reidy noted in his *From Slavery To Agrarian Capitalism In The Cotton Plantation South* that "planters' estates routinely contained individual volumes, if not entire libraries, of ancient classics."[94]

Wade Hampton II's library, constructed within the structure of Millwood itself, matched the greatness of the building, and his quantity of books- estimated at 10,000-overtook two adjoining rooms. Many of these works were on American history, thus reflecting Hampton's affinity for his country. Also of note within this collection were monographs that bore the signature of King George III.[95] Edward G. Longacre noted in his book *Gentleman And Soldier* that Wade Hampton III, the planter's son, "...had benefitted from daily exposure to the ten thousand volumes in the library at Millwood..."[96]

John Manning also had his library built within confines of the actual house. Upon entrance through the front door, the library was positioned immediately to the right. The books sat upon mahogany shelving, and the room itself was adorned with a majestic mirror above the mantle. Milford's library adjoined the dining room.[97] Similar to Milford's design, the library at Fairntosh was also adjacent to the dining

---

[92]Account, Wade II, HFP, SCL, MD.

[93]Dodd, *Kingdom,* 79.; -, "Home Life.".; Letter, James Henry Hammond to M. C. Hammond, May 15, 1832, JHHP, SCL, MD.; General exploration of the library shelves of some of these plantations, like Redcliffe and Rose Hill (Lockerly), along with a now missing official list from Fort Hill, produced these findings.

[94]Reidy, *Agrarian*, 266 [in endnote #82 on page 53].

[95]Perry, *Reminiscences*, 340.; Mackay-Smith, *Race*, 69.; Triad, "Millwood," n.p.

[96]Longacre, *Gentleman*, 20.

[97]Harmon, "Milford Mansion," 27, JLMP, SCL, MD. ; Harmon, "Milford Plantation," 3, MP, RS, SCHC.

room. The library here was the first room to the right of the great center hall.[98]

The library at Fort Hill was detached from the main residence, just south of the big house. Built in the Greek Revival style, the building followed the model of his main residence. This was a private sanctuary for the very public man. Calhoun alone, and no one else, opened his library door, which was frequently a place for reflection. Though not grand in size, it was filled with many of the ancient classics as well as the works of great Americana.[99] Calhoun included his own writings in his library collection. His possession of all of these books, all in all, was clearly denoted by his inscriptions which he placed within them. John C. Calhoun also included a bust of himself, which helped alter the cumbersome impression of the subdued room burdened with its heavy furnishings and drab coloring.[100] In many ways, this building was a memorial as well as an attestation to his career and persona. Theoretically, it was a representation of his egocentrism.

On the occasion when artist William Scarborough arrived to paint the planter's portrait, Calhoun's library served another purpose. John C. Calhoun opened his private sanctuary to be used by Scarborough as his painting area.[101] The fact that Calhoun permitted Scarborough to paint in his library indicated how important the library and art were to him. Perhaps Calhoun believed the artist would produce his best work in his private sanctuary.

James Henry Hammond too maintained an extensive library at Redcliffe. As he had advocated in his letter to his son John Hammond, "read history chiefly..." in addition to encouraging him to also purchase a "...French book...", he felt that books were essential to one's life and character.[102] Constantly striving to learn more, Hammond was an avid

---

[98]Architectural plan of Fairntosh (Plate IV) in Woodhouse, "Architecture in North Carolina 1700-1900," 17.

[99]-. "Home Life," *The Anderson Daily Mail.*; Coit, *Portrait*, 383.; *Charleston Courier*, September 19, 1859.; Scoville, "'A Visit," 529.; Perry, *Reminiscences*, 108.

[100]Ingersoll, "Summer," 894.

[101]*Charleston Courier*, September 19, 1859.

[102]Letter, James Henry Hammond to John Hammond, July 14, 1836, JHHP, SCL, MD.

reader and kept an assortment of reference works so that he could further educate .[103] He also secured a vast collection of monographs from the estate auction of the original owner of the property whereupon he constructed Redcliffe.[104] The journalist who wrote the "Editorial Correspondence if the Courier," who visited Redcliffe on July 6, 1862, detailed his impressions of the house and property, described Hammond's "...library, well stored, as an intellectual larder, with handsomely bound books of varied character and great value, where both mind and heart may be richly feasted and greatly improved."[105]

North Carolina planter William Williams also had a collection of books at Montmorenci. Most treasured among the works was *Lafayette's Travels.*[106] Books and the library in which they were held were important to the planter. Paul C. Cameron designated in his will who would obtain his books following his death.[107]

The interior and the contents within the upcountry cotton plantation Greek Revival house helped to further this distinction of this separate social class. These Georgia and Carolina planters used architectural and aesthetic design within the house to present an image of their social standing, as much as they did through their art and other possessions. Each item was carefully selected and positioned with painstaking detail within the household to display power, authority, and wealth to those welcomed into the house. The cumulative visual effect was intented to display the image and character of the man who owned them. Even though they made efforts to differentiate themselves from their predecessors, they kept items passed down from them, emphasizing the importance of lineage. These factors, in concert with the Greek Revival

---

[103]"Editorial Correspondence," *Charleston Courier.*; Perry, *Reminiscences,* 108.

[104]Letter, James Henry Hammond to William G. Simms, May 13, 1855, JHHP, LOC, MD.

[105]"Editorial Correspondence," *Charleston Courier.*

[106]Bishir, "Montmorenci," 88.; Estate of Gen William Williams 1835, WCER, NCDAH.

[107]Will of Paul C. Cameron, 1881, NCW, CC, NCDAH, 5.

architectural design of the plantation house, fused together to serve as a representation of the status of the upcountry cotton planter.

CHAPTER 7

AT THE VERY CORE IS SLAVERY: PLANTERS AND THEIR POSSESSIONS

There were many factors that helped define the planter; among them were the big house, its contents and the outer buildings of the plantation. The financial resources that enabled their lifestyle came from the successful cultivation of cotton crops, cultivated, harvested, and prepared for market by slaves. Without the slaves, the mansions and estates would not have existed. As these men expanded their holdings within their states and beyond, they continued to build in their favored Greek Revival architectural style. Slaves were the foundation of these plantation homes and the power maintained by these men. These planters wanted to tell their stories of their lives through their main houses as well as through all their possessions. The one aspect missing in their accounts was the contributions made by their slaves.

There were many tangible possessions which the planter used to convey his authority. Aside from their primary residences, these men owned vacation homes and townhouses for seasons of entertaining as refuge from the weather. These houses served as a measure of status and planters competed for who had the most lavish home or could spend the most money on residences that were their primary homes. There was a sort of unsaid competition among the planter ranks as to who made the greatest expenditure on a house that was not a primary homestead. James Henry Hammond went as far as to boast that his place in Columbia set the standards of extravagance and opulence. In his diary entry of June 28, 1841, he proclaimed "...There is a great rage for building fine houses here now. I believe I set the example."[1] Hammond's Columbia house was also built as a Greek Revival home, with

---

[1]James Henry Hammond diary entry, June 28, 1841 in *Secret*, ed. Bleser, 62. Amid scandals of later years, Hammond sold this town house and concentrated on his plantation holdings. The Columbia house was completely destroyed, sans some columns, during the course of Federal occupation of the city in February 1865.

pillars encircling the entire structure. Lavish decorative wood working filled the house.[2] He took the same great pains to furnish this Greek Revival town house as he did his others. Always striving to maintain his image of a member of the wealthy cotton planter elite, he wanted to make sure that his residences reflected this status. During his ventures to New York City, Hammond acquired various furnishings to enhance the appearance of this Columbia home as well.[3]

Lavishly furnishing his Columbia house was important to Hammond because it would better solidify his place in the state capita as a leader in planter society. He wrote his wife Catherine on one such shopping trip in New York that "...I shall find great perplexity in making purchases," continuing "I contracted to day [sic] for 4 marble mantels. 1 Egyptian & 3 white."[4] He carefully selected the furnishings and reported to Catherine in one instance that he purchased chairs "1 doz. handsome mahogany new French pattern of the best quality."[5]

Although Hammond wanted to stay in style, he did show some discretion in spending, remarking that he bought some seating at a lesser price and noted that "the same articles from Phyfe's would have cost $6 or 700."[6] Duncan Phyfe was among the premier furniture makers in New York. His pieces incorporated "...the ancient traditions..."[7] and his "...artistic expression...tended towards delicacy, refinement, and attenuation."[8] Hammond justified his purchase by claiming that "Phyfe who is as much behind the times in style as he is in price. He thinks it is still 1836—French Bedstands [sic] are decidly [sic] going out. They tell me no one buys them South now at all..."[9] Hammond

---

[2]"The Hammonds," HBCFP, SCL, MD, 11 and 12.

[3]Letter, James Henry Hammond to Kate, July 30, 1840, JHHP, SCL, MD.

[4]Letter, James Henry Hammond, to My Dear Wife (Catherine), August 25, 1840, JHHP, SHC.

[5]Ibid.

[6]Ibid.; Hammond meant that the price would have been six hundred or seven hundred dollars.

[7]Cornelius, *Furniture*, 47.

[8]Ibid, 52.

[9]James Henry Hammond to My Dear Wife (Catherine), August 25, 1840, JHHP, SHC.

normally spent his wife's money freely, but in this letter to Catherine, he attempted to legitimize his expenditures, claiming he was being frugal while still purchasing the most popular styles of the day.

Hammond liked his acquisitions for the Columbia house. "I have nearly completed all my purchases & have shipped the greater portion…I have purchased all the furniture."[10] Although he made all of the selections, clearly with the goal of solidifying his reputation and status, he hinted at being concerned as to his wife's opinion. "I hope they will please you" he wrote to Catherine Hammond, continuing on stating "…you will be satisfied I think."[11] Once Hammond was in the Columbia house, he had each article set up swiftly. By the end of November 1840, he wrote his wife that "the drawing room is finished…Nothing hardly to be done now but hang the picture & put the new shelf on the mantel."[12] Though this was not this cotton planter's main residence, it was a symbol of his wealth and power. It was clearly a depiction of the man and his ability to not only own multiple properties, particularly Greek Revival houses, but his capacity to furnish them all as if they were the only residence.

When choosing to construct other houses, many upcountry planters followed along in the same favored building design as the plantation house since Greek Revival was their architectural style. Each home owned by the upcountry cotton planter was built in this same manner. In addition to his families' plantation homes, Paul C. Cameron built his townhouse in Raleigh in the Greek Revival format as well.[13]

Planters also built vacation homes where their families could escape the heat and mingle with members of their social class. One such popular location was White Sulphur Springs, Virginia. The arrangement of all different sized bungalows was done in a neatly organized

---

[10]Letter, James Henry Hammond to Dear Wife (Catherine), September 4, 1840, JHHP, SHC.

[11]Ibid.

[12]Letter, James Henry Hammond to My Dear Wife (Catherine), November 27, 1840, JHHP, SHC.

[13]Photograph in Sanders, *Cameron*, 59.

pattern for comfort as well as representation of status.[14] The Hamptons were but one of the many upcountry planter families who enjoyed their time here so much that they even owned a home.[15] The Calhouns maintained a cottage here as well.[16] In August of 1846, John C. Calhoun wrote to Thomas Clemson, stating "I leave here in the morning tomorrow for the White Sulpher [sic] Springs where Mrs. Calhoun and Cornelia are waiting me [sic] to join them."[17] The vacation home apparently also served as a place in which to spend time with family.

In addition to these other homes, many planters owned supplementary plantations in other parts of the South. Paul Cameron expanded their holdings into Alabama as well.[18] His abilities as a cotton planter were well known throughout the South. Others kept him apprised when plantation lands became available so that he could continue to enlarge his land holdings. In January 1860, W. A. Jones of E. M. Apperson & Co. of Memphis, Tennessee, wrote Cameron while he was in Greensboro, Alabama, about such an opportunity. "We know of a plantation about 150 or 160 miles below here which can he bought at $60 per acre, 960 acres 600 acres cleared, good houses, fine gin house and every thing in complete running order." The letter included an additional venture for the Camerons, for there were "...48 negroes on this place, which probably could be bought." Jones also presented Paul Cameron with the opportunity to expand this particular plantation as well, advising that "adjoining the place is a tract of 600 acres..."[19] Given Cameron's reputation and status, even the deep South planters desired to incorporate Cameron into their realm.

---

[14]Letter, Wade Hampton to Rosa Schulz, December 9, 1840, HFP, SCL, MD.; Featherstonehaugh, "Excursions," 234.; Map of White Sulpher Springs, Virginia, J. Caldwell, Proprietor, 1847, VGMP, SCL, MD.

[15]*Charleston Daily Courier*, February 12, 1858, VGMP, SCL, MD.; Lewis, *Ladies and Gentlemen*, 61.; Map of White Sulpher Springs, Virginia, J. Caldwell, Proprietor, 1847, VGMP, SCL, MD.

[16]Letter, JA Stuart to John C. Calhoun, October 8, 1841 in *Annual Report*, 161.; Meynard, *Venturers*, 170.

[17]Letter, John C. Calhoun to Thomas G. Clemson, August 8, 1846 in *Annual Report*, 704.

[18] Anderson, *Piedmont*, 53 and 97.

[19]Letter, W. A. Jones to Paul Cameron, January 18, 1860, CFP, SHC.

The Hamptons and the Mannings were also included in this classification. Louisiana was one of the other areas where they cultivated the land and built Greek Revival homes. Although Millwood burned during the Civil War, a sort of visual record was left behind from another Hampton plantation. Houmas, built in Louisiana, apparently featured many architectural similarities as well as shared landscape ideas with Millwood. It featured "an avenue lined with trees..." which "...led to the house..." which was graced with "...pillars supporting the veranda."[20] The Louisiana plantation was also filled with an array of outer buildings, inclusive of "...the white lines of negro cottages and the plantation offices..."[21] The familial ties with John L. Manning were clearly represented in Louisiana too, for their plantations were nearby. Visitor William Russel described them as "one plantation is as like another as two peas. He had the same paths..."[22] It was this plantation, however, where Manning generated much of his wealth.

John C. Calhoun also held plantation lands in the deep South. Trying his luck in Alabama to maximize his cotton output, he opted not to supervise the property himself and placed it under the guidance of one of his children.[23] Calhoun's duties in the nation's capital often guided his time frame for personal property management and often prevented him from traveling that great a distance, although he was so inclined. In November 1839, for example, he wrote to politician and journalist Duff Green, "Andrew and Margaret left us for Alabama...I intended to accompany them to look at my interest in that quarter, but the weather remained too warm and dry till [sic] it was too late to make the visit in time to return and be at my post at Washington at the commencement of the session...[24] Calhoun was always concerned and cognizant as to the productive capabilities of his plantation. In the time of "...the most remarkable drought ever known..." around the vicinity of Fort Hill, he had to look to his other lands for good cotton production.

---

[20]Russel, "Hampton," HFP, SCL, MD.

[21]Ibid.

[22]Ibid.

[23] —, "Home Life," *The Anderson Daily Mail.*

[24]Letter, John C. Calhoun to Duff Green, from Fort Hill, November 2, 1839 in *Year 1899*, 433.; Andrew Calhoun was John C. Calhoun's eldest son.

He continued on in this August 12, 1845 letter to proclaim that "my cotton crop with the exception of the part in the fort [sic] Hill field, is surprisingly good…the last account from Alabama was good."[25]

The deep South plantation was always important even if Calhoun himself could not oversee operations. But when he could take breaks from public service, he visited his other holdings. Writing to his son-in-law Thomas G. Clemson, he expressed a hint of hesitancy about leaving his properties to return to public office: "You will have seen, that I have again been elected to the Senate much against my inclination, but under such circumstances that I could not with propriety decline accepting. I am now on my way to Washington with Mrs. Calhoun and Cornelia, after remaining a few days at Fort Hill on my return from Alabama…[26]

Thomas Clemson apparently thought highly of his father-in-law's Alabama lands. Although Clemson claimed of his South Carolina property that "my plantation [in Edgefield District] is the most valuable I know in the State" he went on in the same 1845 letter to praise Calhoun for the number of slaves he accorded his deep South estate. "If my place had equal force to what you have put upon your place in Alabama, my place would give a greater interest, (considering the cost) than yours."[27] The Alabama plantation was not "home" but it was a means of generating, as well as displaying, the wealth of the planter. It clearly was not as relevant as Fort Hill was to Calhoun. Based on his letters, John C. Calhoun never referred to the Alabama plantation by name.

In essence, the productivity of the cotton crop was always critical to the fundamental operations of the plantation, at both the main homestead as well as on the properties of the other states. John C. Calhoun included the status of his crops in his familial letters. Writing from Fort Hill to his son Patrick, who was serving in the United States

[25]Letter, John C. Calhoun to T. G. Clemson, August 12, 1845 in *Volume XXII*, 68.

[26]Letter, John C. Calhoun to Thomas G. Clemson, December 13, 1845 in *Year 1899*, 674.

[27]Letter, Thomas G. Clemson to John C. Calhoun, September 1, 1845 in *Volume XXII*, 105.

Army in Arkansas, he reported as to the yield of cotton he anticipated. "My crop here & in Alabama is very fine, both corn & cotton. We expect to make in Alabama nearly 200,000 pounds of clean cotton, but, I fear, we shall get but little for it, so low is the price."[28]

Wealth for these planters, however, was never accumulated on a continual basis. Factors far beyond the control of these men, such as droughts and floods, impacted cotton cultivation and yield while tariffs regulated prices and profits. As the upcountry regions did not maintain the consistent heat in which cotton crops flourished, the owners of these estates commonly expanded their land holdings beyond their familial property. As W. J. Megginson asserted in his *African-American Life*, "yearly fluctuations occurred in weather and the resulting yields…"[29] Megginson continued the point by specifying the resulting impact on John C. Calhoun: "…in 1837, Calhoun produced 65,000 pounds of cotton, 75,000 in 1842, but 53,000 in 1844. Families such as The Calhouns who owned lands in several areas-Pickens, Abbeville and Alabama-might have a successful crop on one plantation when another suffered from unfavorable weather. Few farmers had this advantage."[30]

The ability to own additional plantations signified the wealth and prosperity of the planter. At times, it was done as an attempt to reclaim financial resources as the cotton market dipped or as their lands on the east coast showed signs of wear. Sometimes they owned supplementary plantations within the same state in which they resided. Most of these planters owned numerous properties. William Williams and Paul Cameron both maintained multiple plantations in their home state of North Carolina.[31] James Henry Hammond also profited from the several plantations that he owned in South Carolina. Although his first

---

[28]Letter, John C. Calhoun to Lt. Patrick Calhoun, October 21, 1842, JCCP, SCL, MD.

[29]Megginson, *Upper*, 47.

[30]Ibid.

[31]Duncan Cameron Will 1835, WCRWISE, NCDAH.; Letter, P. C. Cameron to Duncan Cameron, May 6, 1847, CFP, SHC.; Mordecai Land Survey, Wake County Survey for Duncan Cameron, January 15, 1828, CFP, SHC, 1.; Obituary of Paul C. Cameron, *The News and Observer*, January 7, 1891.; Paul C.

plantations came through marriage, he expanded on that wealth and built Redcliffe with the profits.[32] Wade Hampton II possessed plantations in South Carolina as well as in other regions of the South.[33]

The upcountry cotton planter was a master of his world but was also a paternal figure for those who resided in the vicinity of his plantation. John C. Calhoun, albeit a man of various political offices, was not only a public servant but offered assistance to his neighbors of lesser social and financial standings. George W. Featherstonhaugh observed that of Calhoun,

> all looked up to him as the first man in South Carolina; and many who were embarrassed in their circumstances came to him for advice...he always listened to their stories, gave them the most friendly advice, and frequently referred them to men of business who could assist them if their affairs were retrievable. By persevering in this wise conduct, he was enabled to do good to all, and keep himself free from embarrassment.[34]

James Henry Hammond too permitted outsiders into his upcountry cotton planter world at Redcliffe. "The hospitality of the owner of "Redcliffe" was well known...once a year, like a great feudal landlord, he gave fete or grand dinner to all the country people about, at which he always contrived to have some distinguished guests present."[35] At

---

Cameron Will 1881, NCW, CC, NCDAH.; William Williams Will 1832, WCW, NCDAH.

[32]Billings, "Notes," HBCFP, SCL, MD, 1 and 2.; Harry Hammond, "James Henry Hammond: Little Known Sketch by Late Major Harry Hammond," March 2, 1924, JHHP, SCL, MD.; Letter, James Henry Hammond to My Dear Major, July 8, 1859, JHHP, SCL, MD.; Letter, James Henry Hammond to Mrs. C. E. Hammond, April 6, 1842, JHHP, SHC.; Perry, *Reminiscences*, 326.; "Editorial Correspondence," *Charleston Courier*.

[33]Abstract of Title To All That Tract Of Land..., HFP, SCL, MD.; Harry R. E. Hampton, "Hampton Houses," VGMP, SCL, MD, 1.; Letter, Wade Hampton to Col. Singleton, August 22, 1842, HFP, SCL, MD.; Map of Hampton Family Plantations, Inside Cover of Meynard, *Venturers*.; --, "Visit."

[34] Featherstonhaugh, *Canoe*, 270-271.

[35]Clay-Copton, *Belle*, 217.

these annual affairs, Hammond proceeded to have "…every neighbour [sic], poor or rich, for miles about was present."[36]

Nevertheless, it was the ownership of slaves that defined his paternalism. Without slavery, cotton could not have been cultivated to the extent that it was in the upcountry or the American South.[37] Planters advocated that the holding of men in bondage was an act that had been practiced throughout human existence.[38] Men like James Henry Hammond contended in a nonchalant manner that while the markets sought cotton, all that was needed were the slaves to get it to that point for their masters.[39] The slaves furnished the planters with their social status. It was "the slaves, who enable them to be aristocratic…" who "…stand to them in the relation of vassals to their lords."[40]

The institution of chattel slavery was deeply rooted in the Greek tradition, much like their favored architectural style, thus further tying the planters to this ancient civilization. The upper echelons of ancient Greek society accorded those deemed inferior the status of slaves. Ironically, ironically, the Southern planter considered the Greek system of enslavement to be far harsher and more cruel.[41] The men of both eras believed that they were helping the slave survive in a world he would be unable to do so on his own. Hammond proclaimed in his "Mud-sill" speech that Southerners had enslaved those who had "…a low order of intellect and but little skill" in order to give them a chance "…to perform the drudgery of life."[42] Ultimately, he felt he was echoing Aristotle's ideas of "…the lower sort are by nature slaves, and it is better for them as for all inferiors that they should be under the rule of a master."[43] John C. Calhoun went as far as to proclaim that slavery was a

---

[36]Ibid.

[37]Dodd, *Kingdom*, 7.

[38]R. Collins, "Essay on the Treatment," 205.

[39]Letter, James Henry Hammond to William May Wightman, June 7, 1840, WMWP, SCHS.

[40]Grund, *Aristocracy*, 149

[41]"Slavery in the South States," pp. 352-353, LOC.

[42]Hammond, "Speech on the Admission of Kansas"/ "Mud-Sill" Speech in *Defended*, 122.

[43]Aristotle, *Politics, Book One, Part V.*

"positive good."[44] Decades after Calhoun's death, Alexander Crummel reminded Americans in his *The Attitude of the American Mind towards the Negro Intellect* about this planters beliefs. "That if he could find a Negro who knew the Greek syntax, he would then believe that the Negro was a human being and should be treated as a man."[45]

Those upcountry cotton planters were clearly committed to protecting slavery. Although a rift had grown between the North and South, these planters voiced their concern about protecting this institution. John C. Calhoun recognized the need for Northern merchants to purchase Southern cotton, an economic relationship that secession would destroy. He presented nullification as a different means by which they could protest the high tariffs. Edward E. Baptist addressed John C. Calhoun's doctrine of nullification in his monograph *The Half Has Never Been Told*. He stated that:

> Calhoun offered a viable alternative to the claim that Southern political bullying was protecting an economically backward institution. Southern politicians could now claim that constitutional rights mandated political solutions to their own decline in relative political power. And at the moment when Calhoun made this move, the vision of perpetually expanding slavery as an alternative but still modern economy was once again becoming plausible.[46]

As committed to the institution of slavery as these upcountry planters were, they comprehended all the economic variables associated with it in the market economy.

Two of these upcountry cotton planters delivered among the most famous speeches regarding the need for slavery, thus demonstrating their personal commitment to this institution, but through their professional political careers. When John C. Calhoun delivered his "Speech on the Reception of Abolition Petitions, Delivered in the Senate, February 6th, 1837," through his carefully articulated words, he

[44]Calhoun, "Abolition Petitions," in *Defending*, 59.

[45]Crummel, *Attitude*, https://www.blackpast.org/african-american-history/1898-alexander-crummell-attitude-american-mind-toward-negro-intellect/

[46]Baptist, *Half*, 331.

emphasized that "the peculiar institution of the South--that, on the maintenance of which the very existence of the slaveholding States depends, is pronounced to be sinful and odious..." which seemed to contradict some of his other speeches. Calhoun furthered his beliefs and stated that he was in fact "...the friend of the Union..."[47] Clearly these planters needed the Northern industrial machine to purchase their cotton, so there needed to be a relationship. However, Calhoun emphasized his region's commitment to slavery when he proclaimed that "we of the South will not, cannot surrender our institutions."[48] In the context of this speech, cotton planter John C. Calhoun stood before the Senate, clarifying the opinion of his class. He, unlike others, had the unique power and ability to have an audience before this governing body. Calhoun said.

> I hold it to be a good, as it has thus far proved itself to be to both, and will continue to probe so if not disturbed by the fell spirit of abolition. I appeal to facts. Never before has the black race of Central Africa, from the dawn of history to the present day, attained a condition so civilized and so improved, not only physically, but morally and intellectually. It came among us in a low, degraded, and savage condition, and in the course of a few generations it has grown up under the fostering care of our institutions, reviled as they have been, to its present comparatively civilized condition. This, with the rapid increase of numbers, is conclusive proof of the general happiness of the race, in spite of all the exaggerated tales to the contrary.[49]

Thus the position of the American South was made clear by an upcountry cotton planter. As John C. Calhoun proclaimed, slavery was "positive good."[50] The significance of his statement is clear. The up-

---

[47]Calhoun, "Speech on the Reception of Abolition Petitions, Delivered in the Senate, February 6th, 1837," http://www.stolaf.edu/people/fitz/COURSES/calhoun.html.

[48]Ibid.

[49]Ibid.

[50]Ibid.

country cotton planter had risen in such stature that he voiced the opinion of the American South. Slavery was essential. In this speech, John C. Calhoun made his commitment to this horrific institution clear.

James Henry Hammond also made a poignant speech to the American Senate regarding the need for slavery in the South. As an upcountry planter Hammond was reliant on this institution. With the volatile situation in Kansas, in March 1858, he said "In all social systems there must be a class to do the menial duties, to perform the drudgery of life. That is, a class requiring but a low order of intellect and but little skill." Hammond asserted that one "...class which leads...it constitutes the very mud-sill of society..."[51] In these words, he advocated White supremacy and the inferiority of the American slave. This also echoed the ideas expressed by Aristotle in his *Politics*, as he had discussed the concept of "natural slavery."[52] He declared that "the status in which we have placed them is an elevation...from the condition in which God first created them, by being made our slaves."[53] Through this speech, Hammond made himself the voice for the South. This upcountry cotton planter evoked the passion of those who sought to cling on to the institution of slavery.

Paul E. Johnson, in *The Early American Republic,* explained planters' ultimate control over all aspects of their slaves' lives, yet they were also cognizant that they needed to facilitate their slaves' productive capabilities.

> In law, in census, and in the minds of planters, slaves members of a plantation household over which the overseer exercised absolute authority not only as owner but also as paternal protector and lawgiver. Yet both slaveholder and slaves knew that slaves could not be treated like farm animals or little children. Wise slaveholders learned that the success of a plantation depended less on terror and draconian discipline (though whippings-and

---

[51]Hammond, "*Speech of Hon. James H. Hammond, of South Carolina, on the admission of Kansas, under the Lecompton Constitution: delivered in the Senate of the United States, March 4, 1858.*" http://simms.library.sc.edu/view_item.php?item=133195.

[52]Aristotle, *Book One.*

[53]Ibid.

> worse-were common) then on the accommodations by which slaves traded labor and obedience for some measure of privilege and autonomy within the bonds of slavery.[54]

Theoretically, Johnson made a valid point, that planters needed to foster a sort of relationship with their chattel in order to get the utmost productivity. Planters ultimately kept economics foremost in their minds. Mistreatment of their slaves truly was bad economic practice. Yet, practicality did not always prevail.

Effective management of the slaves was essential to the profitable operation of these plantations. Due to vast holdings, many planters were reliant upon others to oversee the day to day field activities. Many planters, such like John C. Calhoun, tried to be as directly immersed in the roles and usages of slaves.[55] At times the planters recognized the slaves ironically in an almost familial way. In a letter reporting on the status of the cotton crop to his father, Paul C. Cameron clearly mentioned "...the black family..." in the opening of this note and continued on to report on their health, suggesting that he valued them beyond mere property.[56] Still, it was an economic necessity that these slaves were healthy, so Cameron emphasized proper nutrition as well as adequate attire for all of his servants.[57] He also inventoried his slave lists by their names along with their occupations or categorized his servants by age ranges.[58] Regardless of Cameron's motivations—he did not want his slaves to run away, genuinely cared about their welfare, or simply wanted healthy slaves to reflect well on him—his slaves had no voice and their viewpoints are really unknown. Jean Bradley Anderson concluded that "how the slaves felt towards the...Camerons is harder to discover."[59] The reality was that Paul Cameron was a master whose success was dependent upon the labor of these people.

---

[54]P. Johnson, *Early American Republic*, 98.

[55]Megginson, *Upper*, 48.

[56]Letter, Paul C. Cameron to Duncan Cameron, May 6, 1847, CFP, SHC.

[57]Letter, Paul C. Cameron to Mildred and Margaret Cameron, CFP, SHC.

[58]Lists of Negroes of P. C. Cameron, CFP, SHC.; Undated Slave Lists, CFC, SHC.

[59]Anderson, *Piedmont*, 111.

The Cameron family did consider the issue of slaves and their emancipation. Duncan Cameron served one year as president of the North Carolina's Colonization Society.[60] His son Paul C. Cameron, a decade after the end of the Civil War, granted 1600 acres of land in Alabama to his formed slaves.[61] In regard to concern for the overall welfare of his slaves, William Williams explicitly stated in his will that his slaves were to be handled benevolently. He specifically solicited his son to construct new homes for the slaves and to provide them with adequate sustenance and supplies.[62] Perhaps the willingness to provide for both his current and former slaves helped differentiate the upcountry planter from those of the low country and deep South. Most of these planters discussed were present on their upcountry plantations whereas in the deep South, absenteeism was common. These upcountry planters tended to send family members to manage these other plantations that were not located in their native states. For example, Paul C. Cameron had his son-in-law George P. Collins supervise operations in Mississippi[63] and John C. Calhoun had his son Andrew run the Alabama property.[64] But as a whole, these upcountry were in absent at their other plantations because they remained at their upcountry ones. As a result, their slaves were left to the whims of others.

Brutality expressed by these masters was perhaps not always apparent to outsiders. However, in essence, the ownership of human beings was its own innate cruelty. Duncan Cameron, the initial master of Fairntosh, became increasingly more violent with time. One of his slaves accounted for his transition in behavior in 1850. This slave proclaimed that "he did more whipping in two or three days than he had done in eighteen months I am sure."[65]

In essence, the life of a slave was always one lived in cruelty. Though not every White master was physically or sexually abusive, no

---

[60]Lefler and Wager, *Orange*, 104.

[61]Orange County Deed Book, Paul Cameron #3623, NCDAH.

[62]William Williams Will, 1832, WCW, NCDAH.

[63]Abstract, ACCP, SHC.

[64]—, "John C. Calhoun's Home Life."; Letter, John C. Calhoun to Duff Green, from Fort Hill, November 2, 1839 in *Year 1899*, 433.

[65]Nathans, *Free*, 41.

measure of consideration or kindness compensated for the slaves' lack of freedom, agency, and voice. Even slaves who were thought to be loyal did not want to be held in bondage. For example, "...Mary Walker..." was "...a member of the most favored slave-family..." in Duncan Cameron's household at Fairntosh.[66] She served in a variety of intimate capacities and was clearly among the favored and trusted slaves.[67] Although Mary Walker was allegedly "close" to the Cameron family members, the bond was not enough to keep her enslaved. She was denied control over her own life. Events are unclear but most likely the threat of being sold to the deep South led her to run away. With leniency accorded her while they were in Philadelphia, Mary Walker escaped the clutches of the Cameron family's bondage.[68] Ultimately a slave sought freedom; she obtained that independence by sacrificing a life with her own children. The life of a slave was never stable and was filled with unknown horrors.

The institution of slavery, barbaric by its very nature, was integral in the accumulation of wealth that these upcountry cotton planters obtained. What is known of the lives of the slaves on these plantations was primarily recorded by the slaveocracy class and not the slaves themselves, leaving much room for much speculation. Some other slave accounts were recorded by the Works Projects Administration in *The American Slave: A Composite Autobiography* collection decades after slavery was abolished. The accuracy of these cannot be known for not only did they occur decades after slavery was abolished but former slaves were speaking to White interviewers who may have asked leading questions or implied that the former slaves should answer in a certain way. The former slaves may have told the interviewers what they thought they wanted to hear. In the wake of the Civil War and Reconstruction, with the tumultuous nature of the South, the recording of slave accounts or just the preservation of their experiences had not been a priority. Once the effort was made to document the former slaves' stories, many factors impacted what stories they told. Still, this collection is

[66]*Ibid*, 11-12.
[67]*Ibid*, 17, 23 and 25.
[68]*Ibid*, 27 and 30.

one of the few compilations of slave narratives even though the true experiences of these upcountry slaves will never be known. In one statistical report conducted about slavery at Calhoun's plantation, the researcher noted that "...since slaves at Fort Hill left no written record, their perspective is unavoidably voiceless..."[69] As a result, scholars must try to present their stories from what little is known. Thavolia Glymph explained that "the fact that most of the participants of the Federal Writers' Project were young children when freedom came has been cited by scholars as one of the major weaknesses of the narratives for understanding slavery, along with their advanced age at the time of the interviews...These factors are said to account for the sentimentalism in the narratives, the expressions of devotion and love for masters and mistresses."[70]

Walter Johnson also addressed the questionable accuracy of these accounts in his *Soul By Soul.* He contended that "...taking slave narratives for transparent account of reality can be as misleading as dismissing them entirely."[71] Johnson also accounted for the influence of the era in which they were recorded. "The narratives, like all histories," he wrote, "were shaped by the conditions of their own production-the conditions of both Southern slavery and organized antislavery...the narratives are by definition incomplete accounts."[72]

In reading these slave narratives, it was not always clear as to who owned these individuals. However, some referenced their specific masters, i.e. Wade Hampton.[73] In other instances, one can only deduce from the minimal information provided in the account as to who owned them.

In accordance with the W.P.A. collection of stories, many of these slaves held their masters in fond regard. Hence, their stories and the

---

[69]Nixon, "V.P. John C. Calhoun Plantation Slaves." http://files.usgwarchives.net/sc/oconee/history/h-53.txt.

[70]Glymph, *Bondage*, 15.

[71]Johnson, *Soul*, 9.

[72]Ibid, 10.

[73]In these narratives, the slaves did not clearly designate which of the three Wade Hamptons are being discussed and it is left to interpretation and assessment of reference points in the accounts to make that determination.

ones included in the following paragraphs must be read with some discrimination as to their overall validity. Two of Paul Cameron's slaves who were interviewed expressed awe regarding how many he held in bondage and spoke of him in kind terms.[74] Former slave Doc Edwards remained on the Cameron plantation after his emancipation and proclaimed that he would spend the remainder of his days there "…'till [sic] de [sic] good Lawd [sic] calls me home, den [sic] I will see Marse [sic] Paul once more."[75]

A slave who had been brought to James Henry Hammond acknowledged that he rarely saw him but maintained that he had been of age at the time of the Civil War, he "…would surely have gone to the front wid [sic] my white master."[76] Hammond personally held another brutal interest in his slaves, one that was not all that uncommon with a master's treatment of his female slaves. James Henry Hammond and his son Harry debated over the paternity of certain slaves born at Redcliffe as well as on his other plantations. In a letter, Hammond left this son a certain slave and her offspring, contending that "her second child I believe is mine. Take care of her & her children who are both your blood if not of mine…"[77] As a whole, however, Hammond did not think the slaves were competent without the assistance of their masters and overseers. "…The negro race differ as much from our own or that of swine from dog, to say the least—that they are Baboons on two legs gifted with speech—that no faith can be properly placed in any one of them."[78]

Wade Hampton II was referred by a former slave as being "…the kindest of masters…" In response to this treatment "…to the slave the

[74]Daisy Wailey, ed., "Abner Jordan Ex-slave, 95 years" in *North Carolina Narratives Part 2*, 35.; Daisy Wailey, ed., "Doc Edwards, Ex-slave, 84 yrs" in *North Carolina Narratives Part 1*, 296.

[75]Wailey, "Doc," 297.

[76]Stiles M. Scruggs, ed., "Anson Harp: Ex-Slave 87 Years Old" in *South Carolina Narratives Parts 1 and 2*, 237-239.

[77]Letter, James Henry Hammond to Harry Hammond, February 19, 1856, JHHP, SCL, MD.

[78]Letter, James Henry Hammond to William Gilmore Simms, April 19, 1854, JHHP, LOC.

love returned..."[79] It is difficult to judge the authenticity of such sentiments as there were no clear interviews conducted with slaves and it was most likely a romanticized assessment. One of the Millwood house slaves called Uncle Washington reflected that Wade Hampton II "...taught me how to read and to write." He also "...didn't believe in whipping slaves." Uncle Washington went on to proclaim that "he treated me like I was one of the family and not a servant."[80] Assessment of these observations, however, must be taken into consideration as to when they were stated. One must question if these accounts, which were taken from the former slaves in their twilight years, were an embellishment or perhaps a fabrication of what their lives were truly like. Modern day, we struggle figuring out how a man who held human lives in bondage could be thought of as a "good master." The mere ownership of slaves leads one to question such a designation. In researching these planters, however, provisions for slaves were commonly made within the planters' wills. But to many planters, the slaves were mere possessions. The slaves gave them their cotton, their mansions, their lifestyle.

It was the ownership of human life that ultimately gave these men their status, their homes and their way of life. The number of slaves owned by these planters certainly correlated to the production of cotton. Sale of cotton provided them with the financial means to maintain the lifestyle equated with that of a planter. In 1840, John C. Calhoun owned seventy-five slaves, who resided on his South Carolina plantation.[81] In order to effect successful operations on the plantations, planters and their overseers implemented discipline. After all, a disobedient slave threated the successful operations of the plantations; a slave revolt inspired othe slaves who wanted their freedom. When one of Calhoun's slaves attempted to escape and tried "...to kill our overseer...,"[82] the planter deemed that punishment was necessary. Yet Floride and John

[79]Account, Wade II, HFP, SCL, MD.

[80]"Uncle Washington Boasts of Celebrating 104 Birthdays," *The State*, September 1, 1935, HFP, SCL, MD.

[81] U.S. Sixth Census (1840): Pickens District, South Carolina, 23.

[82]Letter, Floride Calhoun to Margaret M. Calhoun, February 8, 1842, JCCP, SCL, MD.

Calhoun did not share the same opinion as to what type. Floride Calhoun wrote that "...Mr. Calhoun, writes me to have him sent out in chains to Andrew, but I think he ought to be sold, or he will do more mischief."[83]

In exploring the experiences and accounts of slaves, Theodore Dwight Weld's *American Slavery As It Is* contains an account about Wade Hampton I's slaves. This was an observation made by a female visitor, who discussed only what the slaves were fed and no other details.[84] There were no further records about this family and their slaves in Weld's book. Edward E. Baptist incorporated the account of a slave, Charles Ball, who was purchased by Wade Hampton I in his *The Half Has Never Been Told.*[85] Ball experienced the brutality of life on a cotton plantation. The experiences in becoming a cotton picker as well as the type of bondage he underwent as a result "...was inherently new."[86] His words were not of fondness for the operations at Wade I's plantation. He recalled that abuse of the slaves became "practised [sic] with...order, regularity and system."[87] One can only assume that Wade Hampton II followed the example set by his father to effectively run a profitable plantation, one in which slaves were solely chattel that produced the man's wealth.

In his own personal letters, Wade Hampton II appeared to be concerned about his slaves' overall well-being. In a letter he wrote to Andrew Jackson in 1810, he mentioned that a couple of his slaves were potential jockeys and as to why he kept them at his plantation. "They are family Negroes, &...the *distance* would create great affliction amongst their relations."[88] However, although this letter seemed to be empathetic to the welfare of these slaves, Hampton was most likely taking a practical and financial, albeit selfish, approach. Hampton revealed that these men were not skilled riders and would not produce the desired victories at the

[83]Ibid.

[84]Weld, *American Slavery*, 74-75.

[85]Baptist, *Half*, 37 and 111.

[86]Ibid, 112.

[87]Baptist, *Half*, 140.

[88]Letter, Wade Hampton to Andrew Jackson, June 1810 in *Jackson, Vol. 2*, p. 248.

racetrack.[89] In essence, the value in the slave was in his ability to generate profits.

The planter class of the upcountry American South was distinct. Various elements helped to account for these differences from their Northern counterparts, among the greatest, slavery. While visiting John C. Calhoun at Fort Hill, George W. Featherstonhaugh recorded his feelings and observations on these points. "What an immense difference there is in the manners of the southern gentlemen, and most of those who are at the head of society in the middle and Northern States."[90] He furthered these explanations by delving into the nature of the relationship of the upcountry cotton planter to his chattel. "I observed a great solicitude here for the welfare of their slaves...there was evidently a great deal of humanity and tenderness exercised to all who were born on the family plantation."[91] This comment causes us in modern times to pause and question. Slavery by its very nature lacked "tenderness." Maybe Featherstonhaugh only saw what he wanted to see, a distorted perception of reality.

As the nineteenth century progressed, the main concentrations of slave holdings shifted. By 1860, South Carolina ranked second in the number of slaves, just behind Louisiana. Seventy years earlier the Palmetto state had the highest slave population of any state in the nation. Though the state still remained in the upper tier of the slave population, she had technically only increased her slave holdings by 2.7%. Georgia and North Carolina had considerably smaller slave populations, ranking sixth and eighth respectively on a national level.[92] The trend of slave holdings had followed the patterns of migration to the deep South, as planters searched for stable, unworn cotton lands. Many of the planters being discussed expanded their holdings and purchased lands in the deep South. But their hearts were in the eastern seaboard states. Perhaps they constructed other homes, but their main residences continued to be their Greek Revival plantation houses in the upcountry regions of Georgia,

---

[89]Ibid.

[90]Featherstonhaugh, Canoe, 270.

[91]Ibid.

[92]Gray, *History of Agriculture*, 530-531.

South Carolina and North Carolina.

To these upcountry planters, their slaves were in many ways the foundation stones upon which they built their Greek Revival plantation homes. Without their forced labor to produce the cotton crops, the planters would not have gained the necessary wealth to attain and maintain their status. Though they never gave their slaves the credit or the recognition they deserved, it was truly their labor that generated the planters' wealth.

These upcountry planters in Georgia, North Carolina and South Carolina strove for generations to attain and surpass the reputation of the low country planters. Their families' social ascendancy was not permanent as they had hoped. The world of the cotton plantation, outfitted with its Greek Revival house with all of its decorative furnishings and details, along with its stables, works buildings, and slave cabins were relatively short lived. Thus, the realm of the upcountry cotton planter, who was so defined by his possessions, especially his slaves, came to a crashing halt with secession, and the ensuing war ended the plantation ownsers' way of life. As the Union armies under Major General William Tecumseh Sherman's command passed through Georgia, South Carolina and North Carolina in 1864-1865, one of his officers reflected upon the status of the wealthy upcountry planters and their fine homes. "These old planters were kings in a way…"[93]

[93]Quoted in Glatthaar, "Union Soldiers," Ph.D. Dissertation, 106.

CHAPTER 8

THE END OF THE UPCOUNTRY COTTON PLANTERS' WORLD

In 1888, Lucy Hampton, Wade Hampton II's granddaughter, proclaimed in 1888, "I think it is queer so many people at the north don't know the broad line of destruction that was left in the south."[1] But the swath that had been cut throughout Dixie was a deep one. The passing of the Union armies under Major General William Tecumseh Sherman brought the war to the home front and some of these planters' majestic estates did not receive clemency. Sherman was not alone in this destruction, for once his troops had passed through South Carolina and moved on to North Carolina, Brevet Major General Edward Elmer Potter took up where he had left off. Potter's men exacted even greater vengeance.[2]

As the tide of the Civil War started to turn, Georgia, South Carolina and North Carolina were exposed to the brunt of the fray. These upcountry planters, who had been reasonably free from the physical destruction of warfare, experienced the gravest of hardships. As the Federal troops trod across these states, battle was not always foremost in their minds. Occasionally the men were engaged in combat, especially in the early stages of their first Georgia campaign.[3] Yet as they plunged deeper into the enemy's homeland, vengeance crept into their thoughts, which in time, for some, became all encompassing.[4] In later years,

---

[1]Letter, Lucy Hampton to Lucy Baxter, February 13, 1888, SSBHP, SCL, MD.

[2]Rev. Wm. W. Mood, "Recollections of Potter's Raid," EEPP, SCL, MD, 50.

[3]Narrative, August 20, 1861- July 17, 1865, Edward Moore, 10th Illinois Infantry Regiment, CWMC, USAMHI.

[4]Fleharty, *Our Regiment*, 135.; Letter, George Shuman to Fannie Shuman, Major George Shuman, January 8, 1865, 9th Pennsylvania Cavalry Papers, HCWRT, USAMHI.; Memoirs, William H. H. Tallman, 66th Ohio Infantry Regiment, Charles Rhodes Collection, USAMHI.; Willison, *Of A Boy's Service*, 116.; Many soldiers wrote of their destruction of plantations in Georgia, South

Sherman reflected on his campaigns in Georgia, asserting "I made them feel the consequences of war, so they will never again invite an invading army."[5] This logic he carried on with greater intensity into the next phase.

The invading forces readily sought the prize possessions of the planter class. Union soldiers stole animals from the plantations, especially the esteemed racehorses, which were sometimes used by the soldiers but were often slaughtered and left to rot.[6] The Greek Revival plantation houses and their valuable contents were attractive targets for the invading armies. For some, punishment for secession equated to destruction.

In *Heart of Dixie: Sherman's March and American Memory*, Anne Sarah Rubin took a new approach in looking at Sherman's campaigns. She asserted that "rather than retell the story..." her book "...explores the myriad ways in which Americans retold and reimagined Sherman's March...from a range of perspectives..."[7] Rubin pointed out that his "...army faced little opposition on its inexorable movement through Georgia and the Carolinas...the devastation wrought along the March's route was extraordinary..."[8] In this work, she acknowledged that there was destruction, albeit "...localized and inconsistent..."[9] and that "...many homes survived Sherman's march, many more than were destroyed."[10] However, she asserted that there had been intensification of the actual impact of these military maneuvers as soldiers waxed nostalgic in the years after the end of hostilities.[11] Just as the slave narra-

---

Carolina and North Carolina but did not include the property names or the owners, since perhaps they probably did not even know.

[5]Dodge, *Personal Recollections*, 26.

[6]G. W. Nichols, "Sherman's Great March," 582.; Mahan, "Forager," 192-193.; Journal (written in letter form to his parents), January 28, 1865—March 13, 1865, William W. Pritchard, 9th Pennsylvania Cavalry Regiment, CWMC, USAMHI, entry February 23, 1865 and February 27, 1865.

[7]Rubin, *Dixie*, 4.

[8]Ibid, 3-4.

[9]Ibid, 23.

[10]Ibid, 52.

[11]Ibid, 98.

tives must be questioned for their validity, one must look with a discerning eye at the accounts, and scholarship, about Sherman's campaigns.

Sherman himself had tried to disavow some of the Southerners' claims that his forces were excessive in their destruction. In his *Memoirs*, he accounted that "...the rebel officers and newspapers represented the conduct of the men of our army as simply infamous...that we burned every thing we came across-barns, stables, cotton-gins, and even dwelling houses..."[12] He furthered these thoughts, claiming "...that Generals Hardees and Smith...knew well that these reports were exaggerated in the extreme...to arouse the drooping energies of the people of the South."[13]

"War is a stern teacher..." proclaimed a soldier from General Joseph Hardee's Signal Corps in Dalton, Georgia, in a piece of correspondence to a Georgian resident as Sherman's armies began their harsh campaign in the state.[14] Once the campaign began, however, Georgians found themselves quickly learning this lesson. As the "..."formidable invasion" of Georgia by the enemy..." commenced the people soon experienced even greater hardships.[15] The Georgians had believed, even held hope, that their state would be left unscathed. The Confederate forces were prepared to die before permitting "...the enemy to occupy one foot of Georgia soil."[16]

En route to the Georgia capital of Milledgeville, Sherman's armies had fair chance to eat the local crops and pillage the homes. "...We reveled in the splendid homes and palatial residences of some of the

---

[12]Sherman, *Memoirs*, 716.

[13]Ibid.

[14]Letter, J. H. Pope to Mr. Barrow, February 20, 1864, CDCBP, HRBML.

[15] Letter, Hon. James A. Seddon to His Excellency J. E. Brown, October 8, 1864, TCC, HRBML.

[16]Army Correspondence (March 30, 1864) copied from *Southern Watchman*, March 30, 1864, EMCHM, HRBML.

wealthy planters."[17] Not too long into the March to the Sea did portions of the army come into the town of Covington.[18] Here the soldiers started to inflict damage sans orders, to which Sherman decided to designate specific individuals to handle the acquisition of necessities. The beautiful city was the recipient of some devastating retribution.[19] White Hall was not burned and there was no clear reason as to why the house was saved. Having been spared of destruction, the house has gone on to be used in television shows such as "In The Heat of The Night" as well as in the cinema.

Among the areas that the army columns passed through was Madison, where The Oaks sat just on the edge of town. Though the area suffered, particularly to the rail line, the plantation house itself was not destroyed even though some of the outbuildings were.[20] The house still stands along a county road. Perhaps the soldiers recognized the beauty that was found in the homes of Madison and the outlying region, but historians can only speculation as to why they were spared. A member of the 102nd Illinois Infantry Volunteers made a record of these "...elegant" structures and that it was clear the people here exquisitely displayed their "...taste and refinement..."[21] Lowther Hall, located south of Madison, survived the war only to succumb to flames in the next century.[22]

Great devastation befell the people, property, and the homes in portions of Georgia.[23] As the forces continued, passing through what a soldier referred to as "...a perfect garden..." on their way to the state

---

[17]Conyngham, *Sherman's March through*, 151.

[18]Dolly Lunt Burge Journal (original), entries November 19, 1864 and November 20, 1864, BFP, EUMARBL.; Sherman, *Memoirs*, 552.

[19]Sherman, *Memoirs*, 657 and 658.

[20]Conyngham, Sherman's March through, 150.; Cox, *March*, 27.; Gleason, *Homes*, 44.

[21]Fleharty, *Our Regiment*, 111.

[22]Nichols, *Early*, 124.

[23]Correspondence, "Letter," *Weekly*, EMCHM, HRBML.; Davis, *Sherman's*, 62 and 63.; Kennett, *Marching Through Georgia*, 296.; Rubin, *Dixie*, 14 and 29.

capital, they relished in living off the land and destroying the plantation structures in particular.[24]

Once in Milledgeville, the soldiers took great delight in raising the Union flag once again over the state house.[25] The Union troops derived pleasure in antagonizing the residents as well as inflicting damage to their property. Cavalry leader Major General Hugh Judson Kilpatrick reveled in his success of purging the liquor supply from a local plantation.[26] Rose Hill survived the Union occupation of the state capital, perhaps due to the fact that the armies withdrew from the city soon after coming to the plantation. Today, Rose Hill, now known as Lockerly, is open for tours in conjunction with the Lockerly Arboretum.

As the March to the Sea started to come to a close, reports about Savannah noted that "Sherman is besieging the place without an attack."[27] Savannah fell into Union hands, thus marking an end to Sherman's campaign in Georgia.[28] With this, both the Union and the Confederacy awaited the next move. South Carolina, of course, was the next logical step.

In many respects, the secession of South Carolina gave impetus to starting the war.[29] Even though most residents' interests were not compatible with the visions of the fire-eaters and disunionists, the people of South Carolina seceded. As a result, all who resided there were seen as having caused the war. It wasn't only Northerners who thought Sherman should punish South Carolina for its role in starting the war;

---

[24]Conyngham, *Sherman's March through*, 150 and 152.

[25]Davis, *Sherman's*, 62 and 63.

[26]Ibid, 63.; It is possible that he was referring to Rose Hill (Lockerly) but is not certain. Based upon Kilpatrick's direct comments as quoted in this book, it seems as though it would be this plantation house.

[27]Letter, R. R. Timill (?) to Col. D. C. Barrow, December 23, 1864, CDCBP, HRBML.

[28]Letter, William T. Sherman to His Excellency Prest. Lincoln, December 22, 1864, in *Sherman's Civil War*, 772.; Oakey, "Marching Through Georgia," in *Battles And Leaders*, 672.

[29]William H. H. Tallman, 66th Ohio Infantry, Regiment Memoirs, CRC, USAMHI, 79 and 87.

Sherman and his men heard pleas from Georgians during their campaigns to "… make those people [South Carolinians] feel the severities of war, we will pardon you for your desolation of Georgia."[30]

Before setting off on this campaign, Sherman wrote to Chief of Staff Major General Henry Halleck "…I think before we are done, South Carolina will not be so tempestuous." Sherman said, "…the whole army is burning with an insatiable desire to wreak vengeance upon South Carolina. I almost tremble at her fate, but feel that she deserves all that seems in store for her."[31]

Crossing into South Carolina was a momentous event. Soldiers recorded their feelings of this taking leave of Georgia into the "hot-bed of secession" for it was an emotional passage.[32] One solder's words were almost simplistic in proclaiming his jubilation. "…for the first time, I touched South Carolina."[33] But others were more direct, stating they "…were therefore more determined to make themselves comfortable. It did not take long to decide how this should be accomplished—they were in South Carolina!"[34] This was a defining moment, a time of just reward. In South Carolina, Sherman unabashedly forged a path clearly noted for its swath of destruction. "His line of march was marked by the light of burning houses."[35] South Carolinians, particularly the cotton planters, who stood as the representatives of secession and the causes of war were to feel the hardships. "They can never forget the day when their homes upon which they had collected many comforts and cherished remembrances, were reduced to ashes."[36]

The Campaign of the Carolinas was similar fashion to the March to the Sea. Because Sherman planned on marching on both Columbia, South Carolina, and on to Raleigh, North Carolina, he knew he needed

---

[30]ORWR, I, 44.

[31]Ibid.

[32]Willison, *Of A Boy's Service*, 116.

[33]Journal, January 28, 1865, William W. Pritchard, 9th Pennsylvania Cavalry Regiment, CWMC, USAMHI.

[34]Fleharty, *Our Regiment*, 130.

[35]Bryce, "The Personal Experiences," 11.

[36]H. T. Cook, *Through South Carolina*, 7.

to employ the element of surprise.[37] The Army columns feigned on Augusta and Charleston but converged on Columbia.[38] Charleston held no strategic value at this point of the war even though it was the birthplace of secession. Due to the course chosen for these two columns of Union armies, areas that happened to house some of these cotton plantations, escaped the wrath of these soldiers. A Union officer spoke of the upcoming campaign quite candidly. "You think the people of Georgia are fairing [sic] badly and they are, but God pity the people of South Carolina when this army gets there, for we have orders to lay everything in ashes." He went on to proclaim that this "...State will be made to feel the fearful sin of Secession before our army gets through."[39]

The great cotton plantations represented slavery and secession. Their possessions were actively sought by the invading Union armies.[40] Amazingly though, Redcliffe, Milford, and Fort Hill were spared. Even though these were the plantation homes of not only the great upcountry cotton planters but also of the men who directly or indirectly helped to lead South Carolina out of the Union, they were not destroyed. South Carolina held a special challenge to the Union armies.[41] It had been South Carolina that had taken the lead in seceding from the Union.[42] John L. Manning attended the secession convention.[43]

By the time of the secession convention both John C. Calhoun and Wade Hampton II had died, but their legacies lived on. Calhoun his-

---

[37]Letter, William Tecumseh Sherman to Ulysses S. Grant, December 22, 1864, in *Sherman's Civil War*, 772.

[38]Letter, William Tecumseh Sherman to Ulysses S. Grant, December 24, 1864, in *Sherman's Civil War*, 773.; Cox, *March*, 164.

[39]Canning, "Georgia," 82.

[40]"A Suffering South Carolina Poet," *The New York Herald*, February 23, 1865, CWC, MCDAH.

[41]Letter, W. T. Sherman to Mrs. Carolina Carson, January 20, 1865, WTSP, SCL, MD.

[42]Epitaph, South Carolina Papers, SCP, SCL, MD.; *Ordinance of Secession*, SCP, SCL, MD.; "South Carolina, A Patriotic Ode," SCP, SCL, MD.

[43]*Ordinance of Secession*, SCP, SCL, MD.; W. Manning, "Sketch," MFP, SCL, MD.

torically has been referred to as the "Father of Secession." It was advocated that the *Fort Hill Address* was from where "the secession doctrine was first openly promulgated by CALHOUN..."[44] In essence, for those who believed that Calhoun desired secession, then his "spirit" was present at the convention. Although John C. Calhoun had advocated some alternatives to secession and proclaimed the notion of "..."masterly inactivity"...", the people of the state chose to leave the Union and there was no longer any talk of compromise.[45]

Fort Hill, the home of the late John C. Calhoun, escaped destruction during the war, if only for the fact that it was out of the line of march. When Sherman's armies converged on South Carolina, neither of which reached the area of Fort Hill's location.[46] His home evaded the ravages of the war, helping to preserve his legacy as a prominent cotton planter and stands as part of Clemson University.

James Henry Hammond was living out the remainder of his life at the time the Civil War broke out. He had long supported disunion and prophesized "...that the matter must terminate in blood..."[47] Hammond never wavered from his belief that South Carolina should leave the Union. "We must go at once, & for good. Nothing half-way...The time has come."[48] However, his sickness caused by his ulcer, combined with his hypochondria, plagued him too greatly for any type of actual physical service.[49]

---

[44]Carroll, "A Secessionist."

[45]Letter, William Van Wyck to Dr. S. M. Van Wyck, January 20, 1861, MVWP, SCL, MD.

[46]Special Field Order No. 19 and Special Field Order No. 25, *Military Orders*, 340-341 and 342-343.

[47]Letter, James Henry Hammond to Cadet MCM Hammond, December 22, 1832, JHHP, SCL, MD.

[48]Letter, James Henry Hammond to Col. B. J. Watts, December 29, 1860, JHHP, SCL, MD.

[49]Letter, James Henry Hammond to Col. B. J. Watts, November 28, 1860, JHHP, SCL, MD.

Hammond died on November 13, 1864 at his home, before Sherman's troops commenced their Campaign of the Carolinas.[50] He did not live to see the destruction of his native state brought on by her act of secession. Even though Sherman's armies were less than twenty miles from Hammond's property, they did not deviate from their course to bring ruin to his estate.[51] Redcliffe was modified by later owners and was eventually taken over by the National Park Service in order to aid in its preservation.[52] The wide oak trees that Hammond had planted along the entranceway stand large and impressive, sweeping over the drive to give that air of mystery and illusion as to the essence of the approaching Greek Revival homestead.

When the alleged "...model of a Southern planter..." Wade Hampton II died in 1858, his son Wade Hampton III inherited his father's great land holdings and slaves.[53] Although Wade III had stood against disunion, he did not turn his back on his home.[54] Wade Hampton III seemed aware that battle would come to South Carolina and advocated during the war that he would "...like to show how Carolinians should fight on their own soil."[55] By 1865, when they had their chance, South Carolinians could offer little resistance. The Hampton legacy of power, slaves, and money, along with loyalty and service to the Confederacy, made the family a target. The Union soldiers wanted to punish this family by destroying their possessions.

Though Wade Hampton II was no longer alive, his properties were actively sought out by the Union troops, especially to due to their association with his son, Confederate cavalry General Wade Hampton

---

[50]Letter, "The Last Moments of James Henry Hammond," Edward Spann Hammond to Harry Hammond, November 13, 1864, JHHP, SCL, MD.; "The Hammonds," HBCFP, SCL, MD, 3.

[51]Ballard, et. al., "Slave Quarters," 8.

[52]Shaw, "Some Notes," RACRF, SCDAH.

[53]Obituary, Col. Wade Hampton, *Southern Christian Advocate*, February 13, 1858, HFP, SCL, MD.; Abstract of Title, August 1, 1879, HFP, SCL, MD.

[54]"Speech of Hon Wade Hampton—Constitutionality of Slave Trade Laws," December 10, 1859, HFP, SCL, MD, 18.; Wade Hampton I and Wade Hampton III, SSBHP, SCL, MD.

[55]Letter, Wade Hampton III to Fisher, December 17, 1861, HFP, SCL, MD.

III. Even though Millwood was in the possession of Wade Hampton II's daughters, it epitomized all that was the world of the upcountry slave owning cotton planter. When Sherman's armies converged upon Columbia, they quickly found this plantation on the outskirts of the city.[56]

Before the Union troops arrived at Millwood and the Woodlands, most of the Edward Troye paintings of Wade II's great race and breeding horses were torn from their frames and taken to safety.[57] Through the efforts of "...Kit Hampton and his sisters, Kate, Ann, Caroline and Mary Fisher," they were able to save these paintings as well as some other valuable items.[58] There were the few items that survived the grand conflagration that engulfed this plantation home.

Not all of the great works of art could be preserved with the impending arrival of Union troops. Household items were stolen or destroyed, and the house was burned.[59] Two of Troye's paintings, *Monarch* and *Fanny*, had not been removed and were destroyed with the house.[60] Reduced to a few remaining columns, the ruins of the house is a haunting reminder of the former world of the cotton planter.[61] After the war, Wade Hampton II's son, although he did not reside at Millwood, wanted to restore the mansion to its previous greatness, but it was not to be.[62] The post-war reality for the planter class was a loss of

---

[56]Cannaday, "Reconstruction's."; -- "Slaves Numerous," WHP, SCHS.; Heyward, "Glowing," WHP, SCHHS, MD.; Millwood, MNRHPHP.

[57]Mackay-Smith, *Race*, 69.

[58]"Possessions Saved, Pillars Remain," *Historically Speaking*, Volume 43, 3.

[59]Letter, Wade Hampton III to General, no date, HFP, SCL, MD.; Blease, *Destruction*, 15, 17, 21 and 58.; Mr. Tucker from Virginia, Congressional Record, House of Representatives, January 21, 1930, HFP, SCL, MD.

[60]Meynard, "Portraits," VGMP, SCL, MD.

[61]Letter, Lucy Hampton to Lucy Baxter, February 13, 1888, SSBHP, SCL, MD.; Letter, Wade Hampton III to General, no date, HFP, SCL, MD.; M B Mer compilation from file of *The State* and personal recollections of Dr. E. L. Green & Mrs. Hagood Bostick, "Wade Hampton Homes," HFP, SCL, MD.; Myers, ed., *When the World Ended*, 44.; Perry, *Volume II*, 340-341.; Photographs of Millwood ruins, WHFP, LOC, MD.

[62]Nelson, *Ruin*, 97.

their property and wealth. Megan Kate Nelson asserted in *Ruin Nation*that "...as Hampton's failed plans for Millwood attest, funds were often scarce and bankruptcy prevalent..."[63] The war had brought an end to the wealth of the Hampton family.

Even before Wade Hampton II 's death in 1858, he had accumulated many outstanding bills.[64] When, the 13th Amendment freed the slaves, the Hamptons-and others like them- faced financial ruin. Wade Hampton III, after his service in the Confederate Army, served as governor, in Congress, and in cabinet posts, in the wake of the financial strains after the war and thereby kept the family's status, if not wealth, inteact.[65] Wade Hampton II ultimately achieved his goal of a permanent legacy, because even in ruin, Millwood remains a testament to the man as a planter.

The Millwood property, the showpiece of its original owners, is all but lost. "the six white columns that mark the site of Millwood..." Nelson writes, "are located on private land, and any inquiries regarding their location are met with vague directions and a warning that the landowner owns a shotgun."[66] I have tried repeatedly to view the property but have been refused at every attempt.

Although James Henry Hammond's plantation houses were spared during the war, his former residence in Columbia, at that points owned by Thomas Clarkson, was burned in February 1865 by Union troops.[67] All that remained following that fateful day of the occupation of Columbia were the battered pillars and the brick foundation. The ruins of both Millwood and this town house symbolized the end of the upcountry cotton planters' world.

Colonel Oscar L. Jackson, who participated in this campaign, recorded his feelings about the destruction of Columbia, writing, "It is no exaggeration to say that the city is burned. I believe it was not done by order but there seems to be a general acquiescence in the work as a fit

---

[63]Ibid.

[64]Longacre, *Gentleman*, 24.

[65]Ibid, 39, 246, 252-253, 267, 271 and 274.

[66]Nelson, *Ruin*, 97.

[67]"The Hammonds," HBCFP, SCL, MD, 12.

example to be made of the capital of the State that boasts of being the cradle of secession and started the war."[68]

As the soldiers roamed the countryside, they took in all that they passed. William Pritchard of the 9th Cavalry, reflected in his journal that in South Carolina, "there are some very nice cotton plantations along the road but the houses are burned..." Later, he wrote that they were "...burning the finer residences..." Pritchard accounted for the great destruction they were inflicting on the people of the South, particularly those who belonged to the upcountry planter class—especially while they were in South Carolina. Clearly he felt that they were doing their duty. "I believe, if there are judgements [sic] inflicted upon men in their "latter days" that Sherman's Army are the avengingangels, [sic] and that they "judgements" [sic] are for the fool cause of slavery."[69]

When it seemed as though a relative calm emerged in South Carolina with the passing of Major General William Tecumseh Sherman's troops on to North Carolina, a new phase of war was on the horizon. Though Sherman had moved on to the final phase of his campaign, he still harbored "an insatiable desire" to give South Carolina her just penance.[70] On directive from Sherman via Brevet Major General Quincy A. Gillmore, Brevet Major General Edward Elmer Potter led his raiders to see to the demolition of portions of a railroad.[71] Taking with him both White and African-American regiments, including the 54th Massachusetts, Potter's Raid was one of vast destruction throughout Sumter County. "The torch was applied to all...with yells...of delight and pleasure."[72]

Potter's forces seemed to relish in their abilities to destroy as well. "The wreck and devastation was complete...their brutality and savage wickedness..." was on full display in South Carolina.[73] At the former Governor John L. Manning's majestic residence Milford, a soldier of

---

[68]Jackson, *The colonel's diary*.

[69]Pritchard journal entry, February 20, 1865 (which was mistakenly written as January 20th).

[70]Hudson, "54th Massachusetts," 181.

[71]Emilio, *Brave*, 289.; Thigpen, ed., *Illustrated*, n.p.

[72]Mood, "Recollection," 49.

[73]Ibid, pp. 49 and 50.

the 54th Massachusetts aimed his weapon point blank while exclaiming "you are a dead man" and stopped the governor at the door.[74] Although Sherman's armies spared Milford, the men conducting Potter's Raid would have been remiss had they too bypassed this great estate. South Carolinians had known when Potter was on his way, just as they had with Sherman, by the impending billowing clouds of smoke on the horizon.[75]

With all of the havoc being wreaked on the people of South Carolina, many local Sumter County ladies gathered at Milford in hopes of being protected. By April 19, 1865, they understood that war had finally reached them.[76] Unverified stories of the army's approach had been told for some time; however, this time it was a reality.[77]

Fighting took place around the area of Milford's location.[78] The former governor was concerned for both the people who sought shelter at his home as well as preserving the estate as well.[79] When Manning met with General Potter, he described how his home had been constructed by a Northern man of the same last name; he assumed it was to be demolished under the guidance of a leader who bore that name as well. The general assured Manning that his men would not burn Milford.[80] Though stories differ as to whether the house was saved because Generals Robert Edward Lee and Joseph Eggleston Johnston had surrendered or because Potter spared the house on a whim, the plantation was preserved.[81]

John L. Manning served in the Eastern Theater of the war in the hopes of standing behind his signature on the Ordinance of Secession of South Carolina. One South Carolina regiment actually bore his

[74]"Continuation of Rev. Wm. W. Mood Accounts" in *Illustrated*, 591.
[75]Mood, "Recollection," 65 and 66.
[76]"Mood," *Illustrated*, 588 and 590.
[77]M. R. R., "Potter's Raid," 291.; Mood, "Recollections," 66.
[78]"Continuation of James G. Ramsey account" in *Illustrated*, 584.
[79]Mood, "Recollection," 66 and 67.
[80]Mood, "Recollection," 68.
[81]Emilio, "Brave," 307.; "Report of Col. Edward N. Hallowell," in *Illustrated*, 627.; M. R. R., "Potter's," 295.; "Mood," *Potter's Raid*, 594-595.

name, the "Manning Guards."[82] Both the former governor and Milford survived the Civil War. After the conclusion of the war, the people of his state elected him to the Senate, an office he was unable to assume due to his service in the Confederacy. In time, he was chosen to represent his district in the South Carolina Senate. When he passed in 1889, he was not buried on his plantation but was interred along with his Hampton relatives in the Trinity Church Yard in Columbia, S.C.[83] Much like he had participated in taking his state out of the Union, he diligently worked towards her re-admittance as well.[84] After Manning's death, ownership of Milford passed through various hands.[85]

Milford plantation was divided into three land tracts, encompassing 326.84 acres, 73.16 acres and 5.00 acres respectively. Richard Hampton Jenrette purchased the lands and the buildings in 1992.[86] Jenrette refurbished the house and before he died, gave it (in 2008) and the property (2017) to the Classical American Homes Preservation Trust before Jenrette's passing.[87]

North Carolina escaped great damage during the initial years of war. With that, life for the Camerons and William Williams' family went on relatively unimpeded. However, when Sherman's armies crossed into North Carolina, the fortunes of the states' people changed. Though Sherman did not exact as much vengeance on the residents

---

[82]Letter, S. Gaillard to Col. J. L. Manning, August 23, 1861, JLMP, SCL, MD.

[83]W. Manning, "Sketch," MFP, SCL, MD.; observations made of Trinity Church Yard, Columbia, South Carolina.

[84]Letter, J L Manning to Henry Storm, January 29, 1877, JLMP, SCL, MD.

[85]Harmon, "Milford Mansion," MP, RS, SCHC, 3.; Milford Plantation, MRSCRF, SCDAH, 10.

[86]Title To Real Estate, State of South Carolina, County of Sumter, SCR, Vol. 542, 391-396.; Survey, February 20, 1992, South Carolina, SCD.; Real Property Characteristic Inquiry, AS1140-02, SCD.

[87]"Richard Hampton Jenrette, Founder," *Classical American Homes Preservation Trust and The Richard Hampton Jenrette Foundation,* https://classicalamericanhomes.org/richard-h-jenrette-founder/#:~:text=Dick%20founded%20Classical%20American%20Homes,land%20and%20outbuildings%20to%20CAHPT.; Sumter County Property Card, Richard H. Jenrette, Prog #AS2006, 1-12, SCRD.; T. Smith, "Living," 740.

here as in South Carolinians, there was still great destruction. Sherman's path "...was a scene of universal desolation. Along all the roads were the remains of burnt farm houses..."[88] As the troops pressed forward, they were "...heralded by the columns of smoke which rose from the burning farm-houses..."[89]

With the Union forces' movement towards the central part of the state, fear spread throughout the Cameron family. Before the Union soldiers arrived, some of General Joseph Wheeler's troops appeared at Fairntosh, questioning the slaves as to the whereabouts of the great possessions of the house. The Confederate soldiers never found the location of most of these goods because Paul Cameron had had the foresight to hide most of the valuables.[90]

Paul C. Cameron lost a good portion of his fortune and lands, and of course all of his slave labor, as a result of the Civil War and the 13th Amendment. Although Cameron had stood against secession, his role in the Confederate government is unknown aside from his purchase of bonds.[91] Fearful of what potentially might happen, Paul Cameron expeditiously reviewed his private papers. In the hopes of protecting himself, before the Union troops arrived, he tossed anything into the flames that potentially tied him to the Confederacy.[92] As a result, historians are left to only speculate about his involvement.

The Union soldiers too sought the valuables that had been hidden on Fairntosh, particularly the silver, and aggressively questioned the slaves as to where it had been hidden. Though the soldiers did not injure any people or damage the buildings, they stole food and horses.[93]

---

88 S. A. Ashe, "Some Reminiscences," CWC, NCDAH, 5.

89 Spencer, *The Last Ninety Days*, 94.

90 "Cy Hart, Ex-Slave," in *North Carolina Narratives Part 1*, 380.

91 Letter, J. T. Swain to His Excellency Andrew Johnson, July 27, 1866, PCCPAF, MCDAH.; Letter, W. J. Holden (?) to His Excellency Andrew Johnson, PCCPAF, MCDAH.; Paul C. Cameron Petition for Amnesty, PCCPAF, MCDAH.; Certificate, Confederate States of America bond purchase, March 1, 1864, CFP, SHC.

92 Letter, R. D. W. Connor to Bennehan Cameron, December 17, 1907, NCHCP, NCDAH.

93 Daisy Wailey, ed., "Abner Jordan Ex-Slave, 95 years," in *North Carolina Narratives Part 2*, 35 and 36.

Before the Yankee soldiers left the plantation, they informed the slaves of their emancipation.[94]

Without slave labor, the life of the great planter with his vast land holdings, wealth, and bountiful crops slaves was gone. This was all that Paul Cameron held dear.[95] Though he recovered financially to an extent, it was in a new era with a different way of life.[96] Navigating the post-war reality was a challenge for these upcountry planters. Paul Cameron lived the remainder of his life encumbered by the antebellum planter lifestyle which he truly had embodied. Jean Bradley Anderson claimed in her book *Piedmont Plantation* that years after the war that Paul Cameron "…bore immedicable wounds, for the world he had loved was gone."[97] This assessment may be a bit of poetic license. Cameron did survive the war and its aftermath relatively unscathed. His house was not burned and he remained a farmer on his own lands.[98] There were times of financial stress for Paul Cameron.[99] In her *Out Of The House Of Bondage*, Thavolia Glymph included a portion of a letter he wrote his daughter in which he clarified that "-I shall have no fortune to be on my children-all will have to make their own way."[100]

By the time of the Civil War, William Williams had been dead for decades. The advertisement for the sale of his estate had been posted in the *Roanoke Advocate* (Halifax, North Carolina) on December 6, 1832. It read "Land And Negroes For Sale. On Thursday the 13th day of December, the residence of the late Gen. William Williams…will be offered for sale…"[101] It is unknown what became of his descendants, if there were any. Montmorenci, which stood so close to

---

[94]Daisy Wailey, ed., "Doc Edwards, Ex-Slave, 84 Yrs" in *North Carolina Narratives Part 1*, 297.

[95]Letter, Paul C. Cameron to his sister, October 18, 1881, CFP, SHC.

[96]S. A. Ashe, et. al, eds., *Biographical History*, 51.; Will of Paul C. Cameron, 1881, NCW, CC, NCDAH.

[97]Anderson, *Piedmont*, 123.

[98]Ibid, 122.

[99]Glymph, *Bondage*, 201.

[100]Ibid.

[101]"Sale of the estates of Gen. William Williams," *Roanoke Advocate* (Halifax, North Carolina) 6 December 1832, http://www.newspapers.com/clip/652308/sale_of_the_estate_of_gen_william/

the Virginia border, was not reached by Sherman's armies. Confederate General Joseph E. Johnston, joined by members of his staff which included Wade Hampton III, met with Sherman on the outskirts of the North Carolina capital of Raleigh to surrender.[102]

With this, the ravaging of the state ceased. Montmorenci survived the war, only to be destroyed by the wrecking ball after years of neglect in the twentieth century.[103] The du Pont family purchased portions of the house, such as the staircase, façade, and moldings for Winterthur. Tragedy struck, however, during the relocation. The staircase fell from the truck and was destroyed. A slightly altered replica now stands in its stead.[104]

Sherman left wide swaths of destruction in parts of Georgia and South Carolina, and the residents pled for assistance in the aftermath.[105] Destruction had been encompassing.[106] People appealed to the governors, the president, the military leaders as well as fellow citizens.[107] This time, however, the planter could not come to the rescue

---

[102]S. A. Ashe, "Some Reminiscences," CWC, NCDAH, 8.; Godfrey, "Johnston's Surrender," 73.; Palmore, *Riding With Sherman*, 27.; Slocum, "Final Operations," 755, 756 and 757.; *Surrender Terms*, Joseph E. Johnston and William T. Sherman, April 21, 1865, CWC, NCDAH.

[103]Bishir, "Montmorenci," 89.

[104]Ibid, 90.; Cantor, *Winterthur*, 188, 189 and 192.; Sweeney, *Winterthur*, 86 and 151.; Denmark Raleigh photographs of Montmorenci moldings and structure, 1J-3—1J-6, 1J-9—1J-17, 1J-23—1J-24, DRPM, WL, WA.; personal observations and meetings with members of the Winterthur staff.

[105]Appeals for Food from Destitute Families, Cumberland County 1865, CWC, NCDAH..; Letter, G. L. Quinn to His Excellency Governor Brown, March 12, 1864, TCCGGP, HRBML.; Letter, Mrs. S. A. Spiers (?) to His Excellency Joseph E. Brown, January 19, 1865, TCCGGP, HRBML.

[106]Aldrich, "In the Track," 201 and 203.; Bryce, "Personal," 11.; Canning, "Georgia," 77 and 83.; Cook, *Through South Carolina*, 7.; Correspondence, "Letter," *Weekly*, EMCHM, HRBML.; Currie, "Back in the Sixties," CWC, NCDAH.; "Personal Reminiscences," CWC, NCDAH..; Tallman, "66th Ohio," CRC, USAMHI.; Trezvant, "Burning," DHTP, SCL, MD.

[107]Letter, W. T. Sherman to Mrs. Annie Gilman Bowen, June 30, 1864, WTSP, SCL, MD.; Letter, W. T. Sherman to Mrs. Carolina Carson, January 20, 1865, WTSP, SCL, MD. Both these letters are responses to pleas that had been sent to Sherman.

or offer financial assistance in a time of despair. It was he who had borne the brunt of the destruction. The world of the upcountry cotton planter with all its luxurious trimmings was no more. Life would not go on as usual. Now the planter sought assistance as well.

In the aftermath of the war, many Southerners solicited reimbursement for destroyed properties and possessions. The key, however, in finding some success in these petitions was the continued loyalty to the United States during the war.[108] Claims were made but many lacked the necessary standing to bring compensation.[109] Some of these planters did not even attempt to seek reimbursement for their losses. They readily stood behind their role as the upcountry cotton planter before and during the time of the Confederacy. Others, like Paul C. Cameron, pursued amnesty after the war, where he met with limited success.[110] Perhaps Cameron endeavored to preserve some of his dignity, but he claimed he maintained his allegiance to the U.S.A. throughout the war and requested a reprieve. Cameron was not alone in trying to find amnesty. On September 12, 1865, Georgia planter J. H. Harris dutifully affixed his signature to the Oath of Allegiance, proclaiming his loyalty to the United States.[111] With their world gone, these men tried to find a place in this drastically changed environment.

Some losses were of an entirely different nature and could not be compensated. These cotton planter families experienced financial, physical, and mental losses. Like many Southern and Northern families, the Hamptons and Hammonds suffered combat deaths during the war.[112] Family members could not be replaced, and their loss only magnified the destruction of their properties and possessions.

For years, in the wake of the aftermath of the Campaign of the Carolinas, particularly that of the burning of Columbia, William Sherman and Wade Hampton III attacked each other's character through

---

[108]Klingberg, *Commission*, 16 and 17.

[109]Views of the South Claim Commission files, National Achieves.

[110]"Petition for Amnesty," Paul C. Cameron Papers, CWC, OC, NCDAH.

[111]Oath of Allegiance, TCC, HRBM. I am not certain that this is the Harris who is the owner of the White Hall, but all the listed statistics appear to coincide with the Harris who owns the lands and house.

[112]Kirkland, *Broken*, 147.

written letters.[113] Hampton put great emphasis in his reports and letters on the loss of Millwood and its contents.[114] Though it was no longer his home, his unwed sisters lived there, and the loss of estate was a blow to the family fortune and prestige that Wade Hampton III took as a personal assault. The world of the great upcountry cotton planter crumbled with the scorching fires that brought the demise of the Millwood plantation.

Though the world of these upcountry slaveholders with their vast tracts of cotton lands that were worked by the hands of those held in bondage came to a crashing halt with the end of the Civil War, there were still attempts to hold on to the legacy. The subsequent generation still took their pride in their "...cotton fields..." and "big wooden white houses..."[115] In many ways, they stayed in the past, unable to fully progress to the new era before them.

The upcountry planters who survived the war had to confront a new reality without their slaves, wealth, and prestige. Many tried, or their families attempted to, rebuild but were unable. Wade Hampton III planned to reconstruct his father's destroyed Millwood but never was able.[116] Wade III was prominent in politics the aftermath of the conflict, even in the wake of initial debt.[117] He maintained the continued prominence of the Hampton family name. Other planter, such as Paul Cameron and J. H. Harris claimed that they had remained Unionists throughout the war. Some of these men lost their homes; all lost their slaves. Thus they lost what they had used to define their status, as slavery had been the foundation stone upon which they had built their worlds. However, many of these men's legacies, much like Hammond, Hampton, and Calhoun, are still focal points in scholarship.

That aura of power and prestige that was found in the antebellum world of the great upcountry cotton planter was gone forever. It had

113Blease, *Destruction*, 18-19 and 22-24.; Letter, Lucy Hampton to Lucy Baxter, February 13, 1888, SSBHP, SCL, MD.; Letter from Genl. Wade Hampton To The Editors Of The Day Book, June 14, 1865, HFP, SCL, MD.

114Letter, Wade Hampton to General, no date, HFP, SCL, MD.

115Robertson, *Red Hills*, 20.

116Nelson, *Ruin*, 97.

117Longacre, *Gentleman*, 246, 252-253, 267, 271 and 274.

been an ambition of these upcountry planters to be recognized on a basis of equality with those of the low country. In addition, they sought to elevate their own status through the building of their homes in the Greek Revival style. Slaves enabled them to accomplish this. This world that had been meticulously created by the upcountry Georgia and Carolina cotton planters was distinctive from that of other Southern planters. From the start they were underestimated regarding their wealth, status, and abilities to climb into the select low country planter ranks. By selecting one of the most elaborate and historical architectural styles, they defined themselves as the elite. Though these upcountry cotton planters are often overlooked for their contributions to the Old South by historians, their legacy endures through their Greek Revival plantation homes. Often lost in telling their stories is the means by which they were able to ascend to such positions of power. Without their slaves, these planters would have never succeeded.

CHAPTER 9

MARRED BY THE STAIN OF SLAVERY

The legacy and lure of the Southern cotton plantation is deeply rooted in White American consciousness. Though the tradition had been cultivated somewhat in the mythology that was generated in the post-bellum era, during a time of both restoration and lost cause ideology, the realities of this lifestyle and operation were at one time factual. Many of the planters described achieved renown in state or national politics; some were perhaps a bit obscure. But these upcountry Georgia, South Carolina, and North Carolina cotton planters left a dramatic mark on American, particularly Southern, history. Their Greek Revival plantation houses were a mark of distinction. These men embraced an architectural style that they reaffirmed was tied to slave ownership and mastery over cotton lands.

The upcountry cotton planters of Georgia, South Carolina and North Carolina were probably much like their counterparts of other regions of the South. They all sought successful crops that would generate wealth for them and their families. Also, there were planters and others who also built in the Greek Revival architectural style in this era as well who did not reside in this region of the South. The men examined here were not alone in their usage of the Greek Revival architectural design. However, they found that this style allowed them to both display their own identities, their status, and separate them from previous generations as well as those who were less successful.

The plantation house, the outer buildings as well as the contents of these structures were all testaments to the men who built them. As White Southerners coped with the loss of their way of life after the Civil War, the "moonlight and magnolias" ideology offered a veneer of nostalgia for past times.

Greek Revival architecture was not unique to the American South. It did, however, take a certain meaning among the upcountry cotton planter class, as it showed that they were just as powerful and wealthy as their low country counterparts. In Georgia, South Carolina, and

North Carolina, the low country planters dominated. Attempting to display their sovereignty and capabilities, the upcountry planters embraced this architectural style with its ties to an ancient slave civilization that they idealized and emulated.

One assessment made within this book was that Greek Revival architecture was a representation of slave-generated cotton wealth. Although this architectural style was clearly found throughout the United States in the private, public, and ecclesiastical spheres, it took on a distinct characteristic in the southern states. In an attempt to distance themselves from their fathers' generation, who primarily built in the Federal or colonial styles, the nineteenth century upcountry cotton planter made Greek Revival a trend of his generation. Whereas the Federal style was symbolic of democratic ideals, Greek Revival conveyed of states' rights.

The low country rice planters around Charleston viewed the upcountry of South Carolina with disdain. But cotton helped to transform the upcountry into a land of the moneyed planter realm as well. The Greek Revival plantation homes of Fort Hill, Redcliffe, Millwood. and Milford helped set the standards of magnificence. These houses were symbols of the men of power who owned them, all of whom dominated in politics/government, agriculture and society. Their plantation homes set the standards and the patterns of the day. These planters desired to, and were successful in, creating an autocratic world in which they prevailed.

It was intended for South Carolina's Greek Revival State House to bear the means of her wealth within the architectural style itself, with slaves to be carved into the pediment.[1] Though war altered this design, the upcountry cotton planters who built their Greek Revival homes had enthusiastically approved these plans.[2] This style was bound with many

---

[1]Letter, Johnson M. Mundy to Mary E. Mundy, February 20, 1861, JMMP, SCL, MD.; Letter, Jno. Niernsee to H. K. Brown, Jan. 19, 1860, HKBBP, LOC, MD.; Photographs, Design for Pediment, State House, South Carolina, Right Hand Fragment and Left Hand Fragment, HKBBP, LOC, MD, Vol. V: 1333A, 1369A and 1369B.

[2]Letter, J R Niernsee to H. K. Brown, March 10, 1860, HKBBP, LOC, MD.

aspects of slavery, that of authority, supremacy, and other horrors. Though Greek Revival was used in the North as well, there was not a single class with which it was associated.

Each home held a specific meaning to the man who owned it. Although each Greek Revival house was symbolic of the upcountry cotton planter class, its significance was more deeply entrenched. James Henry Hammond's motivation in building Redcliffe was in fact two fold. One was to outdo John L. Manning's Milford,[3] while the other was to make Redcliffe a place of solace, even an escape after having been caught molesting his nieces.[4] This plantation home became symbolic of the man, for it was his creation and design, the enduring legacy he sought for future generations to see.

James Henry Hammond was fully dedicated to the principles of the lifestyle of the wealthy cotton planter. He married a woman for whom he held little affinity in order to advance his social rank into the planter class. Taking possession of her properties, he expanded these holdings and began his assent into high society. Building Greek Revival homes, first in Columbia and then his Redcliffe plantation, he further bound himself to this world. So dedicated to the elite planter realm, he advocated and supported disunion. Hammond proclaimed "...whenever she determines to dissolve the union, I shall, without hesitation, go with her fully..."[5]

The stories from the South Carolina planters seemed to make the strongest case of the tie of Greek Revival and slave holding. Their plantation homes stood as the embodiment of the oligarchical world they created. Their plantations appear to be among the most renowned. Even though many letters, papers, and documents were destroyed during the Civil War and afterwards, a fair amount of their stories survived. John C. Calhoun, James Henry Hammond, Wade Hampton II, and John L. Manning are widely recognized not only because of their political stances but because of the enduring legacies of their grand Greek Revival plantation homes. Not as much detail was available on

---

[3]Billings, "Notes," RACRF, SCDAH.; Shaffer, *Gardens*, 184.

[4]Letter, James Henry Hammond to William G. Simms, February 27, 1856, JHHP, LOC, MD.

[5]James Henry Hammond, Speech, 1860, JHHP, SCL, MD.

the Georgia planters who were discussed. Their plantations and homes fit into the model being assessed but many of these men did not leave behind written documents. Of the two planters selected from North Carolina, Paul Cameron left a wealth of documentation whereas most information about William Williams was obtained through his multiple wills and other individuals' written comments.

Though some of these planters, particularly the Georgia ones, did not leave behind detailed accounts of their lives, their Greek Revival homes helped to tell their stories. The magnificence of these houses have been captivated by scholars and have been included, albeit briefly, in works like Mills Lane's *Architecture of the Old South: Georgia* and David King Gleason's *Antebellum Homes of Georgia.* North Carolina planter William Williams left behind primarily tax records and wills in part to tell his story, but the significance of Montmorenci was so great that the du Pont family sought to preserve not only the façade but moldings and the staircase.

When Frederick Law Olmsted made his famous trek from 1852 to 1857 through the South, it was his contention that as a whole "a large plantation is necessarily a retreat from general society..."[6] There is truth in some aspects of this statement. Many of these planters that have been discussed found some comfort in being at their plantations and being in their homes. James Henry Hammond clearly built Redcliffe as some form of escape.[7] Wade Hampton II took great pleasure in being home and made his expansive plantation the center of society.[8] His Millwood was seen as the greatest of plantation houses. Olmsted was also correct in asserting that the plantation was its own world. Here, the owner was master, a ruler over his lands and possessions particularly in his slaves. It was this that truly defined him. Perhaps the general populace never had access to the cotton lands and the grand Greek Revival mansion that was filled with possessions unattainable by the common man. But the people knew of these plantations through

[6]Olmsted, *Kingdom*, 477.

[7]Letter, James Henry Hammond to Col. B. J. Watts, November 28, 1860, JHHP, SCL, MD.

[8]Letter, Wade Hampton II to Mary, August 26, 1857, HFP, SCL, MD.; Cannaday, "Reconstruction's."

stories, articles and general conversation. This was not a life, a property, a house that just anyone could attain. It was created through the possession of a great number of chattel slaves who made the cotton salable. It was the slaves who generated the profits that allowed the planter to build a Greek Revival house, which in turn, stood as a symbol of this life.

The intrinsic union of this architectural style and slave ownership was ever present. The Greek Revival plantation house was a defining factor of the upcountry Georgia, South Carolina and North Carolina planter. It told the tale of his power, his might, and his character. These plantation houses, all grand in stature of varying degrees, were a testament to the legacy of the men who owned them. Built to be lasting legacies of the slave-owning cotton planter, they stood as perpetual reminders of the antebellum era. Though the men died, slavery was abolished, and some of the houses were destroyed, these Greek Revival plantation houses survived in either reality or in story, enabling them to share the legacies of these individuals.

In essence it was the slaves and their labor that generated these upcountry planters' wealth and allowed them to build, maintain and furnish their Greek Revival plantation houses. Slave cabins were built and positioned so as to optimize work levels. Strategically placed on the plantation lands, these cotton planters kept their slaves within an arm's reach but also hidden from general view. There was clear recognition on the part of these planters that the slaves were their source of wealth, hence the paternal relationship that was maintained. However, there was the perpetual acknowledgement that the upcountry cotton planter class was the master and the slaves were just their property. They could be sold at whim.

Homes are in fact historical records. These Greek Revival plantation houses told the story of the men who owned them and their desire to dominate their societal world. The effort placed into the design, construction, modification, and decorations, inclusive of the outlying approach, are accounts of this self-contained oligarchical world they created. Greek Revival was the medium through which these men told their stories. It was their symbol, their essence, their being. Although their voices were muted, their slaves were why they had these homes.

The Southern Greek Revival plantation houses, especially in the upcountry regions of Georgia, South Carolina and North Carolina, were a symbol of this generation's planter class who earned their money from slaves and cotton. These upcountry planters put much of their individual stories in their Greek Revival plantation houses. Each home was a manifestation of the wealth, power and status of the planter. The house, its contents as well as the overall design were illustrative of the man who owned them. Though the root of their wealth, which had been generated by slave labor, became defunct, the status that each man painstakingly tried to preserve was, in the end, attained. Every aspect of the plantation house stood as a measure of the man who had it constructed. It was a testament to his legacy and power, one that was intended to transcend the generations. The illusion of grandeur displayed in these homes masked the reality of how they were built and maintained; it was accomplished by the labor of slaves. The beauty of these homes and their representations of the power of the planter however are forever marred by the stain of slavery.

BIBLIOGRAPHY

ARCHIVES

Adger and Bowen Families Papers, South Caroliniana Library, Manuscripts Division.

Baldwin County, Georgia. Deed Book J.

Colonel David C. Barrow Papers, Hargrett Rare Books and Manuscripts Library, University of Georgia Libraries.

Richard Bennehan Letters Miscellaneous, North Carolina Division of Archives and History.

Burge Family Papers, Emory University Manuscript, Archives, and Rare Book Library.

Bryce Family Papers, South Caroliniana Library, Manuscripts Division.

Henry Kirke Bush-Brown Papers, Library of Congress, Manuscripts Division.

Robert M. Cahusac Papers, South Carolina Historical Society, Manuscripts Division.

Matthew Calbraith Butler Papers. South Caroliniana Library, Manuscripts Division.

John Caldwell Calhoun Papers, South Caroliniana Library, Manuscripts Division.

John C. Calhoun. *The Papers of John C. Calhoun.* 28 vols. Edited by Clyde N. Wilson, W. Edwin Hemphill, and Shirley Bright Cook. Columbia, S.C.: University of South Carolina Press, 1958-2003.

Cameron Family Papers, Southern Historical Collection, University of North Carolina.

Bennehan Cameron Family Papers, Southern Historical Collection, University of North Carolina Press.

Duncan Cameron Will, Durham County, Record of Wills, Vols. A, B. North Carolina Division of Archives and History.

Duncan Cameron Will, 1853, Wake County, Record of Wills. Inventories, Settlement of Estates, 1850-1855. Vols. 27, 28. North Carolina Division of Archives and History.

Paul C. Cameron Papers, Civil War Collection, Orange County, North Carolina Division of Archives and History.

Paul C. Cameron Petition for Amnesty File, North Carolina Division of Archives and History.

Elizabeth S. Winthrop Chandler Papers, South Caroliniana Library, Manuscripts Division.

Civil War Collection, North Carolina Division of Archives and History.

Civil War Collection, Orange County, North Carolina Division of Archives and History.

Civil War Miscellaneous Collection, US Army Military History Institute.
Thomas Green Clemson Papers, South Caroliniana Library, Manuscripts Division. Copies of the original letters that are housed at Clemson University.
Anne Cameron Collins Papers, Southern Historical Collections, University of North Carolina.
Ellis Merton Coulter Historical Manuscripts, Confederate States of America, Hargrett Rare Books and Manuscripts Library, University of Georgia Libraries.
Telamon Cuyler Collection, Hargrett Rare Books and Manuscripts Library, University of Georgia Libraries.
Telamon Cuyler Collection, Georgia Governor's Papers, Hargrett Rare Books and Manuscripts Library, University of Georgia Libraries.
Fairntosh Plantation, National Register of Historic Places Inventory-Nomination Form, Durham County, North Carolina. North Carolina Division of Archives and History.
Fort Hill-Pickens County Research File, South Carolina Archives and History.
Hammond, Bryan, and Cumming Families Papers, South Caroliniana Library, Manuscripts Division.
Harry Hammond Papers, South Caroliniana Library, Manuscripts Division.
James Henry Hammond Papers, Library of Congress, Manuscripts Division, Microfilm.
James Henry Hammond Papers, South Caroliniana Library, Manuscripts Division.
James Henry Hammond Papers, Southern Historical Collection, University of North Carolina.
Harry Hammond Papers, South Caroliniana Library, Manuscripts Division.
Hampton Family Papers, South Caroliniana Library, Manuscripts Division.
Preston Hampton Revolutionary Pension and Bounty Land Warrant Application Files, National Archives Microfilm Publication, Revolutionary Pension and Bounty Land Warrant Application Files 1800-1900, roll #1177 Hamner, Henry—Hancks, Abraham.
Sarah (Sally) Strong Baxter Hampton Papers, South Caroliniana Library, Manuscripts Division.
Wade Hampton Papers, Southern Historical Collection, Manuscripts
Division, University of North Carolina.
Harrisburg Civil War Round Table, US Army Military History Institute.
Historic American Buildings Survey. Ainsley Hall, South Carolina.
Historic American Buildings Survey. Clinton, Jones County. Lowther Hall.
Historic American Buildings Survey. Milford. Governor John L. Manning Plantation.
Historic American Buildings Survey. Milledgeville Vicinity, Baldwin County, Tucker, Daniel R. House (Lockerly), Survey No. GA-1151, Data Sheet #2

Historic American Buildings Survey, "Millwood" (Wade Hampton Mansion) Ruins, Habs No. SC-256, Part I, Historical Information.
James Jones Papers, South Caroliniana Library, Manuscripts Division.
Ledger Papers, South Caroliniana Library, Manuscripts Division.
Manning Family Papers, South Caroliniana Library, Manuscripts Division.
John L. Manning Biographical Information, Compilation for Class of Ex-1837. Preparation Material for General Catalogue of Alumni, Officers and Honorary Graduates of Princeton University, Department of Rare Books and Special Collections, Princeton University Library.
John L. Manning File, Department of Rare Books and Special Collections, Princeton University Library.
John Laurence Manning Papers, South Caroliniana Library, Manuscripts Division.
John L. Manning Paperwork. Filed with Princeton University for the compilation
of the Princeton University General Biographical Catalogue 1746-1916. Princeton University Library.
Maverick and Van Wyke Papers, South Caroliniana Library, Manuscripts Division.
Virginia Gurley Meynard Papers, South Caroliniana Library, Manuscripts Division.
Milford Plantation, Sumter County Research File, South Carolina Department of Archives and History.
Milford Plantation, 1839-1969. Private File of Dr. Rodger Stroup. The South Carolina History Center.
Military Records, American Revolution, North Carolina Division of Archives and History.
Robert Mills Papers, Library of Congress, Manuscripts Division.
Millwood, National Register of Historic Register of Historic Places—Nomination Form, South Carolina Department of Archives and History.
Millwood-Richland County Research File. South Caroliniana Division of Archives and History.
Montmorenci. Winterthur Library, Winterthur Archives.
Johnson M. Mundy Papers, South Caroliniana Library, Manuscripts Division. National Register of Historic Places Inventory—Nomination Form, Fort Hill, Pickens County File. South Carolina Department of Archives & History.
North Carolina Historical Commission Papers, North Carolina Division of Archives and History.
Northampton County, Wills, 1764-1950, Calvert-Clemens. North Carolina Division of Archives and History.

Henry Junius Nott Papers, South Caroliniana Library, Manuscripts Division.
Official Records of the War of the Rebellion (CD-Rom).
Orange County, North Carolina Deeds. Book 28. North Carolina Division of Archives and History.
Orange County Deed Book, North Carolina Division of Archives and History.
Orange County Wills, Book F. North Carolina Department of Archives and History.
Person County, North Carolina Deeds, Book O. North Carolina Division of Archives and History.
Photographs. Montmorenci. Winterthur Library, Winterthur Archives.
Photographs of the Historic American Building Survey. Interiors-Lowther Hall. Online Georgia Tech catalog. http://www.library.gatech.edu/archives/habs/HABS_PH_046.htm.
Polk Papers, North Carolina Division of Archives and History.
Edward Elmer Potter Papers, South Caroliniana Library, Manuscripts Division.
Denmark Raleigh photographs, Montmorenci, Winterthur Library, Winterthur Archives.
Redcliffe, Aiken County, Research File, South Carolina Department of Archives and History.
Charles Rhodes Collection, US Army Military History Institute.
William Tecumseh Sherman Papers, South Caroliniana Library, Manuscripts Division.
Mary Amarinthia Snowden Papers, South Caroliniana Library, Manuscripts Division.
South Carolina Papers, South Caroliniana Library, Manuscripts Division.
Southern Claims Commission Files, National Archives.
Dr. Rodger Stroup Private File. South Carolina Archives and History Center.
Sumter County Deeds.
Sumter County Records.
Sumter County Records and Deeds.
George Tattersall Papers, South Caroliniana Library, Manuscripts Division.
Daniel Heyward Trezant Papers, South Caroliniana Library, Manuscripts Division.
200 Meeting Street File, South Carolina Historical Society, Manuscripts Division.
Wake County Record of Wills, Inventories, Settlement of Estates 1850-1855, Vols. 27, 28, North Carolina Division of Archives and History.
Warren County Estate Records 1772-1940, n.d. (Williams, W.K.A.—Wise), North Carolina Division of Archives and History.
Warren County Wills. North Carolina Division of Archives and History.
R. Wearn Photographs, South Caroliniana Library, Manuscripts Division.

William May Wightman Papers, South Caroliniana Historical Society, Manuscripts Division.

Williams-Chesnut-Manning Families Papers, South Caroliniana Library, Manuscripts Division.

PRIMARY SOURCES

American Historical Association Report, 1899, Volume II.

—. "A Few Facts Of Slavery" As Told by Celeste Avery-Ex-Slave." In *The American Slave: A Composite Autobiography Volume 12 Georgia Narratives Parts 1 and 2*, ed. George P. Rawick, 22-27. Westport, CT: Greenwood Publishing Company, 1976.

—. "Cy Hart, Ex-Slave." In *The American Slave: A Composite Autobiography Volume 11 North Carolina Narratives Parts 1*, ed. George P. Rawick, 380. Westport, CT: Greenwood Publishing Company, 1972.

—. *Memorial Of The Cotton Planters' Convention To the Honorable Senate And House Of Representatives Of The State Of Georgia, In General Assembly Met.* Augusta, GA: Steam Press Chronicle & Sentinel, 1860. Georgia Department Of Archives and History, Rare Books.

1820 Federal Census of North Carolina, Volume LII, Warren County. Tullahoma, N.Y.: Dorothy Williams Potter, 1973.

"Abstract of Title." 1 August 1879. Hampton Family Papers, South Caroliniana Library, Manuscripts Division.

Aldrich, Mrs. A. P. "In The Track of Sherman's Army. In *"Our Women In The War." The Lives They Lived; The Deaths They Died.*, 197-211. Charleston, S.C.: The News And Courier Book Presses, 1885.

Aristotle. *Politics*. Ed, Benjamin Jowett. Books One-Six. http://classics.mit.edu/Aristotle/politics.html

"Articles of Agreement." Signed by Jos. Fenney, C.L. Hampton, Nathaniel Potter and Jn. L. Manning. 6 May 1839. Williams-Chesnut-Manning Families Papers. South Caroliniana Library, Manuscripts Division.

Avirett, James Battle. *The Old Plantation: How We Lived in Great House and Cabin Before the War*. New York: F. Tennyson Neely Co., 1857.

Bierce, Lucius Verus. "The Piedmont Frontier, 1822-23." In *South Carolina the Grand Tour 1780-1865*, ed. Thomas D. Clarke, 61-71. Columbia, S.C.: University of South Carolina Press, 1973.

Beecher, Catherine Esther. *A Treatise on Domestic Economy*. New York: Source Books Press, 1970 [reprint].

Benjamin, Asher. *The American Builder's Companion Or. A System of Architecture Particularly Adapted To The Present Style of Building*. New York: Dover Publications, Inc., 1969. [reprint of 1827 edition].

Blease, Hon Cole L. *Destruction Of Property In Columbia, S.C. By Sherman's Army*. Washington: United States Government Printing Office, 1930.

Bleser, Carol, ed. *The Hammonds of Redcliffe*. New York and Oxford: Oxford University Press, 1981.
Bleser, Carol, ed. *Secret and Sacred: The Diaries of James Henry Hammond, a Southern Slaveholder*. New York and Oxford: Oxford University Press, 1988.
Breeden, James O., ed. *Advice Among Masters: The Ideal In Slave Management In The Old South*. Westport, CT: Greenwood Press, 1980.
Bremer, Fredericka. *The Homes of the New World: Impressions of America*. New York: Harper & Brothers, Publishers, 1853.
Bryce, Mrs. Cambell. "The Personal Experiences of Mrs. Campbell Bryce During The Burning of Columbia, South Carolina By General W. T. Sherman's
Army February 17, 1865." Philadelphia: n.p., 1899.
Buff, Jr., L. H. *The Richland District (SC) 1850 Census*. Lexington Genealogical Association, 2000.
Burke, Emily. *Pleasure and Pain: Reminiscences Of Georgia in the 1840s*. Savannah, GA; The Beehive Press, 1978.
Calhoun, John C. "Further Remarks In Debate On His Fifth Resolution." In *The Papers Of John C. Calhoun XIV: 1837-1839*, ed. Clyde N. Wilson, 80-86. Columbia: University of South Carolina Press, 1981.
Calhoun, John C. "Resolution On The Slave Question." In *John C. Calhoun*, ed. Margaret L. Coit, 51-52. Englewood Cliffs, NJ: Prentice-Hall, Inc., 1970.
Calhoun, John C. "Speech on the Importance of Domestic Slavery." In *Slavery Defended: The Views of The Old South*, ed. Eric L. McKitrick, 16-19. Englewood Cliffs, New Jersey: Prentice-Hall, Inc., 1963.
Calhoun, John C. "Speech on the Reception of Abolition Petitions, Delivered in the Senate, February 6th, 1837." In *Defending Slavery: Proslavery Thought in the Old South, A Brief History with Documents*, ed. Paul Finkelman, 54-60. Boston and New York: Bedford / St. Martin's Press, 2003.
Calhoun, John C. "Speech on the Reception of Abolition Petitions, Delivered in the Senate, February 6th, 1837." http://www.stolaf.edu/people/fitz/COURSES/calhoun.html.
Canning, Mrs. Nora M. "Sherman in Georgia." In *"Our Women In The War." The Lives That They Lived; The Deaths They Died*, 77-85. Charleston, S.C.: The News and Courier Book Presses, 1885.
Cauthen, Charles E., ed. *Family Letters of the Three Wade Hamptons 1782–1901*. Columbia, S.C.: University of South Carolina Press, 1953.
Chambers, Col. James M. "Essay on the Treatment and Cultivation of Cotton" (read in 1852 before the Southern Central Agricultural Association of Georgia). In *The Cotton Planter's Manual: Being A Compilation of the Facts from the Best Authorities on the Culture of Cotton and the Cotton Gin*, ed. J. A.

Turner, 11-20. New York: C. M. Saxton and Company, 1852. Georgia Department of Archives and History.

Charleston Hotel, Charleston, S.C. United States South Carolina Charleston, None. [Photographed between 1861 and 1865, printed between 1880 and 19889] Photograph. https://www.loc.gov/item/2014645931/.

Clay-Copton, Virginia. *A Belle of the Fifties: Memoirs of Mrs. Clay, of Alabama, Covering Social and Political Life in Washington and the South, 1853-66.* New York: Doubleday, Page & Company, 1905.

Clemens, William Montgomery, ed. *North and South Carolina Marriage Records: From The Earliest Colonial Days To The Civil War.* New York: E.P. Dutton & Company, 1927.

Conyngham, David P. Selections from *Sherman's March through the South.* In *Times That Prove People's Principles: Civil War In Georgia A Documentary History*, ed. Mills Lane, 144-153. Savannah: A Beehive Press Book, 1993.

Cook, Harvey Toliver. *Sherman's March Through South Carolina in 1865.* Greenville, S.C.: 1938.

Cox, Jacob B. *The March To The Sea; Franklin And Nashville.* Edison, N.J.: Castle Books, 2002. [reprint of 1882 edition].

DeSaussure, N. B. *Old Plantation Days: Being Recollections Of Southern Life Before The Civil War.* New York: Duffield & Company, 1909.

Dixon, W. W. "Adeline Johnson Alias Adeline Hall Ex-Slave 93 Years Old." In *The American Slave: A Composite Autobiography Volume 3 South Carolina Narratives Parts 3 and 4, Volume XIV. Part 3*, ed. George P. Rawick, 35-39. Westport, CT: Greenwood Publishing Company, 1941.

Dixon, W. W. "Eli Harrison: Ex-Slave 87 Years." In *The American Slave: A Composite Autobiography Volume 2 South Carolina Narratives Parts 1 and 2*, ed. George P. Rawick, 244-246. Westport, CT: Greenwood Publishing Co., 1972.

Dodge, Grenville M. *Personal Recollections of General William T. Sherman.* Columbia: The State Company, 1903.

Downing, Andrew Jackson. *The Architecture of Country Houses.* New York: Da Capo Press, 1961. [reprint of 1850 edition].

Emilio, Luis F. *A Brave Black Regiment: History of the Fifty-Fourth Regiment of Massachusetts Volunteer Infantry 1863-1865.* Salem, N.H.: Ayer Company Publishers, Inc., 1990 [reprint].

Epitaph. South Carolina Papers. South Caroliniana Library, Manuscripts Division.

Featherstonhaugh, George W. *A Canoe Voyage Up The Minnay Sotor with An Account of the Lead and Copper Deposits in Wisconsin; of the Gold Region In The Cherokee Country; and Sketches of Popular Manners, Volume 2.* St. Paul: Minnesota Historical Society, 1970. [Reprint edition]

Featherstonhaugh, G. W. "Excursions Through The Slave States." In *The South: A Documentary History*, ed. Ina Woestemeyer VanNoppen, 231-234. Princeton, N.J.: D. Van Nostrand Company, Inc., 1958.

Fleharty, Stephen F. *Our Regiment, A History Of The 102d Illinois Volunteers With Sketches of the Atlanta Campaign, the Georgia Raid, and the Campaign of the Carolinas*. Chicago. Brewster & Hanscom, Printers, 1865.

"Ga., 1860, physician" in *Advice Among Masters: The Ideal In Slave Management In the Old South*, ed. James O. Breeden, 58-60. Westport, CT: Greenwood Press, 1980.

"Ga., 1860, physician" in *Advice Among Masters: The Ideal In Slave Management In The Old South*, ed. James O. Breeden, 135-139. Westport, CT: Greenwood Press, 1980.

Gallay, Alan, ed. *Voices of the Old South: Eyewitness Accounts, 1528-1861*. Athens: The University of Georgia Press, 1994.

Godfrey, George L. "Johnston's Surrender to Sherman." In *War Sketches and Incidents*. MOLLUS, IA, Vol. 2, 65-76. Wilmington, N.C.: Bradfoot Publishing Company, 1994. [reprint]

Greenough, Horatio. "Structure and Organization." In *Form and Function: Remarks On Art, Design, And Architecture*, ed. Harold A. Small, 113-129. Berkeley and Los Angeles: University of California Press, 1962.

Grund, Francis J. *Aristocracy In America: From the Sketch-Book of a German Nobleman*. New York: Harper Torchbooks, 1959. [reprint of 1839 edition].

Hall, Captain Basil. "These Hospital Planters." In *The Plantation South*, ed. Katherine M. Jones, 95-104. New York: The Bobbs-Merrill Company, Inc., 1957.

Hammond Traveling Accounts, May 1836—November 1837. James Henry Hammond Papers, South Caroliniana Library, Manuscripts Division.

Hammond, Harry. "Sketch of James Henry Hammond." James Henry Hammond Papers. South Caroliniana Library. Manuscripts Division.

Hammond, James Henry. "Hammond's Letters on Slavery." In *Voices of the Old South: Eyewitness Accounts, 1528-1861,* ed. Alan Gallay, 387-404. Athens: The University of Georgia Press, 1994.

Hammond, James Henry. "James Henry Hammond Plantation Records #2, 6 January 1857. South Caroliniana Library, Manuscripts Division.

Hammond, James Henry. "Speech on the Admission of Kansas." / "Mud-Sill." In *Slavery Defended: the views of The Old South*, ed. Eric L. McKitrick, 121-125. Englewood Cliffs, N.J.: Prentice Hall, Incorporated, 1963.

Hammond, James Henry. *Speech of Hon. James H. Hammond, of South Carolina, on the admission of Kansas, under the Lecompton Constitution: delivered in the Senate of the United States, March 4, 1858.* http://simms.library.sc.edu/view_item.php?item=133195.

Hammond, James Henry. "Stud Book, 1833-1839." James Henry Hammond Papers, South Caroliniana Library, Manuscripts Division.

Hammond, James Henry. "Stud Book, 1833-1840." James Henry Hammond Papers, South Caroliniana Library, Manuscripts Division.

Hammond, Harry. "Agriculture in South Carolina." Harry Hammond Papers, South Caroliniana Library, Manuscripts Division.

Hammond, Harry. "The Estate of James H. Hammond Deceased in Account with

Harry Hammond Executor, Account Book 1886-1893." Harry Hammond Papers, South Caroliniana Library, Manuscripts Division.

Hampton, Ann Fripp, ed. *A Divided Heart: Letters Of Sally Baxter Hampton 1853-1862*. Spartanburg, SC: The Reprint Company, Publishers, 1980.

Hampton, Wade v. Catherine M. Hampton, et. al. Judgment Roll No. 994. Office of the Clerk of the Court, Richland County. South Carolina Division of Archives and History.

Haviland, John. *The Builder's Assistant Containing The Five Orders of Architecture, for the Use of Builders, Carpenters, Masons, Plasters, Cabinet Makers and Carvers*. Philadelphia: John Bioren, 1818. Microfilm.

Haweis, H. R. *The Art of American Decoration*. London: Chatto and Windus, 1881.

Hewatt, Alexander. *An Historical Account of the Rise and Progress of the Colonies Of South Carolina and Georgia, in Two Volumes, Vol. I*. Spartanburg, South Carolina: The Reprint Company, 1962. [London: Alexander Donaldson, MDCCLXXIX.]

Horton, C.R.S. "Savannah and Parts of the Far South." In *Grandeur of the South*, ed. Lisa S. Mullins, 9-40. Harrisburg, Pennsylvania: National Historical Society Publications, 1988.

Hundley, Daniel. *Social Relations in Our Southern States.* Baton Rouge: Louisiana State University Press, 1979.

Irving, J.B. *The South Carolina Jockey Club.* Charleston: Russell & Jones, 1857.

Jackson, Oscar L. *The colonel's diary; journal kept before and during the civil war by the late Colonel Oscar L. Jackson...sometimes commander of the 63rd regiment O.V. I.,* ed. David Prentice (reproduction printer from a digital file created at the Library of Congress, 1922).

Jenkins, John S. *The Life of John Caldwell Calhoun*. New York: Hurst & Co., Publishers, 1852.

Jones, Joseph. *First Report To The Cotton Planters' Convention Of Georgia, On The Agricultural Resources of Georgia*. Augusta, Georgia: Steam Press Of Chronicle & Sentinel, 1860.

Johnston, Richard Malcolm. "The Planter Of The Old South." In *Publications of the Southern History Magazine*, bound edition, Volume 1 (1), 35-47. Washington, DC: The Association, 1897.

Klingberg, Franklin. *The Southern Claims Commission*. New York: Octagon Books, 1978.

Lafayette, General. *Memoirs of General Lafayette with an Account of His Visit to America and His Reception by the People of the United States from His Arrival August 15th to the Celebration at Yorktown October 19th, 1824*. Kessinger Publications, n.d. [reprint].

Latrobe, Benjamin Henry. "Anniversary Oration To The Society Of Artists, 8 May 1811." In *The Correspondence and Miscellaneous Papers of Benjamin Henry Latrobe, Volume 3, 1811-1820*, ed. John C. Van Horne, 67-91. Published for The Maryland Historical Society by New Haven and London: Yale University Press, 1988.

Latrobe, Benjamin Henry. *The Journal of Latrobe*. New York: Appleton and Company, 1905.

Letter, Wade Hampton to Andrew Jackson, June 1810. In *The Papers of Andrew Jackson, Vol. 2*. eds. Harold D. Moser and Sharon Macpherson, 248. Knoxville: University of Tennessee Press, 1985.

Letter, John C. Calhoun to Duff Green, 2 November 1839. In *Annual Report Of The American Historical Association For The Year 1899: Volume II. Calhoun Correspondence (Fourth Annual Report Of The Historical Manuscripts Commission Correspondence of John C. Calhoun)*, ed. J. Franklin Jameson, 432-433. Washington: Government Printing Office, 1900.

Letter, JA Stuart to John C. Calhoun, 8 October 1841. In *Annual Report Of The American Historical Association For The Year 1929*, 161-162. Washington, DC: Government Printing Office, 1930.

Letter, Henry Bailey to John C. Calhoun, 30 May 1844. In *Annual Report Of The American Historical Association For The Year 1929*, 236-237. Washington, DC: Government Printing Office, 1930.

Letter, John C. Calhoun to Thomas G. Clemson, 13 December 1845. In *Annual Report Of The American Historical Association For The Year 1899: Volume II. Calhoun Correspondence (Fourth Annual Report Of The Historical Manuscripts Commission Correspondence of John C. Calhoun)*, ed. J. Franklin Jameson, 674. Washington: Government Printing Office, 1900.

Letter, John C. Calhoun to Thomas G. Clemson, 8 August 1846. In *Annual Report Of The American Historical Association For The Year 1899: Volume II. Calhoun Correspondence (Fourth Annual Report Of The Historical Manuscripts Commission Correspondence of John C. Calhoun)*, ed. J. Franklin Jameson, 704-705. Washington: Government Printing Office, 1900.

Letter, William Tecumseh Sherman to His Excellency Prest. Lincoln. 22 December 1863. In *Sherman's Civil War: Selected Correspondence of William T. Sherman,1860-1865*, ed. Brooks D. Simpson & Jean V. Simpson, 772. Chapel Hill & London: The University of North Carolina Press, 1999.

Letter, William Tecumseh Sherman to Ulysses S. Grant. 22 December 1864. In *Sherman's Civil War: Selected Correspondence of William T. Sherman,1860-1865*, ed. Brooks D. Simpson & Jean V. Simpson, 771-772. Chapel Hill & London: The University of North Carolina Press, 1999.

Letter, William Tecumseh Sherman to Ulysses S. Grant. 24 December 1864. In *Sherman's Civil War: Selected Correspondence of William T. Sherman,1860-1865*, ed. Brooks D. Simpson & Jean V. Simpson, 773-774. Chapel Hill & London: The University of North Carolina Press, 1999.

Lossing, Benson J. *A Pictorial Field-Book of the Revolution, Vol.2*. New York: Harper Brothers, 1859.

Mackay, Charles. "General James Gadsden's Rice Plantation." In *The Plantation South*, ed. Katherine M. Jones, 208-217. New York: The Bobbs-Merrill Company, Inc., 1957.

Mahan, Major Samuel. "The Forager in Sherman's Last Campaigns." In *War Sketches and Incidents As Related By The Campaigns Of The Iowa Commandery Military Order Loyal Legion Of The United States, Volume II*, 188-200. Wilmington, 1994. [reprint of Des Moines, 1898 edition].

Maury, Sarah M. "This Great Statesman." In *John C. Calhoun*, ed. Margaret L. Coit, 72-76. Englewood Cliffs, NJ: Prentice-Hall, inc., 1970.

Mallet, John William. *Cotton: The Chemical, Geological, And Meteorological Conditions Involved In Its Successful Cultivation*. London: Chapman and Hall, 1862.

Manning, John L. Account Book, Cost of Construction of Milford. Wiliams-Chesnut-Manning Families Papers, South Caroliniana Library, Manuscripts Division.

Mills, Robert. *Statistics of South Carolina*. Charleston: Hurlburt And Lloyd, 1826.

Mood, Rev. Wm. W. "Recollections of Potter's Raid." Edward Elmer Potter, South Caroliniana Library, Manuscripts Division.

Myers, Earl Schneck, ed. *When The World Ended: The Diary of Emma Le Conte*. Lincoln and London: University of Nebraska Press, 1987.

Oakey, Daniel. "Marching Through Georgia And The Carolinas." In *Battles And*

Leaders Of The Civil War, Volume IV, eds. Robert Underwood Johnson and Clarence Clough Buel, 671-679. Secaucus, N.J.: Castle, n.d.

Olmsted, Frederick Law. *The Cotton Kingdom: A Traveler's Observations on Cotton and Slavery in the American Slave States*. New York: Alfred A. Knopf, 1953. [reprint of 1861 & 1862 editions].

Olmsted, Frederick Law. *The Cotton Kingdom: A Traveler's Observations on Cotton and Slavery in the American Slave States*. New York: The Modern Library, McGraw-Hill, Inc., 1984). [reprint of 1861 & 1862 editions].

Olmsted, Frederick Law. *Journeys And Explorations in The Cotton Kingdom, vol. I.* London: Sampson Low, Son & Co., 1861.

Ordinance of Secession. South Carolina Papers. South Caroliniana Library, Manuscripts Division.

Painting of Wade Hampton II by William H. Scarborough. Historic Columbia Foundation.

Parkes, Frances Byerly. *Domestic Duties.* London: Longman, Hurst, Rees, Brown and Green, 1825.

Parsons, Charles G. *Inside View of Slavery: Or A Tour Among the Planters.* Boston: John J. Jewett and Company, 1855.

Perry, Ex-Gov B. F. *Reminiscences Of Public Men.* Philadelphia: John D. Avil & Co., Printers and Publishers, 1883.

Perry, Benjamin F. *The Writings of Benjamin F. Perry, Vol. I: Essays, Public Letters, and Speeches.* Spartanburg, South Carolina: The Reprint Company, Publishers, 1980.

Perry, Benjamin F. *The Writings of Benjamin F. Perry Volume II: Reminiscences of Public Men*, eds. Stephen Meats and Edwin T. Arnold. Spartanburg, S.C.: The Reprint Company Publishers, 1980.

Plato. *The Republic.* Translated by Desmond Lee. London: Penguin Books, 2003.

Potter, Nathaniel F. House Plans for Milford, Drawings/Prints. Williams-Chesnut-Manning Families Papers, South Caroliniana Library, Manuscripts Division.

Potter, Nathaniel F. "Specifications for a Barn for John L. Manning Esq. to be Erected on his Plantation in Claredon So Ca [sic]." Williams-Chesnut-Manning Families Papers, South Caroliniana Library, Manuscripts Division.

Potter, Nathaniel F. "Specifications for a House to be built in Sumpter [sic] district, South Carolina, for John L. Manning, Esq." May 1839. Williams-Chesnut-Manning Papers. South Caroliniana Library. Manuscripts Division.

Potter, Nathaniel F. "Specifications for the Kitchen for John L. Manning's house." May 1839. Williams-Chesnut-Manning Families Papers, South Caroliniana Library, Manuscripts Division.

M. R. R. "Potter's Raid." In *"Our Women In The War." The Lives They Lived; The Deaths They Died*, 290-295. Charleston, S.C.: The News and Courier Book Presses, 1885.

Ramsey, David. "The Impact of Cotton upon the Older Staples of South Carolina." (1858) In *Cotton and the Growth of the American Economy: 1790-1860*, ed. Stuart Bruchey, 62-66. New York: Harcourt, Brace & World, Inc., 1967. [reprint of 1858 version].

"Revolutionary Incidents of the Hampton Family." June 1843. Hampton Family Papers, South Caroliniana Library, Manuscripts Division.

Richland District, South Carolina Land Records 1785-1865. Columbia, South Carolina: Congree Publications, 1986. Equity Rolls 34 and 85.

Robertson, Ben. *Red Hills and Cotton: an upcountry memory*. Columbia, S.C.: University of South Carolina Press, 1992. [reprint].

Russell, William. "Wade Hampton I—Description of Louisiana Plantation 1861."

Hampton Family Papers, South Caroliniana Library, Manuscripts Division.

Scoville, Joseph A. "A Visit to Fort Hill by "A Traveler."" (1849) In *The Papers of John C. Calhoun*, ed. Clyde N. Wilson, 526-537. Columbia, South Carolina: The University of South Carolina Press, 2001.

Scubbs, Stiles M., ed. "Anson Harp: Ex-Slave 87 Years Old." In *The American Slave: A Composite Autobiography Volume 2 South Carolina Narratives Parts 1 and 2*, ed. George P. Rawick, 237-239. Westport, CT: Greenwood Publishing Company, 1972.

Sherman, William Tecumseh. *Memoirs of General W. T. Sherman*. New York: The Literary Classics of America, 1990.

Slocum, Major-General H. W. "Final Operations Of Sherman's Army." In *Battles And Leaders Of The Civil War, Volume IV*, 754-758. Secaucus, N.J.: Castle, n.d.

Smith, Oliver P. *Domestic Architecture: Comprising a series of original designs for rural and ornamental cottages*. Buffalo: Derby & Co., 1852.

Somma. Thomas P. *The Apotheosis of Democracy, 1908-1916: The Pediment for the House Wing of the United States Capitol.* Newark: University of Delaware Press, 1995.

"South Carolina, A Patriotic Ode." South Carolina Papers. South Caroliniana Library, Manuscripts Division.

Special Field Order No. 19 and Special Field Order No. 25. *Military Orders of General William T. Sherman*.

"Speech of Hon Wade Hampton—Constitutionality of Slave Trade Laws." 10 December 1859. Hampton Family Papers, South Caroliniana Library, Manuscripts Division.

Spencer, Cornelia Phillips. *The Last Ninety Days Of The War In North Carolina.* New York: Watchman Publishing Company, W. H. Chase, Publishing Agent, 1866.

Stuart, James. *Three Years in North America, Vol. II*. Edenburgh: R. Cadell, 1833.

Stuart, James, And Nicholas Revett. *The Antiquities Of Athens, Volume The Second.* New York and London: Benjamin Blom, 1968. [reprint of the 1787 Edition].

Stuart, James, And Nicholas Revett. *The Antiquities Of Athens, Volume The Third*. New York and London: Benjamin Blom, 1968. [reprint of the 1794 Edition].

Stud Book. "Journals." James Henry Hammond Papers, South Caroliniana Library, Manuscripts Division.

Stud Book 1833-1839. "Pedigrees, Purchases, Sales & Raves of Blood Horses Belonging Wholly or in Part to James Henry Hammond, Silver Bluff, Barnwell, S.C. 1833." James Henry Hammond Papers, South Caroliniana Library, Manuscripts Division.

Stud Book 1833-1840. "Journals, Recipees [sic], Expenses & c of Blood Horses Belonging Wholly or in part to James H. Hammond, Silver Bluff, Barnwell,

S.C., 1833." James Henry Hammond Papers, South Caroliniana Library, Manuscripts Division.

Tasistro, Louis Fitzgerald. "A Theatrical View, 1843." In *South Carolina: The Grand Tour, 1780-1865*, ed. Thomas D. Clark, 182-200. Columbia, South Carolina: University of South Carolina Press, 1973.

Tax Lists (1791, 1796, 1798, 1797, 1798, 1802 and 1824, Richard Beenhan. Cameron Family Papers, Southern Historical Collection, University of North Carolina.

Thigpen, Allan D., ed. *The Illustrated Recollections of Potter's Raid April 5-21, 1865*. Sumter, S.C.: Gamecock City Press, 1999.

Thomas, Ella Gertrude Clanton. *The Secret Eye: The Journal of Ella Gertrude Clanton Thomas, 1848-1889*. Ed. Virginia Ingraham Burr. Chapel Hill: The University of North Carolina Press, 1990.

Trezvant, Daniel Heyward. "Burning of Columbia, 1865." Daniel Heyward Trezvant Papers, South Caroliniana Library, Manuscripts Division.

Trowbridge, John Townsend. *The South: A Tour of Its Battlefields and Ruined Cities Before the War, A Journey through the Desolated States, and Talks with the People, 1867*. ed. J.H. Segars. Macon, GA: Mercer University Press, 2006. [reprint of 1867 edition].

Turnage, Elmer, ed. "Stories From Ex-Slaves." In *The American Slave: A Composite Autobiography Volume 3 South Carolina Narratives Parts 3 and 4, Volume XIV, Part 3*, ed. George P. Rawick, 56-57. Westport, CT: Greenwood Publishing Company, 1941.

Turner, J.A. *The Cotton Planter's Manual: Being A Compilation Of Facts From The Best Authorities On The Culture Of Cotton; Its Natural History, Chemical Analysis, Trade And Consumption; And Embracing A History Of Cotton And The Cotton Gin*. New York: C. M. Saxton and Company, 1857.

Tuthill, Mrs. Louisa. *History of Architecture From the Earliest Times; Its Present Condition in Europe and the United States*. New York: Garland Publishing Inc., 1988. [reprint from 1848 edition].

U.S. Sixth Census [1840]: Pickens District, South Carolina.

Wailey, Daisy, ed. "Abner Jordan Ex-Slave, 95 Years." In *The American Slave: A Composite Autobiography Volume 15 North Carolina Narratives Part 2*, ed. George P. Rawick, 34-36. Westport, CT: Greenwood Publishing Company, 1976.

Wailey, Daisy, ed. "Doc Edwards, Ex-slave, 84 yrs." In *The American Slave: A Composite Autobiography Volume 14 North Carolina Narratives Part 1*, ed. George P. Rawick, 295-297. Westport, CT: Greenwood Publishing Company, 1971.

Waitt, Daisy Bailey, ed. "Reverend Squire Dowd." In *The American Slave: A Composite Autobiography Volume 14 North Carolina Narratives Part 1*, ed. George P. Rawick, 263-269. Westport, CT: Greenwood Publishing Company, 1971.

Weld, Theodore Dwight. *American Slavery As It Is: Testimony of a Thousand Witnesses.* Chapel Hill: The University of North Carolina at Chapel Hill Library, A DocSouth Books Edition, 2001. Reprint of the 1839 edition.

Wheeler, John Hill. *Historical Sketches Of North Carolina From 1854 to 1851 Compiled From Original Records, Official Documents, And Traditional Statements*. Baltimore: Regional Publishing Co., 1964. [reprint of Philadelphia, 1851].

White, Rev. George. *Historical Collections of Georgia Containing the Most Interesting Facts, Traditions, Biographical Sketches, Anecdotes, Etc., Relating to its History and Antiquities, From Its First Settlement to the Present Time; Complied from Original Records and Official Documents.* New York: Pudney & Russell, Publishers, 1855.

Whitney, Eli. *Memorial of Eli Whitney, Patent Petition 1793*. National Archives And Records Administration. Records of the United States House of Representatives. Record Group 233. http://www.archives.gov/education/lessons/cotton-gin-patent/#documents

Whipple, Henry Benjamin. *Bishop Whipple's Southern Diary, 1843-1844*, ed. Lester B. Shippee. New York: Da Capo Press, 1968.

Williams, William. Warren County Record of Taxable Property, 1824-1828. North Carolina Division of Archives and History.

Willison, Charles A. *Reminiscences Of A Boy's Service With The 76th Ohio*. Huntington, West Virginia: Blue Acorn Press, 1995. [reprint].

Wilson, Samuel. "An Account Of The Province Of Carolina, In America: Together With An Abstract Of The Patent And Several Other Necessary And Useful Particulars To Such as Have Thoughts Of Transporting Themselves Thither." In *Historical Collections of South Carolina: Embracing Many Rare And Valuable Pamphlets, And Other Documents, Relating To The History Of That State, From Its First Discovery To Its Independence, In The*

Year 1776, Vol. II, ed. B.R. Carroll, 19-35. New York: Harper & Brothers, 1836.

SECONDARY SOURCES

Allen, Letitia D. "Wade Hampton II's Patronage of Edward Troye." In *Art In The Lives Of South Carolinians: Nineteenth Century Chapters*, ed. David Moltke-Hansen, LA-1—LA-27. Charleston, SC: Charleston Art Association, 1979.

Anderson, Jean Bradley. *Piedmont Plantation: The Bennehan-Cameron Family and Lands in North Carolina.* Durham, N.C.: The Historic Preservation Society of Durham, 1985.

Andrews, Wayne. *Architecture, Ambition And Americans: A Social History of American Architecture.* New York: The Free Press, 1964.

Ashe, Samuel A., Stephen B. Weeks, and Charles L. Van Noppen, eds. *Biographical History of North Carolina, Volume III.* Greensboro, N.C.: Charles L. Van Noppen Publishers, MCMVI.

Bailey, N. Louise, Mary L. Morgan and Carolyn R. Taylor, eds. *Biographical Directory Of The South Carolina Senate 1776-1985, Volume I, Abbott- Hill.* Columbia, South Carolina: University of South Carolina Press, 1986.

Baker, Ernest. *The Political Thought Of Plato And Aristotle.* New York: Russell & Russell, Inc., 1959.

Ballard, Rene, et. al. "The Slave Quarters Historic Structure Report: Redcliffe State Historic Site, Beech Island, South Carolina." Columbia: Public History Program, University of South Carolina, 2002.

Baptist, Edward E. *The Half Has Never Been Told: Slavery And The Making Of American Capitalism.* New York: Basic Books, 2014.

Bardaglio, Peter W. *Reconstructing the Household: Families, Sex, & the Law in the Nineteenth-Century South.* Chapel Hill and London: The University of North Carolina Press, 1995.

Bishir, Catherine W. "A Proper Good Nice and Workmanlike Manner: A Century of Traditional Building Practice, 1730-1830." In *Architects and Builders in North Carolina: A History of the Practice of Building in North Carolina*, eds. Catherine W. Bishir, Charlotte V. Brown, Carl R. Lounsbury and Ernest H. Wood III, 48-129. Chapel Hill: The University of North Carolina Press, 1990.

Bishir, Catherine W. *Southern Built: American Architecture, Regional Practice.* Charlottesville, Virginia: University of Virginia Press, 2006.

Bishir, Catherine W. "A Spirit of Improvement: Changes in Building Practice, 1830-1860." In *Architects and Builders in North Carolina: A History of the Practice of Building*, eds. Catherine W. Bishir, Charlotte V. Brown, Carl R. Launsburg and Ernest H. Wood III, 130-192. Chapel Hill: The University of North Carolina Press, 1990.

Bishir, Catherine W. "The Montmorenci-Prospect Hill School: A Study of High Vernacular Architecture in the Roanoke Valley." In *Carolina Dwelling, ed.* Doug Swain. The Student Publication of the School of Design, North Carolina State University, 1978.

Bishir, Catherine W. and Michael Southern. *Guide to the Historic Architecture of Piedmont_North Carolina.* Chapel Hill and London: The University of North Carolina Press, 2003.

Bonner, James C. *Milledgeville: Georgia's Antebellum Capital.* Athens: The University of Georgia Press, 1978.

Bryan, John M. *Creating the South Carolina State House.* Columbia, S,C,: University of South Carolina Press, 1999.

Bulter, Joseph T. *Field Guide to American Antique Furniture: A Unique Visual System for Identifying the Style of Virtually Any Piece of American Antique Furniture.* New York: Holt Paperbacks, 1986.

Burchard, John, and Albert Bush-Brown. *The Architecture Of America: A Social and Cultural History.* Boston: Little, Brown And Company, 1961.

Burton, Orville Vernon. *In My Father's House Are Many Mansions: Family and Community in Edgefield, South Carolina.* Chapel Hill: The University of North Carolina Press, 1985.

Bushman, Richard L. *The Refinement of America: Persons, Houses, Cities.* New York: Vintage Books, 1993.

Caldwell, Wallace Everett. *The Ancient World.* New York: Rinehart & Company, Inc., 1949.

Cantor, Jay E. *Winterthur.* New York: Harry N. Abrams, Inc., Publishers, 1997.

Censer, Jane Turner. *North Carolina Planters And Their Children, 1800-1860.* Baton Rouge:

Louisiana State University Press, 1984.

Coit, Margaret L. *John C. Calhoun: American Portrait.* Boston: Houghton Mifflin Company, 1950.

Collins, Bruce. *White Society In The Antebellum South.* London: Longman Group Limited, 1985.

Collins, Carvel. *The American Sporting Gallery: Portraits Of American Horses From 1839—Spirit of the Times—1844.* Cambridge: Harvard University Press, 1949.

Cornelius, Charles Over. *Furniture Masterpieces of Duncan Phyfe.* Garden City, NY: Published for The Metropolitan Museum of Art by Doubleday, Page & Company, 1923.

Cook, Anna Green. *History Of Baldwin County Georgia.* Spartanburg, South Carolina: The Reprint Company, 1978. [reprint from 1925].

Coulter, E. Merton. *James Monroe Smith, Georgia Planter: Before Death and After.* Athens: University of Georgia Press, 1961.

Dattel, Gene. *Cotton And Race In The Making Of America: The Human Costs of Economic Power.* Chicago: Ivan R. Dee, 2009.

Davis, Burke. *Sherman's March.* New York: Vintage Press, 1988.

Dodd, William E. *The Cotton Kingdom: A Chronicle Of The Old South.* New Haven: Yale University Press, 1919.

Dodd, William E. *Statesmen Of The Old South Or From Radicalism To Conservative Revolt.* New York: The Book League of America, 1929. [reprint].

Fant, Christie Zimmerman. *The State House of South Carolina: An Illustrated Historic Guide.* Columbia, S.C.: R. L. Bryan, 1970.

Faust, Drew Gilpin. *James Henry Hammond and the Old South: A Design for Mastery.* Baton Rouge: Louisiana State University Press, 1982.

Flanders, Ralph Betts. *Plantation Slavery In Georgia.* Chapel Hill: The University of North Carolina Press, 1933.

Ford, Lacy K. *Deliver Us from Evil: The Slavery Question in the Old South.* Oxford: Oxford University Press, 2009. Kindle edition.

Fox-Genovese, Elizabeth. *Within the Plantation Household: Black and White Women of the Old South.* Chapel Hill: The University of North Carolina Press, 1988.

Freehling, William. *The South vs. The South: How Anti-Confederates Shaped the Course of the Civil War.* Oxford: Oxford University Press, 2001.

Gaines, Francis Pendleton. *The Southern Plantation: A Study in the Development and the Accuracy of a Tradition.* New York: Columbia University Press, 1924.

Gates, Paul W. *The Farmer's Age: Agriculture 1815-1860.* New York: Holt, Rinehart, and Winston, 1960.

Gelernter, Mark. *A History of American Architecture: Buildings in Their Cultural and Technical Context.* Lebanon, N.H.: University Press of New England, 2001.

Genovese, Eugene D. *The World the Slaveholders Made: Two Essays in Interpretation.* New York: Pantheon Books, A Division of Random House, 1969.

Glatthaar, Joseph T. *The March To The Sea And Beyond: Sherman's Troops in the Savannah and Carolinas Campaign.* New York: New York University Press, 1985.

Gleason, David King. *Antebellum Homes of Georgia.* Baton Rouge: Louisiana State University Press, 1987.

Glymph, Thavolia. *Out Of The House Of Bondage: The Transformation of the Plantation Household.* Cambridge and New York: Cambridge University Press, 2008.

Gowans, Alan. *Images of American Living: Four Centuries of Architecture and Furniture as Cultural Expressions.* Philadelphia: J.B. Lippencott Company, 1964.

Gray, Lewis C. *History of Agriculture in the Southern United States to 1860, Volume I.* Washington, DC: The Carnegie Institute of Washington, 1933.

Green, Edwin L. *A History of Richland County Volume One 1732-1805*. Baltimore: Regional Publishing Company, 1974.

Hamlin, Talbot. *Greek Revival Architecture in America: Being An Account of Important Trends In American Architecture And American Life Prior to the War Between the States*. New York: Dover Publications, Inc., 1993.

Hennig, Helen Kohn. *Great South Carolinians Of A Later Date*. Chapel Hill: The University of North Carolina Press, 1949.

Hilliard, Samuel. "Plantations and the molding of the Southern landscape." In *The Making of the American Landscape*, ed. Michael P. Conzen, 104-126. Boston: Urwin Hyman, 1990.

Holmes, Alester G. *Thomas Greene Clemson: His Life and Work*. Richmond: Garrett Massie, Incorporated, MCMXXXVII.

Hopkins, George. *Creating Your Architectural Style*. Gretna, LA: Pelican Publishing Company, Inc., 2009.

Hopkins, Laura Jervey. *Lower Richland Planters: Hopkins, Adams, Weston and Related Families of South Carolina*. Columbia, South Carolina: The R. L. Bryan Company, 1976.

Howard, Annie Howady, ed. *Georgia Homes And Landmarks*. Atlanta, GA: Southern Features Syndicate, 1929.

Ingle, Edward. *Southern Sidelights: A Picture of Social and Economic Life in the South a Generation Before the War*. New York: Thomas V. Crowell & Company, 1896.

Jenrette, Richard Hampton. *Adventures With Old Houses*. Charleston: Wynck & Company, 2000.

Johnson, Paul E. *The Early American Republic: 1789-1829. New York and Oxford: Oxford University Press, 2007.*

Johnson, Walter. *River of Dark Dreams: Slavery and Empire in the Cotton Kingdom*. Cambridge, MA: Harvard University Press, 2013.

Johnson, Walter. *Soul By Soul: Life Inside The Antebellum Slave Market*. (Massachusetts and England: Harvard University Press, 1999.

Jones, Mrs. C. J., and Henry T. Williams. *Beautiful Homes: How To Make Them*. Boston: Thompson, Brown & Co., 1885.

Kasson, John F. *Rudeness & Civility: Manners in Nineteenth-Century Victorian America*. New York: Hill and Wang, 1990.

Kennedy, Roger G. *Architecture, Men, Women And Money In America 1600-1860*. New York: Random House, 1985.

Kennedy, Roger G. *Greek Revival Architecture*. New York: Rizzoli International Publications, Inc., 2010.

Kennett, Lee. *Marching Through Georgia: The Story of Soldiers and Civilians During Sherman's Campaign*. New York: Harper Collins Publishers, 1995.

Kirkland, Jr., Randolph W. *Broken Fortunes: South Carolina soldiers, sailors, and citizens who died in service of their country and state in the War for Southern Independence, 1861-1865.* Charleston, S.C.: The South Carolina Historical Society, 1995.

Lancaster, Clay. *Ante Bellum Houses of the Bluegrass: The Development of Residential Architecture in Fayette County, Kentucky.* Lexington: University Press of Kentucky, 2015.

Lander, Jr., Ernest McPherson. *The Calhoun Family and Thomas Green Clemson: The Decline of a Southern Patriarchy.* Columbia, South Carolina: University of South Carolina Press, 1983.

Lane, Mills. *Architecture of the Old South: Colonial & Federal.* Savannah: The Beehive Press, 1996.

Lane, Mills. *Architecture of the Old South: Georgia.* Savannah: A Beehive Press Book, 1996.

Lane, Mills. *Architecture of the Old South: Greek Revival and Romantic.* Savannah: A Beehive Press Book, 1996.

Lane, Mills. *Architecture of the Old South: Louisiana.* Savannah. A Beehive Press Book, 1997.

Lane, Mills. *Architecture of the Old South: North Carolina.* Savannah, Georgia: The Beehive Press, 1985.

Lane, Mills. *Architecture of the Old South: South Carolina.* Savannah, Georgia: The Beehive Press, 1984.

Lane, Mills. *Architecture of the Old South: Virginia.* Savannah: A Beehive Press Book, 1996.

Lefler, Hugh Talmage, and Albert Ray Newsome. *The History of a Southern State: North Carolina*, 3rd edition. Chapel Hill: The University of North Carolina Press, 1973.

Lefler, Hugh T., and Paul Wager. *Orange County, 1752-1952.* Chapel Hill: The University of North Carolina Press, 1953.

Lewis, Charlene M. Boyer. *Ladies and Gentlemen on Display: Planter Society at the Virginia Springs 1790-1860.* Charlottesville and London: University of Virginia Press, 2001.

Linley, John. *Architecture of Middle Georgia: The Oconee Area.* Athens: The University of Georgia Press, 1972.

Linley, John. *The Georgia Catalog: Historic American Building Survey—A Guide to the Architecture of the State.* Athens, GA: The University of Georgia Press, 1982.

Longacre, Edward G. *Gentleman And Soldier: A Biography Of Wade Hampton III.* Lincoln and London: University of Nebraska Press, 2003.

Lounsbury, Carl R., ed. *An Illustrated Glossary Of Early Southern Architecture And Landscape.* Charlottesville: University Press of Virginia, 1994.

Lucas, Marion Brunson. *Sherman and the Burning of Columbia*. College Station: Texas A & M Press, 1976.

Mackay-Smith, Alexander. *The Race Horse of America, 1832-1872: Portraits And Other Paintings By Edward Troye*. Saratoga Springs, New York: The National Racing Museum of Racing, 1981.

Majewski, John. *Modernizing A Slave Economy: the Economic Vision of the Confederate Nation*. Chapel Hill: The University of North Carolina Press, 2009.

Marsh, Blanche. *Plantation Heritage In Upcountry, South Carolina.* Asheville, North Carolina: Biltmore Press, 1962.

Massey, Mary Elizabeth. *Refugee Life in the Confederacy*. Baton Rouge: Louisiana State University, 1964.

Matrana, Marc R. *Lost Plantations of the South.* Jackson: University Press of Mississippi, 2009.

Mayfield, Mark. *Southern Style*. Boston: A Bulfinch Press Book, Little, Brown and Company, 1999.

Mayhew, Edgar de N., and Minor Myers, Jr. *A Documentary History of American Interiors: From the Colonial Era to 1915*. New York: Charles Scribner's Sons, 1980.

Maynard, W. Barksdale. "The Greek Revival: Americanness, Politics and Economics." In *American Architectural History*. Ed. Keith L. Eggener. New York: Routledge, 2004. 132-141.

McFarland, Kenneth. *The Architecture of Warren County, North Carolina 1770s to 1860s*. Warren County Historical Association, 2001.

Megginson, W. J. *African American Life in South Carolina's Upper Piedmont, 1780-1900.* Columbia, South Carolina: University of South Carolina Press, 2006.

Meynard, Virginia G. *The Venturers: The Hampton, Harrison, And Earle Families Of Virginia, South Carolina And Texas*. Easley, South Carolina: The Southern Historical Press, 1981.

Milling, Chapman J., and Carl Julien. *Beneath So Kind a Sky: The Scenic and Architectural Beauty of South Carolina*. Columbia, South Carolina: University of South Carolina Press, 1947.

Mooney, Katherine C. *Race Horse Men: How Slavery And Freedom Were Made At The Racetrack.* Cambridge, Massachusetts and London, England: Harvard University Press, 2014.

Moore, John Hammond. *Columbia and Richland County: A South Carolina, 1740-1990*. Columbia: The University of South Carolina Press, 1993.

Mumford, Lewis. *The South In Architecture: The Darcy Lectures Alabama College 1941*. New York: Harcourt, Brace and Company, 1941.

Nash, Gary B. *First City: Philadelphia and the Forging of Historical Memory*. Philadelphia: University of Pennsylvania Press, 2002.

Nelligan, Murray H. *Custis-Lee Mansion*. Washington, DC: National Park

Service Historical Handbook Series No. 6, 1956.

Nathans, Sydney. *To Free a Family: The Journey Of Mary Walker. Cambridge, Massachusetts and London, England: Harvard University Press, 2012.*

Nelson, Megan Kate. *Ruin Nation: Destruction and the American Civil War.* Athens and London: The University of Georgia Press, 2012.

Nichols, Frederick Doveton. *The Architecture of Georgia*. Savannah: The Beehive Press, 1976.

Nichols, Frederick Doveton. *The Early Architecture of Georgia*. Chapel Hill: The University of North Carolina Press, 1957.

Newton County Historical Society. *History of NEWTON COUNTY Georgia*. Covington, Ga: Newton County Historical Society, 1988.

"North Carolina County Development." Genealogical Services Branch, State Library of North Carolina, Raleigh, North Carolina.

Oakes, James. *The Ruling Race: A History of American Slaveholders*. New York: W. W. Norton & Company, 1998.

Orser, Jr., Charles E., and Annette M. Nekola. "Plantation Settlement from Slavery to Tenancy: An Example from a Piedmont Plantation in South Carolina." In *The Architecture of Slavery and Plantation Life*, ed. Theresa Singleton, 67-94. Orlando: Academic Press, Inc., 1985.

Palmore, John S. *Riding With Sherman: The Civil War Travels of the Fifth Kentucky Cavalry, USA*. Frankfurt, KY: John S. Palmore, 2000.

Peck, Amelia. "The Greek Revival Parlor." In *Period Rooms in The Metropolitan Museum of Art*, ed. Amelia Peck, et. al., 238-243. New York: Harry N. Abrams, Inc., 1996.

Perkerson, Medora Fields. *White Columns In Georgia*. New York: Bonanza Books, 1956.

Perrottet, Tony. *The Naked Olympics: The True Story of the Ancient Games*. New York: Random House Trade Paperback, 2004.

Ravenel, Beatrice St. Julien. *Architects of Charleston*. Columbia, South Carolina Press, 1992.

Reidy, Joseph P. *From Slavery To Agrarian Capitalism In The Cotton Plantation South: Central Georgia, 1800-1880.* Chapel Hill and London: The University of North Carolina Press, 1992.

Reiff, Daniel D. *Houses from Books: Treatises, Pattern Books, and Catalogs in American Architecture, 1738-1950: A History and Guide*. State College, Pennsylvania: Penn State University Press, 2000.

Robert, Joseph Clarke. *The Tobacco Kingdom: Plantation, Market, and Factory In Virginia and North Carolina, 1800-1860*. Gloucester, Mass.: Peter Smith, 1965.

Rogers, Jr., George C. *Charleston in the Age of the Pinckneys*. Columbia, South Carolina: University of South Carolina Press, 1980.

Rogers, Jr., George C. "The Transition To The Nineteenth-Century Economy."
In *Perspectives In South Carolina History: The First 300 Years*, eds. Ernest M. Lander, Jr. and Robert K. Ackerman, 87-93. Columbia, South Carolina: University of South Carolina Press, 1973.
Rubin, Anne Sarah. *Through The Heart Of Dixie: Sherman's March and American Memory*. Chapel Hill: The University of North Carolina Press, 2014.
Sanders, Charles Richard. *The Cameron Plantation in Central North Carolina (1776-1973) and Its Founder Richard Bennehan*. Durham, North Carolina: Charles R. Sanders, private publication, 1974.
Salley, A. S. "Origin and Development." In *Columbia: Capital City of South Carolina*, ed. Helen Kohn Hennig, 1-12. Columbia, South Carolina: The State Printing Company, 1966.
Savage, Kirk. *Standing Soldiers, Kneeling Slaves*. Princeton: Princeton University Press, 1997.
Scranton, Robert L. *Greek Architecture*. New York: George Braziller, 1965.
Seebohm, Caroline, and Peter Woloszynski. *Under Live Oaks: The Last Great Homes of the Old South*. New York: Clarkson Potter Publishers, 2002.
Severens, Kenneth. *Southern Architecture: 350 Years of Distinctive American Buildings*. New York: E. P. Dutton, 1981.
Shaffer, E.T. *Carolina Gardens*. Chapel Hill: The University of North Carolina Press, 1939.
Smith, Alfred Glaze. *Economic Readjustment of an Old Cotton State: South Carolina, 1820-1860*. Columbia, South Carolina: University of South Carolina Press, 1958.
Smith, Alfred Glaze. "The Old Order Changes." In *Perspectives In South Carolina History: The First 300 Years*, eds. Ernest M. Lander, Jr. and Robert K. Ackerman, 95-103. Columbia, South Carolina: University of South Carolina Press, 1973.
Smith, J. Fraser. *Plantation Houses And Mansions Of The Old South*. New York: Dover Publications, Inc., 1993.
Smith, Jane Webb. *Georgia's Legacy: History Chartered Through The Arts, An Exhibition Organized on the Occasion of the Bicentennial of The University of Georgia, 1785-1985*. USA: Georgia Museum of Art, 1985.
Stoney, Samuel Gaillard. *Plantations of the Carolina Low-Country*. Charleston, South Carolina: Carolina Art Association, 1969.
Stowe, Steven M. *Intimacy And Power In The Old South: Ritual in the Lives of the Planters*. Baltimore: The Johns Hopkins University Press, 1987.
Stroup, Rodger. "Up-Country Patrons: Wade Hampton II and His Family." In *Art In The Lives Of South Carolinians: Nineteenth-Century Chapters*, ed. David Moltke-Hansen, Rsb1-Rsb13. Charleston, SC: Carolina Art Association, 1979.

Sweeney, John A. H. *Winterthur Illustrated.* A Winterthur Book, 1963.

Sweet, Waldo E. *Sport And Recreation In Ancient Greece: A Sourcebook with Translations.* Oxford and New York: Oxford University Press, 1987.

Taylor, Benjamin F. "Commerce and Manufacturing." In *Columbia: Capital City of South Carolina 1786-1936*, ed. Helen Kohn Hennig, 315-348. Columbia, South Carolina: The State Printing Company, 1966.

Taylor, Rosser H. *Ante-Bellum South Carolina: A Social And Cultural History.* New York: De Capo Press, 1970.

Truettner, Julia M. *Aspirations for Excellence: Alexander Jackson Davis and the First Campus Plan for the University of Michigan, 1838.* Ann Arbor, MI: University of Michigan Press, 2003.

Vlach, John Michael. *Back of the Big House: The Architecture of Plantation Slavery.* Chapel Hill: The University of North Carolina Press, 1993.

Vlach, John Michael. *The Planter's Prospect: Privilege & Slavery In Plantation Paintings.* Chapel Hill and London: The University of North Carolina Press, 2002.

Watkin, David. *Athenian Stuart: Pioneer of the Greek Revival.* London: George Allen and Urwin, 1982.

Wellman, Manly Wade. *The County of Warren North Carolina 1586-1917.* Chapel Hill: The University of North Carolina Press, 1959.

Wellman, Manly Wade. *Giant in Gray: A Biography of Wade Hampton of South Carolina.* New York: Charles Scriber's Sons, 1949.

Wertenbaker, Thomas Jefferson. *The Old South: The Founding of American Civilization.* New York: Cooper Square Publishers, Inc., 1963.

Whiffen, Marcus, and Frederick Koeper. *American Architecture Volume I: 1607-1860.* Cambridge: The Massachusetts Institute of Technology Press, 1981.

Wiebenson, Dora. *Sources Of Greek Revival.* University Park & London: The Penn State University Press, 1969.

Wieneck, Henry. *Plantations of the Old South.* Birmingham, Alabama: Oxmoor House, Inc., 1983.

Woodman, Harold D. *King Cotton & His Retainers: Financing & Marketing the Cotton Crop of the South, 1800-1925.* Lexington, KY: The University of Kentucky Press, 1968.

Wright, Gavin. *The Political Economy of the Cotton South: Households, Markets, and Wealth in the Nineteenth Century.* New York: W.W. Norton & Company, Inc., 1978.

Wyatt-Brown, Bertram. *Southern Honor: Ethics & Behavior in the Old South.* Oxford: Oxford University Press, 1983.

ARTICLES

--. "A Visit To A Cotton Plantation." *The Scientific American*. February 1860.

--. "American Classic: A Greek Revival Interior Appropriately Furnished." *Antiques* 45 (1944): 23.

--. "Possessions Saved, Pillars Remain." *Historically Speaking*, Volume 43: 3.

--. "Romance of Fort Hill: The Beautiful Old Home of John C. Calhoun, Part 1." *South Carolina Magazine*. September 1955: 14-15 and 25.

--. "Slavery in the Southern States." *Southern Quarterly Review*. 8 (October 1845): 317-360.

Allen, Richard Lamb. "Letters From The South." *The American Agriculturalist*. November 1846: 20-21.

American Turf Register and Sporting Magazine. May 1840: 244.

Bonner, James C. "House and Landscape Design in the Antebellum South." *Landscape* (21) 1077: 2-8.

Cardwell, Guy A. "The Plantation House: An Analogical Image." *Southern Literary Journal* 2(1) 1969: 3-21.

Collins, Robert. "Essay on the Treatment and Management of Slaves." *Southern Cultivator*, 12 (July 1854): 205-206.

Correspondence. "Letter." *Weekly*. Ellis Merton Coulter Historical Manuscripts, Confederate States of America, Hargrett Rare Books and Manuscripts Library, University of Georgia Libraries.

Crummel, Alexander, "The Attitude Of The American Mind Towards The Negro Intellect." https://www.blackpast.org/african-american-history/1898-alexande r-crummell-attitude-american-mind-toward-negro-intellect/.

Draper, Earle Sumner. "Southern Plantations." *Landscape Architecture* XXIII (1932): 1-14.

Draper, Earle Sumner. "Southern Plantations II." *Landscape Architecture* XXIII (1933): 117-138.

Easterby, J. H. "The Three Wade Hamptons: The Saga of a Family of the Old South." *The State*. 4 March 1934.

Eisenberg, John. "Off to the Races." *Smithsonian* 35 (5) August 2004: 98-105.

Ellett, Mrs. E. F. "The Noble Wife." *Godey's Lady's Book* (August 1841): 121ff.

Ellis, Clifton. "Greeking the Southside: Style and Meaning of James C.Bruce's Berry Hill Plantation House." *Journal of Early Southern Decorative Arts* Vol. XXVIII, No. 3 (Summer 2002): 1-51.

Gamble, Robert. "The White Column Tradition: Classical Architecture And The Southern Mystique." *Southern Humanities Review*: 41-59.

Greenough, Horatio. "American Architecture." *US Magazine and Democratic Review* XIII (August 1848): 206-210.

Grootkerk, Paul. "Artistic Images of Mythological Reality: The Antebellum Plantation." *The Southern Quarterly* 32 (4) 1994: 33-44.

Hale, Mrs. S. J. "Domestic Economy No. 1." *Godey's Lady's Book and Ladies' American Magazine*, Vol. XX (Jan. 1840): 42-43.

Hampton, Ann Fripp. "The Hampton Family of South Carolina." *The Caroline Herald, Official Publication of the South Carolina Genealogical Society*, Vol. 3, Number 3: 19-23.

Harmon, G. Thomas. "Milford Mansion." *Southern Architect and Building News.* October 1931. John Laurence Manning Papers, South Caroliniana Library, Manuscripts Division.

Hollingsworth, Kent. "The Equine Art of E Troye." *The Blood Horse. A Weekly Magazine Devoted to the Turf.* 23 December 1967: 3948-3955.

Horton, Frank L. *The Museum of Early Southern Decorative Arts: The Rooms and Their Furnishings.* [reprinted from *Antiques,* January, 1967].

Hudson, Leonne M. "The Role of the 54th Massachusetts Regiment in Potter's Raid." *Historical Journal of Massachusetts*, 30 (2002): 181-197.

Ingersoll, Ernest. "The Calhoun Summer House." *Scribner's Monthly.* Vol. XXI (5) March 1881: 892-895.

Joseph, J.W. "White Columns and Black Hands: Class and Classification in the Plantation Ideology of Georgia and South Carolina Lowcountry."

Historical Archaeology 27 (3) 1993: 57-74.

May, Bridget A. "Advice on White: An Anthology of Nineteenth Century

Design Critics' Recommendations." *Journal of American Culture* 16 (4) 1993: 19-24.

Lero, Nicole. "The History of Horse Racing In North America." 2008. http://ezinearticles.com/?The-History-of-Horse-Racing-In-North-America&id=1075530.

Mattson, Richard L. "History And Architecture Of Orange County, North Carolina." September 1996.

http://www.hpo.ncdcr.gov/surveyreports/orangecountysurveypubmanuscript-1996.pdf.

Mitchell, Mrs. J.H. "The Romance of Fort Hill." *South Carolina Magazine.* Vol. 20, Sept. 1955: 14-15 and 24.

Morse, Samuel F. B. "The Fine Arts." *The Southern Review* Vol. IV (August and November, 1829): 70-86.

Nichols, Brevet Major George Ward. "Sherman's Great March." *Harper's New Monthly Magazine* Volume XXXI, October 1865: 571-589.

Nixon, Angela Snyder. "V.P. John C. Calhoun Plantation Slaves." http://files.usgwarchives.net/sc/oconee/history/h-53.txt.

Patrick, James. "Ecclesiological Gothic in the Antebellum South." *Winterthur Portfolio* 15 (2) 1980: 117-138.

Pendleton Agricultural Society. *Southern Cultivator*, Volume III (7) July 1845: 97-99.

"Richard Hampton Jenrette, Founder," *Classical American Homes Preservation Trust and The Richard Hampton Jenrette Foundation,* https://classicalamericanhomes.org/richard-h-jenrettefounder/#:~:text=Dick%20founded%20Classical%20American%20Homes,land%20and%20outbuildings%20to%20CAHPT.

Signourey, Mrs. L. H. "The Perception of the Beautiful." *Godey's Lady's Book and Ladies American Magazine.* Vol. XX (January 1840): 9-11.

Smith, Harry Worcester. "Edward Troye (1808-1874) The Painter of American Blood Horses." *The Field, The Country Gentleman's Newspaper.* 21 January 1926: 96-98.

Smith, Harry Worcester. "The Best Of These War Troye." *The Spur.* January 1919: 41, 47-48.

Smith, Thomas Gordon. "Living With Antiques: Millford Plantation." *The Magazine Antiques.* May 1997: 732-741.

Sweet, Ethel Wylly. "The House that Cotton Built." The Sandlapper-The Magazine of South Carolina, January-February 1975: 19-22.

Tucker, George. "On Architecture." *Port Folio* IV (1814): 559-569.

Vosburgh, W. S. "Horse Portraiture in America." *Daily Racing Form.* 18 March 1919.

Walter, Thomas U. "Architecture." *Journal of the Franklin Institute* XXXII 1 January 1841: 12.

Woodhouse, Lawrence. "Architecture in North Carolina 1700-1900." *North Carolina Architect.* November December 1969: 9-28.

PERIODICALS

--. "A Suffering South Carolina Poet." *The New York Herald.* 23 February 1865. Civil War Collection, North Carolina Division of Archives and History.

--. "John C. Calhoun's Home Life." *The Anderson Daily Mail.* 23 October 1926. [reprint from August 1848 Baltimore newspaper article].

--. "Hampton's Slaves Numerous." *The News and Courier.* 8 May 1952 [reprint from *Age-Herald*, 8 May 1902]. Wade Hampton Papers, South Caroliniana Library, Manuscripts Division.

--. "The New State House, The Capital Of South Carolina-From a Sketch By Our Special Artist." *Frank Leslie's Illustrated Newspaper. 17 August 1861.*

--. "Personal Reminiscences of the Spring of 1865." Civil War Collection, North Carolina Division of Archives and History.

--, "The Rev. Dr. Storrs on the Influence of Climate on Civilization." *The New York Times.* November 1858.

--. "The South Carolina Turf." *The News and Courier.* 27 September 1844.

--. "Sale of the estates of Gen. William Williams." *Roanoke Advocate* (Halifax, North Carolina) 6 December 1832. http://www.newspapers.com/clip/652308/sale_of_the_estate_of_gen_william/.

--. "Uncle Washington Boasts of Celebrating 104 Birthdays." *The State*. 1 September 1935.

Alison, Archibald. "Architecture." *The Daily Orthopolitan*, Nashville, Tennessee, 8 January 1846.

Cannaday, Ralph Jerome. "Gen. Wade Hampton-War And Reconstruction's Hero." *The News and Courier*. 30 March 1961.

Carroll, Anna Ella. "John C. Calhoun A Secessionist. A Letter from a Granddaughter of Charles Carroll, addressed to Edward Everett. July 13, 1865." *The New York Times,* July 23, 1861.

Charleston Courier. 27 September 1844 and 19 September 1859.

Currie, R. M. "'Back in the Sixties" South Carolina." Civil War Collection, North Carolina Division of Archives and History.

Easterby, J.H. "The Three Wade Hamptons: The Saga of a Family of the Old South." *The State-Columbia, South Carolina, 4 March 1934.*

"Editorial Correspondence of the Courier." *Charleston Daily Courier*. 10 July 1862.

Heyward, Ex-Gov. D.C. "Glowing Tribute to Wade Hampton By Former Governor D.C. Heyward." *Charleston Evening Post*. 10 July 1929. Wade Hampton

Papers, South Carolina Historical Society.

Ingmire Frances T. "Citizens of Baldwin County" (n.d., n.p.), Georgia Department of Archives and History. (This work is merely a copy of the 1860 census.)

Irving, John B. "Sporting Epistle From South Carolina." *The News and Courier*, Charleston, South Carolina. 27 September 1844.

Marriages. *The Macon Georgia Telegraph*. 4 February 1832.

Miller, J. L. "The Hampton Family." *The Times Dispatch*, Richmond, Virginia. 26 Nov.—11 Dec. 1911. Virginia Gurley Meynard Papers, South Caroliniana Library, Manuscripts Division.

Morgan, Kerri. "Proposed Design in Razed." *The News and Courier*. 29 June 1989. 200 Meeting Street File, South Carolina Historical Society.

Obituary of Hon. Paul C. Cameron. "The Death Of Mr. Cameron." *The News and Courier*. 7 January 1891.

Obituary, Wade Hampton II. *Charleston Daily Courier*. 12 February 1858.

Obituary, Col. Wade Hampton. *Southern Christian Advocate*. 13 February 1858. Hampton Family Papers, South Caroliniana Library, Manuscripts Division.

Pendleton Agricultural Society. "Report Of The Committee On Farms Made To the Society On The 10th October 1844." *Southern Cultivator* (2) July 1845: 97-99. Library of Congress, microfilm.

Pendleton Agricultural Society. *Southern Cultivator*. Vol. III (7) July 1845: 97-99.

Pendleton Correspondent. "John C. Calhoun's Home Life." *The Anderson Daily Mail*. 23 October 1929. [reprint from August 1849 Baltimore article].

Raleigh Register. 28 July 1806. North Carolina Division of Archives and History, microfilm.

Raleigh Register And North Carolina State Gazette. 18 February 1825, 13 March 1825 and 25 March 1825. North Carolina Division of Archives and History, microfilm.

Roanoke Advocate. 8 November 1832, 14 November 1832, 22 November 1832.

Strong, Willard. "Charleston Hotel Reflected Antebellum Glory." *The News and Courier*, Charleston, South Carolina. 3 March 1986. 200 Meeting Street File, South Carolina Historical Society.

Spirit of the Times. 23 March 1839, p. 39.

Warrenton (North Carolina) Reporter. 2 March 1827 and 9 May 1837.

UNPUBLISHED WORKS

--. "VP John Calhoun." http://www.senate.gov/artandhistory/history/common/generic/VP_John_Calhoun.htm

--. "Fort Hill History." http://www.clemson.edu/about/history/properties/forthill/

--. "List of Paintings Collected by James Henry Hammond." James Henry Hammond Papers, South Caroliniana Library, Manuscripts Division.

--. "The Hammonds." Hammond, Bryan and Cumming Families Papers, South Caroliniana Library, Manuscripts Division.

--. "Prices in Rome of Art, 21 February 1837." James Henry Hammond Papers, South Caroliniana Library, Manuscripts Division.

--. "Wade Hampton II and Artists." Virginia Gurley Meynard Papers, South Caroliniana Library, Manuscripts Division.

Account—Wade II. Hampton Family Papers, South Caroliniana Library, Manuscripts Division.

Ashe, S. A. "Some Reminiscences of the Beginning And The End of the War." Civil War Collection, North Carolina Division of Archives and History.

Billings, John Shaw. "Some Notes On The History Of Redcliffe." Redcliffe, Aiken County Research File. South Carolina Division of Archives and History.

Bonner, James C. "Lockerly." (pamphlet) (n.p., 1967), n.p

Cunningham, J. Whitney. "South Carolina Architecture." Maverick and Van Wyke Family Papers. South Caroliniana Library, Manuscripts Division.

Edmunds, Jr., John B. "A Biographical Sketch of John L. Manning." John Laurence Manning Papers, South Caroliniana Library, Manuscripts Division.

Glatthaar, Joseph Thomas. "Union Soldiers and Their Attitudes in Sherman's Savannah & Carolina Campaign." Ph.D. Dissertation. University of Wisconsin, Madison, 1983. Edward M. Coffman, Major Professor.

Hammond, Harry. "James Henry Hammond: Little Known Sketch by Late Major Harry Hammond." 2 March 1924. James Henry Hammond Papers, South Caroliniana Library, Manuscripts Division.

Hampton, Harry R. E. "Hampton Houses." Virginia Gurley Meynard Papers, South Caroliniana Library, Manuscripts Division.

Hampton, Harry R. E. "The Second Wade." Virginia Gurley Meynard Papers, South Caroliniana Library, Manuscripts Division.

Mackay-Smith, Alexander. "Comments on Letitia Adams "Wade Hampton II's Patronage of Edward Troye." Virginia Gurley Meynard Papers, South Caroliniana Library, Manuscripts Division.

Manning (?), Wade Hampton. "The Hampton Family of South Carolina." Hampton Family Papers, South Caroliniana Library, Manuscripts Division.

Manning, Col. Wyndham. "Sketch of Manning Family." Manning Family Papers, South Caroliniana Library, Manuscripts Division.

Meynard, Virginia. "Portraits Of Horses By Edward Troye and Henri DeLattre Owned By Col. Wade Hampton." Virginia Gurley Meynard Papers, South Caroliniana Library, Manuscripts Division.

Miller, Dr. J. L., et. al. "Partial History of the Hampton Family in the State of Florida." Hampton Family Papers, South Caroliniana Library, Manuscripts Division.

Rockman, Seth. "The Future of Civil War Studies: Slavery and Capitalism." http://journalofthecivilwarera.com/forum-the-future-of-civil-war-era-studies/the-future-of-civil-war-era-studies-slavery-and-capitalism/

Seale, William. "Diagram of Interior Sketch; Conjectural Diagram at Millwood as it was Prior to its Destruction in February 1865." Millwood-Richland County Research File. South Carolina Division of Archives and History.

Sublette, Julia Wright. "The Letters of Anna Calhoun Clemson. 1833-1873. Volume I. Chapters 1-3: 1883-1850. Volume II: Chapters 4-5: 1855-1873," Ph.D. Dissertation, The Florida State University, Fall Semester1993, Major Professor, Elisabeth Muhlenfeld, Ph.D., South Caroliniana Library, Manuscripts Division.

The Triad Architectural Associates (John W. Califf). "Millwood: Its Architecture And Ambiance." Draft Copy. Columbia, S.C. 1982.

Williams, Marshall W. "A Documentary History Outline of "The Oaks" Plantation."

Volz, Candace M. “An Analysis of the Interiors of Fort Hill, The John C. Calhoun. House.” http://www.volzassociates.com/Calhoun_House_Files/JohnCCalhoun_Excerpt.pdf, pp. I-2—I-3.

ART

Troye, Edward. Argyle. Whitney Collections of Sporting Art. Yale University Art Gallery. http://artgallery.yale.edu/collections/objects/argyle

Troye, Edward. Pocahontas. Whitney Collections of Sporting Art. Yale University Art Gallery. http://artgallery.yale.edu/collections/objects/pocahontas

INDEX

ABOUT THE AUTHOR

Heidi Amelia-Anne Weber earned her Ph.D. in 19th Century American History at Kent State University. She hold the rank of full professor of history in the Department of Global Studies at SUNY: Orange, where she was awarded the SUNY: Orange President's Award for Excellence in Teaching and the New York Chancellor's Award for Teaching Excellence. Heidi wrote a chapter in the *Handbook of Military Administration* and has written entries for *The Encyclopedia of the Reconstruction Era (Two Volumes):Greenwood Milestones in African American History* and the *World of Antebellum America: A Daily Life Encyclopedia*. In addition, she has published various articles and book reviews and is the past co-editor and editor of *The Journal of America's Military Past.*